THE TRANSCENDENTAL METHOD

THE TRANSCENDENTAL METHOD

OTTO MUCK, S.J.

Translated by
William D. Seidensticker

HERDER AND HERDER

1968
HERDER AND HERDER NEW YORK
232 Madison Avenue, New York 10016

Original edition: *Die Transzendentale
Methode in der Scholastischen Philosophie der Gegenwart,*
Innsbruck, Verlag Felizian Rauch.

Nihil obstat: Leo J. Steady, Censor Librorum
Imprimatur: ✠Robert F. Joyce, Bishop of Burlington
February 26, 1968

CONTENTS

PART ONE
THE ADOPTION OF THE
TRANSCENDENTAL METHOD BY JOSEPH MARÉCHAL

CONTENTS

PART THREE

TRANSCENDENTAL SYSTEMATIC OF PHILOSOPHY

7

FOREWORD

It would not be entirely proper for me to say too much in praise of this scholarly book because I approached it with full conviction of its significance. Nevertheless, it is obvious that if there is such a thing as a transcendental method in scholastic philosophy, and if anyone who would be a philosopher should at least know in what this method consists, then a book which gives a thorough and objective treatment of how this method has been received in Catholic philosophical circles during the last fifty years is without a doubt a useful work and an important document for all Catholic philosophers and theologians.

Perhaps, though, I might be permitted to say just a few things and thereby to recommend this book at least indirectly. The author discusses the transcendental method in contemporary "*scholastic* philosophy," i.e., he sketches the history of the reception of a mode of thought which so alters the receptive "system" that it becomes an entirely new and different one. The reception of the transcendental method means the end of "neo-scholasticism" in the historical sense of the word. This is not to say that this reception rejects the substance of the heritage of the traditional philosophy of the middle ages (especially that of Thomas of Aquin) as false or insignificant. This, of course, from a variety of points of view, is simply not the case.

Nor does the transcendental turn mean merely the adoption of a brand new doctrine in an otherwise stable and static "system," but an entirely new conception of the "system" itself. This is what leads us to speak confidently of the end of neo-scholasticism as it has been understood since the second half of the nineteenth century. Through this "turn," Christian philosophy has become the first of the ecclesiastical disciplines to have attained the urgently needed capacity for dialogue which the Second Vatican Council has made the task and the duty of each and every aspect of the Church in dealing with the "world."

The transcendental method finds its deepest meaning in *theology*. We cannot avoid *thinking*, viz., doing philosophy, in theology. A theology, as *intellectus fidei,* must view its object through all the methods and within every horizon which it encounters in the intellectual activity of its time. The transcendental method can play an important role in such an approach to theology. This is true especially in "fundamental theology," which, to be contemporary, must not merely demonstrate the "objective" authenticity of the event of divine revelation, but must come to understand man, much more precisely and reflectively than before, as the hearer of a possible revelation. This requires the reflection of the transcendental conditions of possibility of hearing a revelation. Moreover, this mode of framing questions also extends to dogmatic theology, especially with regard to the doctrine of grace and Christology. We cannot understand what we call sanctifying grace, the gift of faith, divinely infused virtues, etc., ultimately as (unique) "categoreal" determinations of man, but as the *a priori* determination of man's "transcendentality" (in grace) as such. Likewise, in the area of Christology we can think of a "transcendental Christology," i.e., the reflection of the nature of man, "elevated" by grace, as open for a confrontation with the absolute God in *history,* or a doctrine of the Incarnation expressed in the concepts of a transcendental anthropology. These are merely glimpses, but I am convinced that because of the reception of the transcendental method in Catholic philosophy a similar turn is taking place in theology, so much so that it can no longer be called neo-scholastic in the historical sense. Consequently, the history of this reception is clearly of immense significance for Catholic theology.

KARL RAHNER

PREFACE

The question concerning methodology is an indication of a crisis. The access to reality most familiar to us appears to have been called into question with regard to its fundamental validity (or at least with regard to its ability to counteract a very pressing problem). Reflection which is focused on the *way,* i.e., which brings it to awareness, determines its suitability and thereby either adapts the way to the goal or suggests new ways, is a reflection on methodology.

Reflections on methodology are often undertaken with some degree of uneasiness. This uneasiness may be partially grounded in the fact that we do not want to recognize the crisis which constitutes the need for reflection. It may partially stem from an impatience that would prefer to set out straight for the goal rather than to get involved in discussions about the way thereto. Yet even in philosophy a method projected from the very beginning arouses distrust since this can easily lead to the danger of approaching the fullness of reality from a one-sided point of view—which spells the death of philosophy. Methods, however, can also be approached from the point of view of the reciprocal relations which constitute the questful efforts of the way to the goal since this procedure is bound up with the discovery of further relations which lead to the goal. The reflection on methodology accompanies inquiry, but it does not project a complete and adequate description of the way *a priori.*

This does not make a reflection on methodology superfluous, because apart from this reflection we cannot test to what extent the goal of scientific knowledge is attained and how, in terms of the insights it leads to, the goal can be properly striven after. A determination of the finality of the attempted or possible steps necessary for the attainment of the direction of further steps is itself a reflection on methodology.

This explains why, especially since the beginning of the modern era, discussions on the method of philosophy have appeared in much more explicit form and why they have assumed a fundamental significance for philosophy. Different philosophical systems can only be understood in terms of their methodical stance, but the conflicts between them compel us to approach systems from the point of view of their respective methods and to evaluate methods with regard to their fruitfulness in, limitations for and adaptability to philosophy.

The concrete problems of philosophy also make a reflection on methodology indispensable. The various special sciences, with their unique methods, offer a variety of approaches to reality. However, what is known through these methods and what contributions the results of the various sciences can make to philosophy's goal in knowledge is only possible through a reflection on the methods of the special sciences and their relations to the methods of philosophy. This involves philosophy in the wider question concerning the ways which, independently of the methods of the special sciences, are open to it for the attainment of its goal.

The question concerning its methods is imposed upon philosophy, but the clarification of the method is connected with the actuation of the method. The more the method corresponds to the goal, the closer philosophy comes to its goal through the actuation of its method. This, however, involves the possibility of coming to a better understanding of its own method as well as to an improvement of the method. Thus actuation and reflection mutually stimulate each other, but by the same token the results that can be expected from an examination of a philosophical method are limited. The reflection on methodology attains its goal if it clarifies and advances the process of philosophy. The advance achieved in this way makes a more complete reflection on methodology possible which surpasses the previous method. This indicates the scientific use which a preliminary reflection on the methodology of philosophy involves.

This work should be approached from this point of view, viz., as a reflection on the so-called transcendental method as it has evolved during the past several decades in the area of neo-scholasticism, i.e., in that area of philosophy which is committed to the scholastic tradition. It is hoped that through a reflection on the discussion which has focused on this method in the area of contemporary scholastic philosophy, the nature of this method can be clarified and expanded into a broader application of this method for the needs of philosophy. This work is thus a contribution to this discussion currently under way, which deals with the synthesis of the Graeco-scholastic heritage with the contemporary demands of philosophy.

INTRODUCTION

Neo-scholasticism does not consist in a compendious relation
to the philosophical positions of medieval thinkers. The philosophical topics discussed in books, journal articles and confer-
ences manifest the scientific earnestness with which neo-
scholastics approach all the areas of contemporary philosophy.
This testifies to two facts. First, the obvious relation with the
scholastic tradition does not imply a mechanical reproduction
of the latter. This tradition has proven itself to be a useful tool
for philosophical exposition and inquiry, but the aim has been
the transformation of the problems which confronted high
scholasticism in the middle ages for the present times. This
leads to a second point, viz., that the contemporary philosophical positions which have emerged in the post-scholastic eras
are the very positions of non-scholastic contemporary philosophy. Consequently, neo-scholastic philosophy comes into
immediate contact with other philosophical traditions.

The dialogue with these traditions would not attain its goal
if it were restricted to a purely negative context which was only
interested in the "true" viewpoint in opposition to all the
others. This approach could, of course, be useful since such
opposition (insofar as it is openly considered) draws attention
to problems which may have been overlooked and stimulates
self-criticism and the needed clarification of personal points of
view. But besides this there must be a positive confrontation
which reveals the relations of different traditions to each other
and thereby establishes an acquaintance with the philosophical
efforts of others. The adoption and re-development of the
results of others is ultimately necessary for true scientific
cooperation. Even though it may be impossible to accept an-

other philosophical point of view because of its illegitimate one-sidedness, this does not completely exclude the possibility of cooperation because the investigations carried on from this point of view cannot be entirely worthless (often relations come into focus through a narrowed perspective which otherwise would pass notice but which are nonetheless important). However, in order that these results might be properly adopted and re-developed (while avoiding the dangers of mere syncretism), this endeavor must be joined together with a fundamental clarification of the relations between these viewpoints.

The very nature of philosophy and its claim to scientific status require that each philosophical tradition seek out such a positive confrontation with the other traditions. Philosophy, in order to be what it claims to be, cannot afford to limit itself to a specifically restricted point of view (to the *a priori* exclusion of others). To the extent that some sort of limitation is methodically justifiable we do not have *the* philosophy, but parts of philosophy which are (and often must be) related to the other parts. Just as a concrete expression of philosophy cannot be *the* philosophy, it also ceases to be philosophical if it is not prepared to draw the necessary conclusions from the main objectives of philosophy.

This positive relation among the traditions and the parts of philosophy is not unilateral, but reciprocal, and consists in the relation of scholastic disciplines to each other as well as in the relation of these disciplines to other philosophical traditions. If another tradition should not recognize this relation (thereby rejecting the very nature, and scientific status, of philosophy), this would be no reason to commit the same mistake.

This helps explain the development of neo-scholasticism in the last century. The more it has become aware of the philosophical potentialities which can be drawn from the rediscovery of its heritage, the more it has recognized both the possibility and the necessity of entering into a fruitful dialogue with other philosophical traditions and with the current philosophical problems. Its philosophical-historical researches into the middle ages, and other epochs, made it possible to attempt a re-development of the valid insights of its own tradition within the context of contemporary conditions. This makes it easier to understand to what degree questions posed by contemporary philosophy can find their solutions through a redevelopment of the traditional synthesis, viz., how these questions relate to the questions of classical scholasticism. This end is also served by a positive confrontation with the various traditions of modern and contemporary philosophy from the point of view of scholasticism, because insofar as these encounters begin from a position which is different from scholasticism and which is imposed by the contemporary problematic, the confrontation prepares the way for a development of philosophy which begins with today's problems and proposes answers which are not limited to the scholastic synthesis (and yet establishes relations which are unavoidable for neo-scholastic thought).

Both approaches are of prime importance, viz., starting with the contemporary problematic and maintaining a connection with classical scholasticism. The connection with classical scholasticism is necessary because otherwise philosophy would not do justice to the problems which involve the whole of human knowledge. The Christian who philosophizes, for example, is of the opinion that philosophy, despite its self-sufficiency and logical independence from Christian revelation, should not be disinterested in questions which are philosophical but whose answers are important for a theological understanding of Christian revelation (even though the development of this understanding is not philosophy, but theology). Furthermore, because (especially for Catholic theology) the historical tradition and the revelatory understanding which evolves in it are decidedly important, and because this understanding is expressed in distinct philosophical formulations, theology requires a philosophy which stands in vital connection with this philosophical tradition and which presents the theologically relevant philosophical insights and modes of expression not only historically, but systematically. Therefore, the Catholic is interested in a philosophy which is truly philosophical, but in a way that does not by-pass tradition but grows from it and attempts to re-develop it in terms of the contemporary problem-

17

atic. Whoever would not accept these presuppositions will nevertheless be confronted with this problematic since he cannot, as a philosopher, neglect the forces which determine our contemporary intellectual climate. Moreover, scholastic philosophy, as true philosophy, is not theology and is therefore intrinsically independent of the personal ideas of individual philosophers concerning Christian revelation. By the same token, however, neo-scholastic philosophy must begin with the contemporary problematic because this will lead, it is hoped, to the resolution of the necessary preliminary questions for contemporary theology, viz., that which pertains to the understanding of belief in the contemporary world. Theology would be unable to complete this task if philosophy did not involve itself earnestly in the contemporary problematic and (from its own point of view) attempt to clarify it in such a way that its relation to the traditional problematic of scholasticism stands out distinctly. A mere "application" of the tradition to the contemporary situation is not sufficient because the problematic includes not only obvious questions which are easily answered, but also a distinct way of posing questions and requirements which any answer must satisfy if it is to be accepted. Only if these requirements are illegitimate does this first have to be explained, and then only so that a way to an answer can be found. However, this approach to the contemporary situation is not restricted to content. It also establishes a basis for dialogue with other philosophical traditions which are grounded in this problematic and mode of questioning. Therefore, the more neo-scholasticism draws closer to its own tradition and (with regard to what is required of the contemporary world by the tradition) also to the contemporary problematic, the more vital and fruitful will its dialogue with other philosophical traditions become—i.e., fruitful for itself because in this way it can make better use of the particular approaches of other traditions for its own confrontation with the contemporary problematic, and fruitful for the other traditions because the philosophical heritage of the tradition is transmitted in such a way that it can be integrated into their problematic thereby facilitating a needed contact with the philosophical tradition

18

which can be a help toward the solution of their own problems.

This should make clear what the discussion of the transcendental method in neo-scholasticism is dealing with. During the last forty years the numbers of neo-scholastics have grown who consider the so-called "transcendental method" the way to reach the goal set by contemporary neo-scholasticism, viz., a response of the scholastic tradition to the contemporary philosophical problematic.

What are the grounds for this expectation? Kant's transcendental position was not a haphazard discovery. It was a result of the intellectual development which distinguishes modern thought from the middle ages. With the accent on methodical specialization and the classification of the special sciences, along with the disregard for a direct and universal relation to reality, the question concerning the unity of the various noetic relations and modes becomes a pressing one. It cannot be answered by referring to the order of reality because this total order is no longer experienced as unproblematically given. Yet the necessity of explaining this total relation consists in the fact that the lack of such an explanation leads to the invalid generalization and absolutization of partial domains and special methods. This constitutes the need for a method which, through a reflection on the various modes of knowledge and relation, determines their properties, demonstrates the validity of their limits and defines them (as far as possible) in relation to the total order (thereby disclosing and clarifying this order). This is, basically, nothing but the transcendental stance as it has been developed in modern philosophy, not only by Kant but by those who followed him.

A thorough and attentive study of Kant's position shows that the transcendental method is by no means restricted to the concrete conclusions of Kant's *Critique of Pure Reason*. The subsequent evolution of philosophy itself indicates that transcendental analysis as such contains the power of pushing beyond incomplete expressions of this method.

A comparison of this position with the philosophical approaches of the scholastic tradition results in the realization that a complete disclosure of the total order of reality is possible from the transcendental point of view. The exponents of the transcendental method in neo-scholasticism attempt to work out a proof of this fact. They show that the faithful pursuit of this method leads not only to answers to questions which are drawn from transcendental reflection, but that these answers are arrived at primarily through a transcendentally grounded metaphysics which agrees in its essentials with the Aristotelian-Thomistic metaphysics. The difference between them basically consists in the fact that this metaphysics is independent of the specific points of view and historical conditions of the ancient and middle ages in its foundations as well as in its results, i.e., it can be understood as such and at the same time be open to the contemporary problematic without succumbing to a non-historical absolutization.

The transcendental stance is sufficiently foundational and universal to be capable of establishing a relation to other philosophical methods. The exponents of the transcendental method in neo-scholasticism can therefore expect that this approach to philosophy directly promotes the task of developing philosophy through the contemporary problematic and thereby achieving the required clarification. This philosophy is at one and the same time a re-development and yet a fresh advancement of the philosophy of the scholastic tradition, such that it attains the fulfillment of the basic problems of scholasticism with regard to theology. The approach to this philosophy, however, is such that it makes possible a fruitful dialogue with contemporary philosophers, to the distinct advantage of both parties.

Not to let our expectations run too high, it must be said that not everyone shares this optimistic point of view. Some regard the entire affair as an unwarranted compromise with modern thought. Others insist that the transcendental turn includes epistemological presuppositions which are irreconcilable with the natural (and traditional) approach to knowledge. These misunderstandings are expressed concretely in the dispute between insight (or the receptive character of the knowledge) and the *a priori* (or the positing character of knowledge). There is also no lack of critics of the concrete procedure, viz., of the development of the proof. Thus an intense discussion of this method has emerged in neo-scholasticism which is still raging and which has already led to the eradication of the original defects and inexact formulations of this method and to the clearer conception of its structure and domain of applicability. It is our belief that a careful reflection of the progress of this discussion would be a fruitful contribution to it. This is the aim of our work.

This treatise, then, will attempt to present the structure of the transcendental approach as it is to be found among its exponents in neo-scholasticism and to examine the most important objections raised against it. It will also serve as an exposition of the publications of the authors dealt with, since a knowledge of the relationships between the various exponents of the transcendental method and of the viewpoints from which they can be understood will help us view the results of their efforts in the proper light, i.e., neither overestimating them nor rejecting them through a misunderstanding.

The individual philosophers discussed here not only make use of the transcendental method, but evaluate the extent of the validity of its procedure. No one philosopher answers all the questions, and taken together they do not all answer all the possible questions. But at least the questions that are answered will help the reader to an understanding of what the transcendental method involves. To some it may seem that the important questions are still to be posed and therefore are not answered here (and are not capable of being answered through the fuller development of what is said here) because to them the problem is more than the problems posed by the philosophers dealt with here. But we also hope to assist such readers by drawing the disputed points into sharper focus and by making it possible for them to understand better the efforts of the exponents of the transcendental method, even if they have no intention of agreeing with them. This would advance the continuing discussion and concrete explanation which is required if philosophy is to attain scientific status.

Only one technical point need be mentioned. The various thinkers dealt with here will be considered in terms of their contribution to the understanding of the structure of the transcendental method. In the presentation of the individual thinkers we shall use the tehnical expressions which they themselves use. Foreign quotations have been translated and, in order to reduce the number of footnotes, have been identified with abbreviated references.

LIST OF ABBREVIATIONS

I–V	J. Maréchal, *Le point de départ de la métaphysique. Leçons sur le développement historique et théorique du problème de la connaissance,* vols. I–V.
Abstr.	J. Maréchal, "Au seuil de la métaphysique: abstraction ou intuition."
Cr.	J. de Vries, *Critica.*
Dyn.	J. Maréchal, "Le dynamisme intellectuel dans la connaissance objective."
EE	A. Marc, *L'être et l'esprit.*
Fin.	G. Isaye, "La finalité de l'intelligence et l'objection kantienne."
Gf.	E. Coreth, *Grundfragen des menschlichen Daseins.*
GW	K. Rahner, *Geist in Welt.*
HH	E. Coreth, "Zum Verhältnis Heideggers zu Hegel."
HK	E. Coreth, *Heidegger und Kant: Kant und die Scholastik heute.*
HW	K. Rahner, *Hörer des Wortes.*
Id.	J. Defever, "Idée de Dieu et existence de Dieu."
Ins.	B. J. F. Lonergan, *Insight: A Study of Human Understanding.*
IT	A. Grégoire, *Immanence et transcendance.*
Jug.	J. Maréchal, "Jugement 'scolastique' concernant la racine de l'agnosticisme kantien."
MA	E. Coreth, "Metaphysik als Aufgabe."
MD	A. Marc, *Méthode et dialectique.*
Mel.	*Mélanges Joseph Maréchal.* I: Oeuvres; II: Homages.
MK	M. Casula, *Maréchal e Kant.*
MO	J. B. Lotz, *Metaphysica operationis humanae methodo transcendentali explicata.*

Mp.   E. Coreth, *Metaphysik*.
Pr.   J. Defever, "La preuve réelle de Dieu."
Prem.   J. Maréchal, "Le point de départ de la métaphysique. Première rédaction."
Priv.   G. Isaye, "Le privilège de la métaphysique."
Ret.   G. Isaye, "La justification critique par retorsion."
Sent.   J. Maréchal, "A propos du sentiment de presence chez les profanes et les mystiques."
US   J. de Vries, "Urteilsanalyse und Seinserkenntnis."
Ver.   A. Pechhacker, "Vérités de fait—vérités éternelles."
Wd.   E. Wingendorf, "Das Dynamische in der menschlichen Erkenntnis."

PART ONE

THE ADOPTION OF THE TRANSCENDENTAL METHOD BY JOSEPH MARÉCHAL

It is impossible to think of the transcendental method in neo-scholasticism without mentioning Joseph Maréchal (1878–1944), and rightly so. He was the first member of that school of thought deliberately to adopt the transcendental method as a fruitful tool for the aims of scholastic philosophy. It is true that he had sympathetic contemporaries, such as Pierre Rousselot (1878–1915),[1] and was indebted to Pierre Scheuer

[1] G. van Riet, *L'Epistémologie thomiste,* Louvain, 1946, pp. 301–313. The similarities between these two thinkers can be explained through their common dependence on Maurice Blondel. Rousselot was thoroughly caught up in the metaphysics of knowledge. He did not apply the transcendental method as such.

(1872–1957)[2] for some important ideas, but Maréchal was the first to see the connections between the Thomistic metaphysics of knowledge and transcendental philosophy. Furthermore, he was able to develop the transcendental method to such an extent that it served as a means of demonstrating these connections, thus overcoming deficiencies in Kant and the idealists with their own method. This is the aim of his five volume work, *Le point de départ de la métaphysique: Leçons sur le développement historique et théorique du problème de la connaissance.*[3] This work gave such a thorough and fundamental examination of the transcendental method and its connections with the Thomistic metaphysics of knowledge that it became the immediate focus of attention, either arousing enthusiastic acceptance, acting as a stimulus for other fruitful developments or meeting with bitter criticism. This is the origin of what will be discussed in this book.

[2] A brief selection of some of his basic ideas can be found under the title "Notes de métaphysique," *Nouvelle Revue Théologique,* vol. 53 (1926), pp. 329–334, 447–451, 510–525. These thoughts on the nature of metaphysics, the apriority and finality of reason and the meaning of the principle of identity are fundamental for Maréchal. However, we shall not take up the question of dependency here. Cf. the testimony by G. Isaye in *Nouvelle Revue Théologique,* vol. 79 (1957), pp. 798–815. The pages following (817–827) present some heretofore unpublished texts.

[3] Cahier I: *De l'antiquité à la fin du moyen âge: la critique ancienne de la connaissance* (1922, 1927, 1944); cahier II: *Le conflit du rationalisme et de l'empirisme dans la philosophie moderne avant Kant* (1923, 1942, 1944); cahier III: *La critique de Kant* (1923, 1942, 1944); cahier IV: *Par dela le kantisme: Vers l'idéalisme absolu* (posthumously in 1947); cahier V: *Le thomisme devant la philosophie critique* (1926, 1949); cahier VI: *Les épistémologies contemporaines* was planned but was never published.

1. MARÉCHAL'S OBJECTIVES

THE ABSOLUTE AFFIRMATION OF BEING
AS THE STARTING POINT OF METAPHYSICS

Maréchal insisted that he was not engaged in constructing a traditional, detailed theory of knowledge (vols. I and II). His primary concern is clearly expressed in the title: *Le point de départ de la métaphysique—The Starting Point of Metaphysics.* This starting point is the derived metaphysical affirmation of being (I, p. 11; V, p. 13). The problem of the derivation of this affirmation, of course, is tightly linked with most of the other fundamental epistemological questions, but they are only dealt with insofar as they elucidate the possibility of the metaphysical affirmation of being (V, p. 184). In order to understand properly how this problem is posed, we must bear in mind how Maréchal conceives metaphysics. He defines metaphysics, along with Aristotle, as "the human science of the absolute" (Prem., p. 289).[4] "Following the definition of Aristotle, which Thomas refers to time and again, the object of metaphysics is being (*l'être*) as being, *ens in quantum ens,* being without regard to this or that difference, being taken in such generality that it excludes no other being. Since the logical properties of generality and necessity are correlative, when dealing with perfect, all-encompassing being [*l'être*], we are dealing with unlimited, necessary being as such, or, in other words, with the absolute of being" (Abstr., p. 104).[5] "*Per*

[4] *Le point de départ de la métaphysique, première rédaction,* appeared in 1927 in Louvain. Extracts were published in *Mélanges Joseph Maréchal,* vol. I, Bruxelles-Paris, 1950, pp. 288–298.
[5] "Au seuil de la métaphysique: abstraction ou intuition," *Revue néoscolastique de philosophie,* vol. 31 (1929), pp. 27–52, 121–147, 309–342 (reprinted in Mel. I, pp. 102–180).

definitionem, those objects are called metaphysical which have the absolute properties of generality and necessity" (*ibid.*). Metaphysics, for Maréchal, is always understood as an "objective, noumenal science which excludes the contingent and unique as contingent and unique from its formal object, but which admits contingent and unique objects under its material object, only, however, insofar as they are invested with a generality and necessity which grounds them in the wholly unconditioned absolute" (Abstr., p. 117).

This does not mean that he restricts the nature of metaphysics to the super-sensible or that he is concerned only with separated realities, but rather that everything must be viewed in relation to the ultimate, non-relative order of being, and in the last analysis to the ultimate, unlimited ground of this order. "An object is metaphysical only through its implicit relationship to absolutely absolute being [*l'être absolument absolu*], or, in other words, only in this way does it convey the absolute properties of what is intelligible, or a 'noumenon' " (Abstr., p. 115).

According to Maréchal, we do not attain this absolute order by the mere application of metaphysical principles to the given if the given is not already contained in an implicit relationship to the ultimate order and affirmed as such. This application, therefore, "presupposes that the term to be subsumed is already constituted as an 'intelligible object,' is, in its relationship to being, already homogeneous to the principle which we wish to apply to it" (Abstr., p. 122). If this were not so we would be faced with the unjustified transposition from one order to another, for the middle term of the syllogism would not be taken in the same sense. We could not reach the metaphysical order if the starting point, what is immediately given, were not already present in this order and if it were not understood and affirmed that the relation to the ultimate order, to the absolute of being, is already contained in it. Maréchal must be approached in this way, because the starting point of metaphysics for him lies in the possibilities of affirming an object in terms of the ultimate order—the order of being.

THE VINDICATION OF THE AFFIRMATION OF BEING

We are, however, confronted with data which indicate a certain relativity to our knowledge and which would seem to call into question the relationship of our affirmation of an object to the absolute order of being. The reality of the objects of knowledge is not itself the object of direct and immediate perception, and only in this way could the possibility of deception and error be explained (Sent., pp. 76ff.).[6] Our knowledge is directed to sensible experience, but the viewpoint under which our senses are related to reality is extremely relative. Is, then, metaphysics at all possible (Abstr., p. 103)? Is it not the case that knowledge is closed off from the realm of the absolute? Would not knowledge break up into antinomies and fall into a multitude of contradictory systems the moment it left the realm of experience?

Some theories of knowledge try to make allowances for these factors through a uniform explanation of knowledge. They specify the range of knowledge in conformity to the theories which they propose, but by ignoring certain characteristics of knowledge through their own prejudiced interpretations, they open the door to opposing theories of knowledge. For example, empiricism defines knowledge in such a way that our relationship with reality is possible only through the senses, Consequently, anything which cannot be explained through the data of the senses cannnot be accepted as valid knowledge. Ontological rationalism tries to make room for hyper-empirical elements of knowledge which necessarily force themselves upon us, and this eventually leads not only to a distrust of experience but eventually also any such hyper-empirical elements of knowledge. Kant attempted to resolve this contradiction by analyzing the necessary structural elements of the constitution

6 "A propos du sentiment de présence chez les profanes et les mystiques," *Revue des questions scientifiques,* vol. 64 (1908), pp. 527–563, and vol. 65 (1909), pp. 219–249, 376–426 (reprinted in *Études sur la psychologie des mystiques,* vol. I, 1924, pp. 69–179), ET *Studies in the Psychology of the Mystics,* New York, 1966.

of knowledge. He developed a theory of knowing which, despite the fundamental importance of sense experience, demonstrated the possibility of universal knowledge which could not be completely explained through the data of the senses. However, this was achieved only at the price of setting a yardstick to all human knowledge, reducing its value to the realm of possible experience. His conclusion is that theoretical knowledge is not related to the absolute order of being, the noumenal realm, but only to the relative, phenomenal realm. This theory also has its inner tensions, and from the effort to resolve them stems idealism. This ultimately tends toward an inadequate monism of spirit which cannot do full justice to the particulars given in knowledge.

"We must admit that the natural viewpoint for human reason, more fundamental than the deceptive divisions suggested by abstraction, is that of absolute affirmation" (Prem., p. 291). But is this valid? What is the meaning of the affirmation performed in knowing? Does the acknowledgement of being possess an absolute signification or, basically, only a purely phenomenal or relative one? (Cf. Abstr., p. 292.)

> 1. "Granted that the absolute affirmation of the object, i.e., metaphysical affirmation, reflects a natural and basic state of the human mind, why do philosophers demand a critical vindication of this basic affirmation? Or in other words, how does the critical problem originate?"
> 2. "To what degree is such a vindication possible? Or in other words, can the critical problem of knowledge be solved?"

THE MODES OF VINDICATION

How does Maréchal propose to answer these questions? The demonstration of the vindication of the affirmation of being could be worked out in the four following ways:

(1) In terms of the metaphysical "classical critique" (I, pp. 23–29, 51–92; V, pp. 49–51, 81–99). This operates in two ways: (a) It vindicates the metaphysical affirmation of

being by showing that the very doubt about its vindication presupposes its validity. Such retorsion demonstrates that the validity of the affirmation of being is an absolute necessity for every kind of intellectual knowing. (b) It solves the difficulties which emerge from the doubt concerning the vindication of the affirmation of being by developing a differentiated metaphysics which reconciles the antinomies of the one and the many and of motion.

(2) Whereas the first way indirectly arrives at the possibility of the affirmation of being from the necessity of its vindication, the second way tries to prove the fact of a critically vindicated affirmation of being directly. This *direct critique* does not exclude reflection, rather it seeks to isolate all those elements of the affirmation of being in reflection which lend a relativity to knowledge. It completely ignores any knowledge of things different from ourselves and of the self conceived as a substance, concentrating rather on the immediate and evident data of consciousness. The immediate openness of the structure and reality of our own act of knowing vindicates the value of our knowledge of this act. The same goes for the direct insight into the necessary and essential interrelationships between the contents immediately given, but since these relations are themselves grounded in the contents and are seen to be absolutely necessary (e.g., the metaphysical principle of causality), their validity is not concluded from what is immediately given. Gradually, one can discover all that is required for the explanation of the contingent act and structure of consciousness. Through this reconstruction of the elements of natural knowledge, our knowledge of these elements is critically vindicated and we begin to evolve a differentiated metaphysics.[7] This direct way is vitally dependent upon what is objectively evident as an insight into what is directly given and the function of such evidence as the ground of the justification of the absolute affirmation of what is given.

(3) The *historico-comparative* way investigates particular epistemological attitudes and seeks to understand their unique

[7] This way is followed consistently and ingeniously by J. de Vries in *Critica*, Freiburg i. Br., 1954.

positions in the history of ideas. It tries to determine to what exent the viewpoints of thinkers can be understood in terms of the historical and personal conditions in which they found themselves. It also attempts to show which positions (which are explainable only through the necessity of the subject itself and the insight of the thinkers into reality) have been points of convergence for philosophical development throughout the course of history. This is how Maréchal, especially in the first four volumes of his work, *Le point de départ de la métaphysique,* tries to show how the aristotelian defense of metaphysical affirmation, as a "classical critique," emerged as the most comprehensive solution to the epistemological discussions of antiquity and was further developed in the Thomistic metaphysics of knowledge. He also indicates the background against which the struggle in modern philosophy between empiricism and rationalism can be understood, showing how Kant was once again on the way to a harmonized view of knowledge. Since, of course, further developments were to lead to idealism, Kant did not attain this goal—but he indicated the way.

(4) A *critico-systematic* examination of insufficient theories of knowledge exposes the unresolved antinomies implicit in them. The imbalance of a theory, then, can be demonstrated and resolved in terms of the theory's own principles. In the fifth volume of his work, Maréchal tries to show that it is only because of inconsistencies and unresolved antinomies that Kant, by means of the transcendental method, reaches a phenomenalism that excludes the theoretical vindication of metaphysical affirmation. If, however, the transcendental method is logically applied, the vindication of the metaphysical affirmation of being is shown to be the very condition for the possibility of experiential knowledge, and thus Kant is overcome with his own premises and with his own method.

AN ASSESSMENT OF THE VARIOUS WAYS

How does Maréchal evaluate these ways? (1) The method employed in the classical critique is objectively sufficient as a reflection of the natural way in which we think, but it has certain drawbacks vis-à-vis the contemporary philosophical situation: (a) Retorsion demonstrates the fact that we cannot apprehend an object without implicitly affirming the absolute order of being. This necessity, however, is only shown to be necessarily implied; it is not yet explained. This is saying a lot, but more can be expected. "If we submit to the necessity of affirmation, we can also hope to know more exactly the rational basis for this necessity. Or, to be more precise, we are perhaps only prepared to admit the necessity of absolute affirmation if we can first know its causes. Modern critical philosophy is dedicated to this more acute rational vindication. Within its historical context . . . the modern critique of knowledge concentrates on discovering the ground for the objective validity of the *a priori* conditions which regulate the incidence of objectified thought" (Prem., p. 292). (b) If an explanation is presupposed for the foundation of the metaphysical explanation of knowledge, i.e., for the proof of the vindication of the metaphysical affirmation of being, then the explanation founded on the affirmation of being is groundless. Since it proceeds metaphysically from the very beginning, a common basis is lacking for fruitful confrontation with other theories of knowledge.

(2) The same can be said with reference to the way which seeks the vindication of fundamental truths in immediate evidence. Marechal expressly admits: "In the last analysis, the attainment of metaphysical truth takes place by means of direct, objective evidence" (I, p. 12). But we must avoid the simple reference to evidence in grounding the assertions which we raise against other theories of knowledge. Evidence can, of course, give us certainty in the vindication of assertions, but it is far from advantageous in discussions with others, for many philosophers, as history shows us, have referred to what is evident setting up opposing views. Others reject evidence altogether, or see it in some other function than the apprehension of reality (I, p. 12f.). Therefore, a way must be found to overcome the relativization of evidence as an ultimate criterion of truth, and in a way that is accessible to those theories of knowledge which reject or relativize evidence in their explana-

tions of knowledge. Ultimately, we must apply the principle: "We do not really overcome an error until we can point to a contradiction" (I, p. 13). At the very beginning of the vindication of knowledge, false interpretations of knowledge must necessarily be corrected, but also from the very beginning, a theory of knowledge must be striving toward an explanation of knowledge and not merely toward a confirmation of what can be claimed as vindicated knowledge through the proof of immediate evidence. We can thus agree with the opinion of B. Jansen when he writes: "Maréchal, like Aristotle, the philosopher of sound human understanding, recognizes objective evidence from the start, grounded in things, as the ultimate norm of truth. Objects, seen in their calm, impersonal light, are real for him also. What he wants is a reflective demonstration of this validation of the criterion of science, the scientific foundation of its claim to validity, an exposition of the conditions and laws of the intelligible light which emerges in the mind and produces the mysterious image."[8]

(3) This is where Maréchal extends his historical and systematic investigations. The aim of these investigations is to demonstrate the vindication of metaphysical affirmation, which can be done by referring to what is evident (the direct critique) or by showing the undeniable necessity of its acceptance (in the indirect critique, through retorsion). The proof, however, ought to take epistemological viewpoints into consideration which seek more than what the direct critique or retorsion can offer. Such an historico-comparative investigation seeks to clarify the essential features of positions on the problem of knowledge and to discover their logical premises (I, p. 7). This critical comparison brings out the insights which are valid, because "there is no absolute error. Every error contains a part of the truth" (II, p. 245). The sources of partial conceptions and erroneous interpretations of knowledge also gain clarity, for one-sided viewpoints lead to contradictory positions and develop into the dialectic which lies beneath the historical succession of systems (II, p. 8). It would be correct to say

8 B. Jansen, "Transzendentale Methode und thomistische Erkenntnismetaphysik," *Scholastik,* vol. 3 (1928), pp. 341–368, 354f.

that Maréchal "seeks the solution to the general problem of objective knowledge, i.e., the vindication of our absolute affirmation of objects in the context of the history of epistemological systems" (Prem., p. 296). This is precisely the way in which Maréchal offers an historical proof for the Aristotelian-Thomistic theory of knowledge. He shows that it provides a solution whose rejection leads to a disintegration into contradictory theories of knowledge. This also prepares the way for an insight into the actual relations which form the object of systematic investigation.

(4) The critico-systematic investigation demonstrates the vindication of the affirmation of being by beginning with the principles of theories of knowledge which argue against such a vindication, accepting their viewpoint insofar as it is valid, and overcoming their bias and false interpretation on their own terms. Since the historical examination has put forth Kant as the chief opponent to the affirmation of being, Maréchal begins with him. He accepts the procedure of the transcendental analysis of object-oriented consciousness and asks, "Why, despite the lack of an intellectual intuition of objects, is this incomplete knowledge able to pose an object over and against the subject at the level of intellectual knowledge?" (Abstr., p. 177). Transcendental reflection, first of all, relates "the conceived object to various *a priori* rules which constitute it in its reality in consciousness" (V, p. 507). The deduction goes on to show which of these *a priori* conditions of possibility are indispensible for the consciousness of an object (V, p. 98). Kant is overcome by showing that the valid metaphysical affirmation of being is a constitutive condition of the possibility of every object of thought. "We must consider the object in its entirety [*intégralement*], as it is immediately given to consciousness, i.e., not merely as an abstract and rigid 'form,' but as the actualization of a possibility—as movement" (Prem., p. 294) and "not only as a movement already linked with the inchangeable, but a self-perfecting movement, as self-moving movement. The whole of metaphysics springs from this concrete givenness and its critical validation" (Prem., p. 295). The analysis of this aspect of knowledge ultimately leads to the demonstration of the dynamic

relationship between knowing and the absolute order of being, and, further, to the awareness that this relationship is fundamental for the human consciousness of objects. "Through the deduction of the *a priori* conditions of object-oriented thought, considered in terms of the dynamism which is essential to it, we reach the very starting point of metaphysics" (Prem., p. 295). For, "critical deduction furnishes us with the '*a priori* conditions of objective thought.' If these are at all determined through the co-efficiency of the absolute, then they become 'constitutive forms of whatever is' " (Prem., p. 296). Kantian agnosticism is not only not irrefutable, it is refutable through its own principles (V, pp. 33f.). This analysis of knowledge and the vindication of the absolute affirmation of being set up "many points of contact . . . between the scholastic theory of abstraction and the significant advances of modern philosophy" (Abstr., p. 178), which prepares the way for fruitful dialogue and discussion, because the critical problem, from the start, aims at the clarification of knowledge without first having to presuppose the validity of metaphysical explanation.

Now, let us turn to these investigations of Maréchal. We shall particularly emphasize those points which will help us understand his evaluation of the transcendental method. Although we shall proceed historically for the most part, in correspondence to the ever deeper crystalization of the transcendental approach in Maréchal's writings through the course of his life, the aim of our work is not to give a complete historical presentation of his thought.

The Basic Framework
of Maréchal's Thought

2. THE PREPARATION OF THE FUNDAMENTAL CONCEPTS

GIVENNESS AS A PRESUPPOSITION

In a work of Maréchal's appearing in 1908 and 1909 on the problem of the givenness of reality,[9] we find him using a notion which is fundamental for his later epistemological studies, i.e., that our knowledge basically rests upon a dynamic conjunction with the absolute. According to A. Milet,[10] this was Maréchal's prime concern in this early work, the main theme being nothing but a convenient means. He takes up the problem of the "truth of sense knowledge," examines the various attempts at a solution and shows their insufficiency. Judgment, which affirms the reality of an object in experience, can neither be considered as a valid syllogistic proposition, nor as the psychological terminus of a certain grouping of representations, nor as the exclusive result of the drive of affective tendencies. All of these attempts cannot succeed because they have posed the problem incorrectly, viz., as the question about the bridge leading from the ideal to the real, from doubtful to certain affirmation, from subjective experience to the objective knowledge of reality. Actually it is the other way around: "We must put the real, affirmation and objectivity forward as fundamental [*fait primitif*] and ask how they can pass into the non-real, doubt and subjectivity. Here, in conjunction with a number of modern psychologists and under the stamp of experience, we find (almost point for point, but not completely analyzed) the viewpoint of the

9 See footnote 6.
10 "Les premiers ecrits philosophiques de P. Maréchal," Mel. I. pp. 23–46, 25.

38

old Thomistic psychology" (Sent., p. 118). Maréchal holds that we must distinguish between the content of a representation [*contenu*] (which is also present in deceptions) and the character of reality [*caractère réel*], which is given to what is represented through the proposition. The apprehension of the character of reality, however, cannot simply be derived from the formal determinations of the noetic image. We must also take the dynamic orientation of reason into consideration, which explains the relationship between knowledge and reality as well as the formal determinations of the content of knowledge as constituted through the active assimiliation of what is given to the senses. Maréchal is seeking here to do away with the vain attempts at constructing the whole of knowledge from secondary and partial elements of knowledge by showing that they truly are secondary and therefore presuppose the whole—the primary elements of knowledge. The primary element is the absolute affirmation of being, which is objective and related to what is real. This orientation of reason admits what is sensibly given as the material of affirmation and goes on to affirm it in accordance with the fundamental principle of intellection—the principle of contradiction. Insofar as it converges toward a total unity of the whole of knowledge, it is asserted as real, and insofar as it diverges from it, as unreal. Through the power of the principle of contradiction to order and divide, we are led to a differentiation and classification of the secondary elements of knowledge, viz., to the distinction between reality and appearance, certainty and doubt (Sent., pp. 121f.).

Although this work is primarily concerned with a clarification of psychological data, viz., the experience of reality, still there are notions here which are fundamental to Maréchal's later works, e.g., the distinction between content and reality, which later recurs as the distinction between form and act, between a formally static and a dynamic conception of knowledge; the dynamic conception according to which the ultimate ground of affirmation is seen as the orientation of reason toward the absolute order (ultimately toward God); the comprehensive explanation of the nature of the content of the noetic image which brings the object of representation through an immanent reconstruction of the object from what is sensibly given, actuated by the dynamism of the intellect.[11]

KANT'S BASIC ERROR

Maréchal used these reflections in his confrontation with Kant and developed them further in a paper written in 1914 which criticized the starting point of Kantian agnosticism in terms of scholastic philosophy,[12] and in the first edition (*Prem*) of *Le point de départ de la métaphysique,* published in 1917.

The assessment of Kant, put in thesis form, would be: "Kantian agnosticism arises from certain basic defects in the *Critique* itself" (Jug., p. 273). The defect could be put this way: "Kant deceives himself by accepting only the pure synthesis of what is empirically given in the activity of the mind" (Jug., p. 274). Maréchal would insist rather that "the human intellect is, at one and the same time, an empirical faculty and a possibility for the absolute. The author of the *Critique of Pure Reason* could not fully grasp this second point" (Jug., p. 274). To show this, Maréchal approaches judgment—"the only activity of our intellect in which 'objects' of knowledge are represented to us" (Jug., p. 274)—from the dual viewpoint of absolute unity (which is expressed in each judgment) and absolute affirmation (which is assumed in each judgment). Maréchal agrees with Kant that each judgment expresses a synthesis of what is sensibly given, but this synthesis is not purely "categorical" in the Kantian sense, i.e., it is not restricted to the universalization of conditions which are related to space and time (Jug., p. 274). Analysis shows that each judgment (as distinguished from mere conceptual representation) intrinsically or expressly refers the categorical synthesis which it produces to being (or reality) in general. Only in this way is the essential characteristic of judgment (to be either true or false) possible. This relation to being breaks beyond the

[11] Cf. G. van Riet, *L'Epistémologie thomiste,* 1946, pp. 269f.

[12] "Jugement 'scolastique' concernant la racine de l'agnosticisme kantien" (Romiley, 1914), first published in Mel. I, pp. 273–287.

restrictive conditions which premiss the Kantian category of "reality"—namely, the localization of what is given in time. This relation also breaks beyond the restrictive conditions of its *terminus ad quem,* for its terminus is absolute reality, i.e., absolute unity (Jug., p. 275). This leads to an analysis of the logical functions which the term "is" symbolizes (Jug., p. 276). The result of this is "that absolute unity enters into the constitution of each judgment as the end-point of a relation determining the multiple as given" (Jug., p. 278). Thus while for Kant absolute unity is nothing but an external condition for the classification of previously constituted objects of consciousness, nothing but a regulative "idea," for Marechal it becomes a constitutive function. "Partial, categorical synthesis can be conceived in the understanding *only* as the relation to a total synthesis, to absolute unity" (Jug., p. 281).

Kant neglected the relationship of "absolute unity" to the form of each judgment because he regarded the act of judgment too exclusively as the "synthesis" of what is given, disregarding the "affirmation" which inevitably accompanies this synthesis and places it in the order of finality. "In effect, the relation of 'synthesis' to absolute reality is particularly evident in 'affirmation' " (Jug., p. 278). Maréchal therefore examines judgment under the viewpoint of affirmation.

Judgment is not only a speculative relationship to the absolute unity of being in which logical truth is already contained, although only materially, but also a kind of attitude (*adopter une attitude*) toward the object, insofar as it is fixed in the order of possible pre-conditions of the activity and insofar as it is "posited" or "affirmed" as the measure of synthetic unity. Only in this way can logical truth be grasped formaliter, "*tamquam cognita in cognoscente*" (Jug., pp. 279, 281).

"Actually, in the judgment, 'this is,' the attribute 'is' is a symbolic transcription of the *primitive, total reaction* of an intelligent subject confronted with something given" (Jug., p. 279). Internal analysis attests to the fact that the intelligent subject does not merely react receptively to objects, but also actively. The word "is" therefore expresses both the intellectual reception to an object and the primal reaction of a striving toward what is given. The heart of this direct, dual relationship lies in the fact that the intellectual subject in activity is directed toward the synthetic character of what is given. The mental reception of what is given, which has become an object in the strict sense, can only be taken as a more or less immanent norm of activity, as the specification of a natural or conscious willing.

"Abstraction," according to the scholastics, or "pure categorical synthesis," is nothing but the awareness of the relationship which naturally occurs in us between the multiplicity of what is concretely given and the formal unity of active tending or willing. The synthesis itself is produced in terms of the principle of finality (Jug., pp. 279f.). The partial ends of striving are ordered under the ultimate, universal end, the natural finality of the knowing subject. Willing, which is the expression of this finality, is not limited to any particular givenness, but it presupposes an end in the positive sense and therefore is related to the absolute final and unconditioned end, being itself, as posited end. This is how the absolute end of the intelligent subject enters into each judgment as a constitutive element (Jug., p. 280). "Partial or categorical synthesis is possible as affirmation only insofar as it fixes it as a goal that is essentially subordinated to the absolute goal" (Jug., p. 281). "Pure being—or the absolute—is thus comprehended in every judgment as universal unity and posited as absolute end" (Jug., p. 282).

Kant's failures now become more undestandable. The too radical separation of phenomenon and noumenon leads to agnosticism, i.e., to the limitation of objective value to objects of experience. An underestimation of the role which active finalty plays in the constitution of the object itself leads to the radical phenomenalism of theoretical reason (Jug., p. 282).

If these deficiencies can be avoided, theoretical reason—the faculty which constitutes objective consciousness—not only can attain the absolute, but inevitably attains it. This allows us to avoid relativism without depending upon intellectual intuition in the strict sense. If, however, we were to exclude finality from theoretical reason, this arbitrary limitation would make it impossible for it to attain absolute being and it would thus cease to constitute objective knowledge (Jug., p. 283).

Maréchal goes on to show that this is the fundamental solution to the problem of knowledge. Since the orientation toward the absolute (which is an element of every judgment) is not merely thought, but affirmed, completed and actively introduced into the ordering of ends which initiate the act, the problem of knowledge cannot be reduced to mere appearance. The distinction between absolute and phenomenon loses its meaning in the finality of activity (Jug., p.284). Reflecting back, we can see how the basic notions which we encountered in the work by Maréchal referred to earlier (Sent.) were used here for a confrontation with Kant. He also introduces several notions which are significant in his later works: the analysis of the constitutive elements of every object of knowledge through an analysis of judgment; emphasis on the dynamic aspect of judgment as opposed to the static; the close connection between knowing and willing (without confusing the two), since the dynamism of the intellect is a natural striving; the demonstration that the orientation toward the absolute supports every judgment, even one that would deny this; the derivation of the fundamental, real value of knowledge from the fact that in the order of active finality the end which determines actuation must be real and that the partial end must be subordinated to the final end.

THE VINDICATION OF KANT

This view of Kant is then developed into a positive confrontation with him. We have already dealt with the basis of this approach in the outline completed in 1917 (Prem.). By means of historical and theoretical investigations, Maréchal sought to reach this simple conclusion: "Proceeding from a point of view which is peculiar to the whole modern critique, i.e., from the point of view of 'appearance,' we feel that this starting point must be validated and that we must establish that 'objective appearance' can only be determined in relation to an absolute.

The viewpoint of pure appearance is evidently artificial and full of contradiction" (Prem., p. 291). The completion of this plan is found within the conceptual framework with which we have already become familiar, but the critique of Kant's position is not conducted externally, rather the primary aim is an internal critique of his procedure. Several points should be emphasized in this connection: (1) He tries, right from the very beginning, not only to demonstrate the inevitability of the validity of knowledge, but also to link this demonstration with an elucidation of knowledge which (a) is necessarily imposed, (b) does not assume any metaphysical presuppositions before the vindication of the absolute affirmation of being is made evident, but rather is entirely grounded on the direct data of consciousness and their structural relationships, and (c) opens the way for the acceptance of the necessity of the absolute affirmation of being as a constitutive element of the consciousness of objects, implying the utter untenability of pure phenomenalism (Prem., pp. 288, 292f.).

(2) The object of thought is considered primarily as appearance (with no other necessary predicates attributed to it as such), the necessity of which turns out to be a condition for the possibility of each and every object of thought as such (Prem., p. 293).

(3) The object of thought is studied in terms of the *a priori* conditions which determine the occurrence of objectified thought (Prem., pp. 292f.).

(4) "The conditions of possibility which determine the essential structure of the object of thought *a priori* are precisely what we term 'faculties of knowledge' " (Prem., p. 293). These faculties are not understood primarily in an ontological sense, rather only as the demonstrated *a priori* determinations of objective consciousness.

(5) The starting point, as with Kant, is the consciousness of objects as given directly. However, in contrast with Kant, this is considered universally, viz., not as abstract, rigid form, but as act—as the actualization of a potentiality (Prem., p. 294). Here again, judgment is not only considered as the moment of

44

synthesis, i.e., of the relation of the matter of judment to the absolute unity of thought (later called "concretive synthesis" by Maréchal; cf. V., p. 520; Prem., p. 289), but as the transcendental moment of affirmation, i.e., of the relation of the matter of judgment to the absolute end of activity (later called "objective synthesis"; cf. V., p. 520; Prem., p. 289).

(6) The immediate structure of knowledge indicates that the power to think objects is not intuitive. This suggests that a non-intuitive power, which is nevertheless confronted with objects, is not possible if it is not the fruit of a dynamic orientation toward the absolute of being, as involved in the thinking of every object and which, when in act, can only lead to what is real (Prem., p. 295).

(7) Not only is the absolute affirmation of being vindicated with one stroke through this derivation (transcendental deduction), but this also explains the occurence of knowledge (Prem., p. 295).

(8) Critical deduction can be extended to metaphysical deduction, for since the a priori conditions for the possibility of objective knowledge, as demonstrated through critical deduction, contain an absolute co-efficient, they yield absolute forms of being. This furnishes the bare framework of metaphysics and anticipates the more precise formulation which follows (Prem., p. 296).

The main point of the five volume work, especially the fifth volume, is clearly expressed viz., the overthrow of Kant's phenomenalism by showing, by means of Kant's method, that the phenomenal object is absolutely impossible unless it is contained in a knowledge which transcends the phenomenal level.

In conclusion, Maréchal ennumerates the elements of the metaphysics which naturally result from the completion of the critical reflections which he has worked out. Thus the critical vindication of the constitutive function of the absolute affirmation of being in knowledge indicates that an empirical content is contained in the proper object of the understanding, which can be objectified only if it exhibits the character of a partial end subordinated to the ultimate and absolute end. This means that the empirically given object, the *"quidditas rerum materialium,"* is affirmed as a contingent object through a necessary relation to absolute being. Consequently, objective knowledge must contain the following elements:

(1) The *absolute,* God, is implicitly given in every object as the transcendental focal point of the relationship which constitutes every object (corresponding to the scholastic notion of knowledge by analogy).

(2) The objects which we affirm are *contingent* and related to absolute being through a multitude of objective relations (metaphysical contingency in scholasticism). These relations are distinguishable in knowledge through the diversity of the empirical element (intentional function of the empirical element in direct knowledge).

(3) The universal *analogy* of being is given in the tension between the relational terms which constitute objects as such.

(4) Being is manifested as objective only in the inner, essential finality of the object. This finality, considered in itself, is just as unlimited as being itself and therefore signifies the transcendental *finality* of being (the *"bonum"* of scholasticism).

(5) Being is given only as objective, i.e., as the terminus of a relation of logical truth. The possible extension of the relation of logical truth, however, is no less than the infinite extension of being. This yields the transcendental "truth" of being (the *"verum"* of scholasticism).

(6) Finally, by extending the deduction to the attributes which accompany everything which is materially given to objective consciousness, we arrive at the fundamental condition for the unique relativity of subject and object—*quantity.*

With this basis, Maréchal derives the complete system of the categories of being. It is also possible to develop a theory of the empirical sciences which would permit the application of this metaphysics to what is empirically given (Prem., pp. 296–298).

Maréchal's aims and purposes, as we have discussed them so far, find their full development in his five-volume work, *Le point de départ de la métaphysique.* Let us turn now to this, Maréchal's main work. Since some of the ideas in this work were clarified in later articles, we shall also refer to these articles, showing how the idea and technique of the transcendental method present themselves.

3. THE FOUNDATION FROM THE VIEWPOINT OF HISTORY

The method of the first four volumes is essentially historico-comparative. They attempt to show how the "classical critique of knowledge," i.e., the Aristotelian-Thomistic theory of knowledge, offers an harmonious and balanced solution to the problems which arise from the complexity of human knowledge (I). Further, Maréchal shows how the dissolution of this theory of knowledge degenerated into the antinomies of nominalism in the late middle ages, viz., on the one hand between sensibility and discursive understanding (I, p. 245) and on the other hand between discursive understanding and reason as the faculty of transcendental being (I, p. 247). These antinomies provide the rationale for the epistemological struggles of modern philosophy and the tension between empiricism and ontological rationalism which prevailed in pre-Kantian philosophy (II). Kant, it is true, sought to overcome this tension, but since he was so immersed in the general presuppositions of his predecessors he only succeeded in solving the first of the two antinomies (despite several indications of going beyond this) (III). The overcoming of these limits is thus already prepared for in Kant's own late writings and is completed in the movement from Kant to German idealism, above all in Fichte (IV). However, all things considered, the synthesis cannot be considered to have fully succeeded here. The fifth volume seeks to recapture this synthesis (which can be found in its essentials in the Aristotelian-Thomistic theory of knowledge) through a more critico-systematic method, with specific reference to the modern mode of inquiry. Thus the Thomistic metaphysics of knowledge is developed by transposing it into the form in which Kant would have posed the problem, and it is developed from Kant's starting point and with his transcendental-philosophical method.

In order to clarify and develop the main points of this work, Maréchal wrote several articles after its publication. "Le dynamisme intellectuel dans la connaissance objective"[13] took up an objection against the fifth volume by Roland-Gosselin and attempted to show, in Thomistic terminology, that a purely static and formalistic conception of the noetic image, the "species," does not suffice. In order to understand the relation to objects in knowledge, reference must be made to the natural orientation of the human intellect to the ultimate end. This is the only way in which there can be a confrontation with an object, viz., as a partial end. The knowledge of objects, of course, is specified through the species, but without the dynamic element of the contrast between object and subject is inexplicable.

A lecture by Maréchal in 1928, "Au seuil de la métaphysique: Abstraction ou Intuition" (Abstr.), developed the dynamism of knowledge as a solution to the problem: whether sensible experience attains metaphysics immediately, or not. If it does, how can there be a problem about the foundations of metaphysics? If not, how do we come to a metaphysics? Maréchal particularly examines the objection that he has excluded any kind of intuition and has simply "postulated" dynamism. The basis of dynamism, for Maréchal, is precisely an inner experience, the immediate, reflective awareness of the unique "becoming" which characterizes knowledge.

His contribution to the Geyser-Festschrift[14] placed dynamism between two extremes: Edmund Husserl, who, in his early writings, inclined toward a rather static and formal conception, and Maurice Blondel, whom he regards as too voluntaristic. A

[13] *Revue néoscolastique de philosophie*, vol. 28 (1927), pp. 137–165 (reprinted in Mel. I, pp. 75–101).

[14] "Phénoménologie pure ou philosophie de l'action?," *Philosophie Perennis*, Regensburg, 1930, vol. I, pp. 377–400 (reprinted in Mel. I, pp. 181–206).

response to Edouard Le Roy[15] examines the dynamism of knowledge in order to explain our knowledge of God and to show how this leads to a realist solution to the idealist position. Dynamism is not creative, but self-assimilative. The horizon of the divine (l'horizon du divin), of which God himself is the condition of possibility, is already revealed in the immanence of the act. An article[16] published with the German translation of the fourth volume, which had not yet appeared at that time. He shows how, in the writings of Kant, the tension between the predominant static-formal consideration of knowledge and certain conflicting statements converge toward a more and more dynamic view. Maréchal here seeks to show that the development of the transcendental method from the viewpoint of dynamism is not foreign to this method but rather lies in the very lines of its development. We find certain indications of this idea already in Kant, and in Fichte they reach their full completion. How then does the transcendental method function in these works? To show how, let us examine several important notions: the classical critique of knowledge, the turn toward the subject in modern philosophy, the transcendental method of his fifth volume by Wingendorf[17] attempted to fill in the gap according to Kant and Fichte, the *a priori* and the dynamism of knowledge in the Thomistic metaphysics of knowledge and finally the transcendental deduction of the metaphysical affirmation of being.

THE METAPHYSICAL CRITIQUE
OF KNOWLEDGE

The "classical critique of knowledge," the solution to the problem of knowledge according to Aristotle and Thomas, consists

[15] " 'Le problème de dieu' d'après M. Edouard Le Roy," *Nouvelle Revue Théologique,* vol. 58 (1931), pp. 193–216, 289–316 (reprinted in Mel. I, pp. 207–259).

[16] "L'aspect dynamique de la méthode transcendentale chez Kant," *Revue néoscolastique de philosophie,* vol. 42 (1959), pp. 341–384.

[17] Engelbert Wingendorf, *Das Dynamische in der menschlichen Erkenntnis,* Bonn, vol. I (1939), vol. II (1940).

basically of two aspects: (1) a general theory of affirmation as the absolute positing of being, and (2) an ontological critique of the constitution of absolute affirmation. Here especially we find the critical function which is open to metaphysics (I, pp. 45f., 254).

The *general theory of affirmation,* according to Maréchal, corresponds "basically to what, in Kantian terms, would be called a 'transcendental proof' of absolute affirmation. It transcends the Kantian 'transcendental proof' only insofar as it achieves the absolute of the object" (I, p. 254). In other words, it achieves the "fundamental identity: being is—i.e., being (the object of thought) is (belongs to the absolute realm of being)" (Prem., p. 292). Kant would see it differently, interpreting the identity this way: "being (the object of thought) is (as phenomenal reality)" (Prem., p. 293). The first principle (the principle of excluded contradiction, or identity; cf., I, p. 23) is set up as the basis because any form of knowledge which can be brought under judgment through the first principle is consequently related to the absolute of being. Pure relativity in knowledge is excluded by virtue of the necessity expressed in the first principle (I, p. 87). The first principle itself can in no way be objectively demonstrated—by the very fact that it is first. However, its necessity can be definitely shown for each knowing subject. Thus, the first principle is not capable of an analytic, but only of a transcendental proof (I, p. 87).

Maréchal conceives the fundamental idea of this transcendental proof, as found in Aristotle and Thomas, in the following way (I, pp. 254f.): the necessity of acting imposes itself *a priori.* The refusal to act is itself an act. Thus, the necessity of acting implies logically the necessity of objective affirmation, of judgment. Where there is volition, we inevitably find affirmation, for each volition implicitly includes an end and a means to the end (I, pp. 46f.). The presupposition of the end of an act which, by its very nature, is in the order of reality (V, pp. 367, 371), already exercises the logical function of judgment (V, pp. 383, 392, 408), even when referring to an end which only leads us to doubt or to abstain from definite judgment

(I, p. 48). The necessity of judgment, of objective affirmation, implies a corresponding necessity in the affirmed object, insofar as it is an affirmed object. This necessity is at least identity with itself (the first principle), which has no meaning outside of a reference to the absolute necessity of being.

Insofar as the absolute necessity of being is included in human activity as an ultimate condition of possibility, this absolute necessity of being completely frustrates the attempt to deny, through an activity (doubt, denial), the activity itself (condition for the possibility of doubt and denial) (I, p. 254). When the skeptic denies truth or champions universal doubt, he contradicts himself (I, p. 25). It need only be pointed out to the skeptic that when he says, "I reject assertion," that he asserts something (I, p. 46). The most extreme effort of the human mind to rid itself of affirmation is itself an affirmation. Affirmation is inevitable (I, p. 49), and thus the absolute affirmation of being (*l'être est*) imposes itself upon us under the force of logical contradiction, as the following proposition imposes itself upon us under the force of both theoretical and practical necessity: Each object of affirmation, precisely because it is affirmable, is related to the absolute of being, and therefore is, in one way or another (I, p. 255).

According to Maréchal, this proof (that every affirmable object, every object of thought, is being [*est de l'être*] in a real and absolute sense) is the ground (I, p. 255) and starting point of metaphysics (I, pp. 77f.) and the defense against universal skepticism (I, pp. 25, 48f.).

This proof was not attained through reference to the evidence of the first principle or the affirmation of being, but through reflection upon the necessity and fundamental irrefutability of them both. Their validity is presupposed in the very attempt to deny them or call them into question. Thus there is neither an objective proof (referring back to other principles), nor a direct reference to what is evident, but a transcendental proof, which reflects on the act of knowledge and the indispensable conditions of this act insofar as they are manifested in it, and, from this point of view, draws conclusions about the necessary nature of this act, viz., that it must be fundamentally related to the absolute order of being. Whoever does not acknowledge these conditions of possibility and their ramifications rejects, through the force of his thought, denial or doubt, that whereby he can think, deny or doubt at all. We shall go into this area later in more detail.

Although the starting point of metaphysics may have been attained and skepticism overthrown, and although it may have been shown that every act of affirming objects must be related necessarily to the absolute of being, we must still show what relationships individual objects have to the absolute of being, how being belongs to them (I, p. 255) and how the vindicated position can confront the skeptic, i.e., how the antinomies, the apparently self-destroying contradictions, which threaten to annul affirmation, can be resolved (I, pp. 26f., 45).

This is the function of *the ontological critique of what constitutes* absolute affirmation. It distinguishes and classifies the possible meanings which can apply to the necessary bestowal of being. It is impossible to avoid contradiction while holding that being always applies to all objects in the same way, that every possession of being is always true in one and the same manner. This is the problem of the one and the many, the reduction of the multiplicity of affirmation to the unity of a rational system (I, pp. 78, 255). This problem can be found in the pre-Socratic philosophy in terms of the analysis of becoming and the "truth" of appearances (I, pp. 26f.). Aristotle offers his solution in the distinction between act and potency, through which neither the perception of movement nor the incontravertible and absolute nature of the affirmation of being must be abandoned. Thus the structure of metaphysics emerges in which the affirmation of being is formulated through the logical relations of its constitution and through the norm of the first principle.

Such a metaphysics, which originated with Aristotle and was later developed by Thomas, deserves to be called a *critique of knowledge,* because it determines the legitimate meaning of the affirmation of being with reference to necessary norms (I, p. 255). Of primary concern is not finding the passage from the order of thought to the order of reality, but developing the manifold character of the relations in which essences stand to the reality which supports them. These relations are required because of the affirmation of being. The kind of relation is therefore capable of variation: subjective or objective, direct or indirect. The problem of such a differentiation of what is affirmed belongs to a critique of knowledge, even to one which is already formulated in metaphysical concepts (I, p. 90).

The structure of metaphysics, however, becomes a "critique of knowledge" in yet stricter sense. In ordering all objective elements in terms of being, it also includes *the* element which is the object of reflective knowledge: the tension between the knowing subject and the object known. This cognitive relationship is also an "object" of consciousness (although of reflective consciousness) and therefore must have a place in the system of being. Thus the ontological relations between subject and object must be determined. They characterize the subjective and objective elements of the psychological relations of both to each other and outline the limits and depth of knowledge itself. We can, then, no longer speak merely of the internal differences between "objective categories," but also of a distinction between a *"modus mentis"* and a *"modus rei"* in each objective predicate (I, p. 255). According to Maréchal, this viewpoint can perhaps be the key to the adaption of theories of knowledge to both metaphysical and critical "modes of expression" (I, p. 256). We shall soon see what this means.

Maréchal derives another conclusion from this critical function of metaphysics which is significant for the historico-comparative method. Since metaphysics, in order to attain its full critical meaning, must present an all-embracing system of being which includes a metaphysics of knowledge as an organic part, both imply each other to the extent that a shift in the fundamental principles of being also alters the ontological theory of knowledge. Therefore, it is not at all surprising that, in the history of philosophical systems, the totality of metaphysical theses has shifted in accordance with theories of concepts (I, p. 256).

54

History also shows that it is not very easy to include in one coherent system the totality of interconnections which, without exception, relates everything that constitutes consciousness to being, as Aristotle and, above all, Thomas were able to do. Other systems have always misinterpreted some element of the constitution of consciousness and let it pass as an antinomy. These systems remain incomplete and labor under implicit contradictions (I, pp. 256f.).

Maréchal has shown this especially to be true for ancient philosophy before Aristotle and for medieval philosophy after Thomas, particularly in Duns Scotus and Occam. The early dissolution of the synthesis of the high middle ages forced the lines of development for modern philosophy (I, p. 257). The equilibrium of realistic metaphysics and the vitality of the classical critique of knowledge are intimately bound up with an epistemological premiss which is a central thesis of Thomistic Aristotelianism. Its elements are a synthetic theory of the concept, as opposed to an intuitive or analytical theory, and a theory of the *universal directum,* which is the fruit of a total abstraction actuated through the senses. Thus the abstract essence of a material thing is seen as the proper object of human reason. Corresponding to all this is a theory of the essential participation of the senses in intellectual knowledge, which is made possible through the substantial unity of body and soul. That which is first given to us through the natural exercise of knowledge is not an opposition of antinomial elements which we vainly try to join together again, but a systematic unity which we grasp in its essential inseparability. Only later can the relative opposition of the constitutive principles of this act be posited (II, pp. 9f.).

In the later middle ages, however, this basic synthetic unity of our fundamental concepts was lost. Correspondingly, the strong substantial unity of the human compositum was denied (without which the synthetical unity of the concept cannot be understood) (I, p. 257). This led to an oscillation between extreme positions—in epistemology, between ontologism and narrow empiricism, with its agnostic consequences, and in psychology, between exclusive spiritualism and gross materialism, or some other unresolved dualism. There is also a disintegration of the proper unity and reciprocal dependence of the understanding and the will, which is evident in Occam (I, pp. 268f.) and results in a separation into static-formal and dynamic aspects of knowledge.

THE TURN TOWARD THE SUBJECT

In the history of modern philosophy, the problem of knowledge was taken up from a new viewpoint—the turn toward the subject. We find here a more direct epistemological use of the self, of the subject, and, according to Maréchal, not without reason. With Descartes, and with the empiricists, this turn is by no means complete. Maréchal contends that Descartes was really not yet aware of the specific viewpoint under which the self must be grasped in order to be able to ground a really strong critique. The Cartesian self remains I-substance, a part of the ontological object. It is merely the "presentedness" of an object among other objects, characterized as directly evident. In empiricism, the self cannot ground the objective value of knowledge because, although it appeals to the subject, it is only to the psychological subject, the producer of and comprehending bond between associations and sensible representations (II, p. 247). Leibniz goes further in his *Nouveaux Essais*. He distinguishes reason as an objective, apperceptive function. This function, however, is not simply a formal analysis corresponding to the principle of contradiction, but dynamic, in that sensible material is dealt with in terms of transcendence, i.e., worked out in accordance with the absolute affirmation of "sufficient reason." Thus being, in these two functions of reason, is presented through both of its irreducible aspects—as the identical measure of representations and as the intelligible ground of representations. Under the first aspect, according to Leibniz, man is capable of mathematics, which is developed analytically, and under the second aspect, of physics and metaphysics. Nevertheless, Leibniz does not escape dogmatism (II, pp. 147f.) because he does not attempt to vindicate his dynamism critically (II, p. 147). Only with Kant does the new concept of the subject appear which treats the transcendental subject as an inner and constitutive function of the object of thought and which permeates the whole of critical philosophy (II, p. 247).

In order to overcome the opposition between empiricism and rationalism and the antinomy between sensibility and understanding, Kant begins with the unity of sensibility and understanding in what is objectified in human knowledge (V, p. 36). The content of knowledge, however, is not considered as the realization of an ontological object, as in the "classical critique," but rather as purely given to consciousness, whose relation to a represented object must be investigated. This is a decisive difference with the classical metaphysical critique, which began with the ontological object, whose affirmation was proven as valid knowledge to critics through the demonstration of its necessity and unavoidability. Other critical problems were then solved with the help of the metaphysics attained through the differentiation of this affirmation of being. As Kant poses the problem, he finds it necessary to accept the vindication of knowledge only if, in contrast with the empirical critique, it can be shown how this knowledge can take place. This does not mean that he presupposes a psychology of association, which by no means sufficiently explains the occurrence of knowledge. Rather, he starts from the fact of knowledge itself. He not only ignores the relation to a psychological subject, as in metaphysical psychology, but also in the relation (taken as already vindicated) to a represented ontological object (III, p. 109; IV, pp. 341f.).

Insofar as the consciousness of objects, as an activity of consciousness, ignores the relation of the phenomenal object to the ontological object, Maréchal calls it *phenomenal in the precisive sense*. However, if a vindicated relation of the phenomenal object to an ontological object represented through it is fundamentally excluded, then we have a phenomenalism which treats the phenomenal object *in the exclusive sense* (V, p. 517).

TRANSCENDENTAL ANALYSIS

The consciousness of objects is now examined in terms of the conditions through which it can be understood. The analysis of the conditions of the consciousness of objects ought to elucidate the validating characteristics and noetic value of the consciousness of objects. The analysis of conditions is not, however, a logical analysis, which analyzes and classifies the properties of objects of thought. Kant works rather with the structural elements which posit these objects precisely as objects of consciousness. He is not concerned with logical connections between the represented objects as known, but with the necessary connections which pertain to the objects known insofar as they are objects of consciousness (and thus in this sense with the necessary structural elements which constitute an object in consciousness). Maréchal, following Kant's terminology, distinguishes this mode of analysis from the logical as *transcendental* (III, p. 111; IV, p. 19; V, pp. 52f.).

The transcendental analysis of objects immanent to consciousness leads, according to Kant, to the *a priori conditions of knowledge*. Kant refers to that knowledge as *a priori* "which determines something about objects before they are given to us" (B, XVI).[18] This priority is, of course, not temporal, but logical. "In terms of time, we have no knowledge previous to experience; rather, all knowledge begins with it. However, if all knowledge commences *with* experience, this by no means implies that it all comes *from* experience" (B, 2). "Despite the temporal priority of experience, there is still room in knowledge for something that is not purely and simply derived from experience" (II, p. 121). "Thus the Kantian conception of apriority is founded on the classical priority of certain designations of objects over and against the concrete and individual experience of objects. This is the priority of the necessary over and against the contingent" (III, p. 121). This concept of the "*a priori*" receives a special meaning within the transcendental

[18] *The Critique of Pure Reason* is cited in the usual way, viz., A refers to the first edition, B to the second edition.

viewpoint. Basically it designates that which necessarily belongs to the object-oriented content of knowledge, a necessary characteristic of an object independent of contingent experience. Such necessary characteristics of objects receive their logical expression in judgments which formulate these essential connections, or in Kant's terminology, in synthetic judgments a priori. Transcendental analysis, however, does not consider the object in and for itself, but only insofar as a subject is conscious of the object. It follows that thought cannot claim validity for objects if it does not take *a priori* characteristics into consideration. The occurrence of truly object-oriented consciousness stands under conditions which are expressed in *a priori* terms and which present a law not only for the object considered in itself, but also for the occurrence of the act of object-oriented consciousness. The *a priori* receives its transcendental meaning as a condition which is given with the knowing subject and which defines the necessary characteristics of the structure of the act of object-oriented consciousness (and this not from the subjective-psychological side, but in terms of the content of the intentional object). In order to understand this concept properly, we must keep in mind that the act of knowledge is not only, generally speaking, an act of the subject, performed and determined by the subject, but also an act of the subject in its ultimate determination. Whatever constitutes the act of knowledge also belongs to its ultimate determination, and therefore the necessary constitution of this act is necessarily connected with the conditions in the subject which determine that the act of knowledge can take place at all. The contingent elements of this constitution, of course, are not referred back to the conditions which determine each act of knowledge except insofar as it is necessary that they be present to give an ultimate determination. Rather, insofar as they are contingent, they are referred back to the contingent and changeable ultimate determination of the subject insofar as it knows and is determinable through the receptivity of the senses.

Thus "according to Kant, the complete knowledge of experience which absorbs sensible experience into the object of thought is arranged *de facto* and *de jure* according to conditions

59

which logically exist before the entrance of what is sensibly given, i. e., according to *a priori* conditions. In Kant's terminology, these *a priori* conditions define 'cognitive subjectivity' " (III, p. 121). Maréchal also points out that on closer examination Kant's critique is only dramatically expressing a platitude when it holds "that we can only know *a priori* in things precisely what we put there" (B, XVII). This contribution is, of course, not meant to be a conscious and arbitrary addition, but a necessary structural element of activity which is determined through the nature of the knower and is the law for the positing of the act of knowledge.

It is quite significant for the further understanding of Maréchal's viewpoint how he compares Kant's *a priori* with the notion of formal causality. Kant himself was aware that his understanding of the concept of apriority relates to a classical concept which was forgotten no less by the Cartesians than by the empiricists, viz., that of *formal causality*. The *a priori* element is present in knowledge as a determination imposed on what is given. It does not enrich the manifold of what is given, but it unifies it and invests it with a higher logical quality. In this synthesis of the manifold and unity at the heart of the object of thought, Kant, like the scholastics, sees a direct application of the notions of "matter" and "form." "The first indicates that which is determinable in some way, the second, the determination" (A, 266; B, 322), givenness and *a priori* principle, which form the unity of the object in consciousness (III, pp. 121f.).

From this way of looking at the *a priori,* we can understand more precisely what "transcendental" means. Kant defines it thus: "I call all knowledge transcendental which is not directly concerned with objects, but with our *a priori* concepts of objects as such", (A, 11f.), or "with our mode of knowing objects, insofar as this is possible *a priori*" (B, 25). "The difference between transcendental and empirical, therefore, belongs only to the critique of knowledge and does not concern the relation of knowledge to its objects" (A, 56f.; B, 80f.).

The transcendental, therefore, is related to the *a priori,* but does not entirely coincide with it. With respect to this, Kant makes the remark "that not every *a priori* knowledge, but only one through which we know that and how certain representations (perceptions or concepts) are applied purely *a priori,* or can be . . . may be called transcendental" (A, 56; B, 80). In connection with all this, Maréchal traces the use of the word "transcendental" in Kant's critical period to two fundamental attributions, from which all the others are derived (III, pp. 116f.):

(1) The *a priori* condition for the possibility of knowledge, i.e., the subject, insofar as it is a condition of the object and determines it internally.

(2) The knowledge of this *a priori* condition of possibility, i.e., consciousness, which the subject has of itself as an *a priori* determination of the object, or the actualized knowledge of the object as determined *a priori* by the subject.

This *a priori* condition for the possibility of knowledge, therefore, should emerge from transcendental analysis. We can thus appreciate Kant's question: how are synthetic judgments, such as those in the pure sciences (mathematics, mathematical physics), possible? This has nothing to do with *whether* they are at all possible, since their existence is a fact. It has only to do with *how* they are possible, to which *a priori* conditions of possibility the objective necessities which are expressed in these judgments and sciences refer.

The premiss for this process of transcendental analysis is simply that the object of thought (*intelligible in actu*) is directly present in reflection, not as something rigid and lifeless, but as a becoming, as a phase in the movement of mind, as something that has passed from possibility to actuality (*intelligible in actu*). "In order for the transcendental method to be applicable to the critique of knowledge (since apriority contains a dynamic character as a form-producing condition), we must be able, through reflections, to perceive the immanent activity of our thought precisely where this activity permeates and actuates the contextual elements of our representations" (V, p. 61). This does not require that the knowing subject be taken as an ontological cause, as the metaphysical principle of this activity. It is sufficient for the Kantian transcendental anal-

61

ysis that the immanent object of reflection be discovered as the actuation of an activity and not merely as a lifeless form. "It follows that a philosopher, who recognizes in man a capacity for reflection which can determine an actuation of the subject in objectified thought, can raise no basic objection against the procedure of transcendental reflection" (V, p. 6). For why should we not question the fundamental potentiality of the act and understand the necessary characteristics of the act in terms of the corresponding potentiality?

"Analytical reflection, which extends to the objective contents of consciousness, discovers there . . . a hierarchy of relations which relate these contents of consciousness to *a priori* conditions which ground their possibility in the knowing subject. At the head of the *a priori* conditions stands the formal unity of consciousness with all its necessity, the 'I think' " (IV, p. 19). This mutuality of the accompanying self-consciousness with the consciousness of objects (analytic unity of apperception) is, however, not possible if each concrete consciousness of objects is not previously unified through the self, viz., if the manifold of representations is not united with the self through the actuation of a universal power of synthesis. "I am, therefore, conscious of myself as identical with myself while considering the manifold of the representations given to me in perception because I call them entirely *my* representations, which determines them as *one*. That, however, is so much as saying that I am conscious of a necessary synthesis *a priori* of my representations which is called the fundamental synthetic unity of apperception under which all the representations given to me stand, but under which they must be brought through a synthesis" (B, 135). This indicates how, according to Kant, reflection itself points to the fact that the consciousness of objects must be conceived as the result of a synthesis. This also indicates how transcendental reflection arrives at *a priori* conditions of possibility from the identification of a necessary element in the consciousness of objects. Likewise, the hierarchical ordering of other *a priori* conditions for the possibility of an immanent object is derived from the subordinated necessary structural elements of the consciousness of

62

objects. The notion of the analytical unity necessary for *every* consciousness of objects, however, as well as the synthetic unity of apperception presupposed by it, leads immediately to the second part of transcendental analysis—transcendental deduction.

The transcendental analysis of the immanent object in terms of the *a priori* conditions for the possibility of the consciousness of objects in the subject, according to Kant, takes place precisely through direct reflection and through transcendental deduction.

Direct reflection frees the unifying and necessary forms in the object known from empirical and non-conscious content, which they make use of and which they raise to conscious objectivity. Reflection thus succeeds in identifying certain faculties which determine the act of the consciousness of objects and which constitute the object in consciousness. By "faculty" (avoiding the definition of a metaphysical entity) is meant a power of conception, proper to each subject, to grasp a given manifold under the various *a priori* conditions which are present in the object (III, p. 117). Transcendental reflection thus attains for us "the consciousness of the relations of given representations to the various sources of knowledge in us, through which alone their relations to each other can be properly determined" (A, 260f.), i.e., "to various possibilities or *a priori* conditions whose hierarchical totality determines our cognitive subjectivity." "Reflective analysis permits us to comprehend the whole structure of our faculties, through which we observe the operation of their parts" (III, p. 117; cf. A, 65f., 260f.).

If we reflect in this way upon a concrete consciousness of objects, we attain the identification of the *a priori* which is necessary for this actually represented object, but we do not attain the necessity of the so determined *a priori* for *every* consciousness of objects. "The transcendental method, however, as a critical method, should not only expose the *fact* of an *a priori* in the objects truly present in our consciousness (thus not only necessity for particular cases), but the *universal necessity* of this *a priori* as the condition for every possible object (of a non-intuitive understanding)" (V, p. 59).

63

This means that an *a priori* indicated through particular contents of knowledge depends upon whether those contents of knowledge are recognized. Thus for Kant the existence of synthetic judgments *a priori* and the pure sciences is an incontrovertible fact, but an empiricist would not agree. If Kant shows that the denial of the *a priori* leads to a rejection of the apodictic character of mathematics and pure physics, an empiricist would gladly see this apodictic character go (V, pp. 53f.). If, therefore, one wishes to produce various classes of synthetic *a priori* judgments without first of all presupposing something, another way must be chosen. Kant himself not only refers to these judgments, but, in the development of the aesthetic and analytic, goes the other, direct way (V, p. 54; cf. III, pp. 119, 151).

There he refers to the principle "that every unified plurality (*a fortoriori,* every synthesis) presupposes an *a priori* as a unifying principle. For example, the grouping of four points on a piece of paper (spatial position) could never be derived from the distributive plurality of each of these particular points, for the plural as such never signifies a unifying element. It follows that the unity of a plurality must be logically presupposed, i.e., *a priori* (in this case, space, as the logical possibility of position). This is valid for every form in the formation of multiple matter, and is equally valid for each object of knowledge in direct sensible experience, because this unquestionably involves a synthesis (unification) of a unified plurality. Kant finds a gradual *a priori* unification of the manifold of the sensibly given in our consciousness of objects, first of all in the perceptions of space and time, then in the categories as strict objectifying a priori conditions, and finally in the unity of apperception as the unifying principle for every object whatsoever" (V, p. 55; Wd. I, pp. 28f.).

This way is no longer dependent upon presupposed synthetic judgments *a priori,* rather simply on the necessary synthesis of a manifold for all experiential knowledge. Not only is the *a priori* element as such considered (this in itself would not be a transcendental analysis), but the faculty of the knowing subject manifested in the *a priori* unifying elements linked to this unity.

The question concerning the inner conditions of possibility of an object thought, insofar as it is an object, is imposed not only through the determination of synthetic judgments *a priori,* but also to the extent that the objective content of consciousness presents itself as a differentiated unity, as a synthesis of a manifold, and is possible only as such. On the one hand, a definite conscious content of knowledge is possible only if it is a definite unity, which ultimately stands under the unity of the "I think" common to all consciousness—the "unity of apperception." On the other hand, this content, as distinct from others, is possible only to the extent that the unity is differentiated through the relation to a contextual manifold demanding unification and distinguishable through content. This, however, means that no complete object of thought can be an object of thought, viz., is not possible as such, if it is not conditioned through something which presents multiplicity and something which unifies the multiplicity. Therefore, the question concerning the conditions of possibility of objective knowledge, viz., concerning the principles and functions which are logically prior to particular knowledge and determine it internally, which activate that fundamental unification whose result we discover in the unified manifold of the immanent object, imposes itself necessarily. The synthesis present in the object is thus broken up into its necessarily presupposed elements. This reveals the unifying functions of cognitive subjectivity in their hierarchical interconnections and at the same time clarifies the necessary structure of the object as object, for if certain functions are necessary for something to be an object, then every object as such is determined through these functions, i.e., cast under the regulations of their interactions and the resulting synthesis, and structured accordingly.

This search for the conditions of possibility of an object as such, according to Maréchal, is, through what is characteristic of this procedure, "easily referred to the logical schema of rational synthesis, which unites the opposing terms" (IV, p. 343). If the question concerning the conditions of possibility of this confrontation with the object as such imposes itself through the tension between unity and multiplicity in the object of knowledge, then the conclusion of the procedure is formed by the opposing terms, which, in themselves, do not yet satisfy the demand for a rational harmony immanent to thought. We must, therefore, find a higher point of view which will resolve this disharmony, which turns out to be the *a priori* conditions of possibility. Thus "every step of the transcendental analysis can be related to the triadic form of a synthesis which reconciles a thesis with an antithesis" (IV, p. 343). With this statement in the fourth volume, Maréchal prepares for the transition to Fichte.

The second step of the transcendental analysis, which does not merely indicate the *a priori* conditions of possibility proceeding from particular, asserted contents of thought, but rather leads to the necessity of definite *a priori* conditions of possibility for every object of knowledge whatsoever is *transcendental deduction* (III, p. 119). Thus while transcendental reflection is a "reflective dialectic which clarifies the *a priori* conditions of possibility of an object present to consciousness" (IV, p. 342), transcendental deduction proceeds in the opposite way. It is, therefore, "more than a simple extension of the previous way. It seeks to derive the conditions of the real actuation of the principle of apperception in the object known in the very terms of this formal principle. Until now, the *a priori* conditions of possibility were signified in terms of a hypothetically given object of thought. Now we are looking for the necessary properties of the object of thought in terms of *a priori* conditions of possibility. We thereby receive pure and apodictic knowledge of consciousness" (IV, p. 344). This opens the way to an understanding of the critical function of transcendental deduction, with which both Kant and Maréchal are principally concerned. In posing the question in the transcendental critique, we are not concerned with whether we can identify the givenness immanent to consciousness, whether in consciousness there is actually some noetic content which claims to make objects present, whether we have insight into certain essential relations and whether the law of excluded contradiction is an indispensable norm of thought. This is all taken as evident. We are rather concerned with clarification of

66

the noetic value of these evidently certain aspects of knowledge inherent in the characteristics of objective thought. This is where transcendental deduction begins. It ascertains which elements must necessarily belong to every such conception of an object. We then derive implications for the noetic value of such a conception. "Since we accept the 'conscious phenomenon' or the 'object in thought' in the critique as unavoidably and initially given, we thereby also accept all the conditions of possibility, all the necessary 'constitutive conditions,' and we accept them—no more, no less—as they are present in the analysis of the object. If they include the objective existence of an absolute, then we thereby know this absolute, and if they only indicate the relativity of phenomena, then we thereby deal with them as simple functions of the phenomenal object" (V, p. 53). This statement advances Maréchal's opposition to Kant's transcendental analysis. For Kant, this relation to the unconditioned does not operate constitutively in the object known, but only regulatively, and thus the categories remain bound to phenomena and have no relation to the absolute order of the unconditioned. Knowledge remains phenomenal. Maréchal, with the help of transcendental analysis, tries to show that the relation to the unconditioned is constitutive for the phenomenal object and that knowledge thus reaches the fundamental order of being. This means that the phenomenal object cannot be viewed as phenomenal in the exclusive sense. Before pursuing this point in detail (which we have already reviewed briefly in connection with the first edition of *Le point de départ de la métaphysique*), we must complete Maréchal's presentation of Kant's transcendental method.

Transcendental deduction can take on the form of a subjective or an objective transcendental deduction (III, pp. 118, 172; V, p. 98). *Subjective* deduction depends upon the consideration of the subject in the critical sense as a function constituting the object as immanent to consciousness, viz., upon the dialectical self-conditioning of the various functions of knowledge, and works out the necessity of the function of a subject. *Objective* deduction, on the other hand, is principally concerned with consideration of the given object and its intrinsic rational possibility. It results in the postulation of the necessity of a structure for the object and this structure is then shown to be the *a priori* condition of possibility of *every* object of thought.

Of course, the transcendental point of view is common to both since they conceive the immanent object from the point of view of the a priori conditions of possibility of its constitution. The one form, however, works more with the functions of knowledge as such, while the other works more with the necessary characteristics of the immanent object as grounded in them. Insofar as the investigation of the *a priori* functions of the transcendental subject indicates that these functions imply *a priori* determinations or unifying forms of the object as thought, these two points of view actually coincide. It is, therefore, understandable that for Kant the subjective and objective elements are mixed together in the transcendental deduction of the categories, because, according to Kant, the categories, as opposed to the ideas, constitute the immanent object from within and therefore necessarily result in definite characteristics of the object. The mixing of subjective elements in a way confuses the deduction, but in itself it is legitimate (III, p. 172). Maréchal here (III, pp. 170–172) tries to show that, for Kant, the deduction of the categories is an objective deduction, although certain elements enter into the deduction which also belong to a subjective deduction

In this deduction of the categories, Kant begins with the highest unity under which each form of consciousness must stand—the pure unity of apperception. From here he attempts to derive the categories. They are the subordinated unities with whose help the manifold can be drawn into the universal unity of consciousness, for the pure unity of the "I think" alone does not yet achieve the unity of an object of thought. This requires a function of the understanding which confers the unity of an object of thought to the sensible representation unified under the forms of space and time. "We can, then, refer all the operations of the understanding to judgments so that the understanding can be presented entirely as a power to judge, for, in terms of what was just said, it is a power to think. Thinking is knowing through concepts. Concepts, however, as predicates of possible judgments, are related to some representation of a still undetermined object. . . . The functions of the understanding, therefore, can be fully discovered if the functions of unity can be completely represented in judgment" (A, 69; B, 94). Kant tries to accomplish this representation through the table of judgments, which he accepts as a complete division of all the kinds of judgment, and from which he derives the corresponding categories, the pure concepts of the understanding, viz., functions of judgment which, as *a priori* functions, give to phenomena the unity of being objects.

Kant holds open yet another way to the discovery of the categories. This begins with appearances which are to be unified through the concepts of the understanding. Since concepts can only be applied to appearances, appearances must merge with the categories in some kind of homogeneity. Kant calls "this pure and formal condition of sensibility, to which the understanding is restricted in its use, the schema of this concept of the understanding" (A, 140). It is thus possible to work our way up from the fundamental complexification of the schemata to an equal number of *a priori* unifying functions of the understanding, whose application is regulated through the schemata. This way begins with the *a priori* differentiation of sensibility in order to attain just as many categories or functions of judgment. In any case, Kant does not complete this way since he derives the schemata from the categories which he has discovered from the table of judgments (IV, pp. 24–26).

Kant then evaluates the transcendental deduction of the categories in terms of its critical implications. Since the categories, as *a priori* conditions of possibility, necessarily constitute every objective content of knowledge, they must have objective value, for if one denied these functions to the categories not only would synthetic judgments *a priori* and the absolutely certain pure sciences be impossible, but all knowledge of experience would be invalidated. If one does away with these *a priori* principles, thought falters and fails to grasp objects because it lacks a perceived object (III, pp. 119, 150; IV, pp. 26f.).

69

On the other hand, these *a priori* determinations directly show themselves to be formal determinations of a given manifold. The categories, however, can only exercise their functions of constituting objective knowledge if they are applied to perceptions. According to Kant, therefore, the objectively valid and vindicated use of the categories and synthetic judgments *a priori* is restricted to the realm of possible experience.

This agnostic conclusion of Kant's centers on the principle: "A formal principle includes a content, a matter, that is either *a priori* or *a posteriori*." He goes on to draw the conclusion that if it is given *a priori,* then we have intuition. Since we do not have such an intuition, something given is required. This illustrates the application of the categories to experience and shows that an object of knowledge, which does not bear something given in itself, is impossible for our non-intuitive knowledge (IV, p. 344).

The premiss for this consideration is that, with respect to the impossibility of an intellectual intuition in Kant's sense (content given *a priori*), the content of an objective representation must come entirely from sense intuition, viz., from the reception of something given. Kant does not prove that there can be no medium between sensible and creative intuition, but from 1772 on this two-part disjunction is fixed. The third term, which is offered through the scholastic theory of analogy, taken in its true meaning, is excluded (III, p. 307; IV, pp. 81f.). It should be noted here that Maréchal, even in his earlier writings, insisted that Kant's fundamental error was a too static conception of the functions of knowledge. "Kant . . . reduces the critical subject to a frame of unmoving 'forms,' which regulate sensible matter and thus constitute 'objects'" (Prem., p. 293). This is why he holds only for a purely subjective deduction as possible for the ideas, positing them as regulative principles for the ordering of the already completely constituted objects of knowledge and for the advancement of knowledge. An objective deduction, on the other hand, which would prove the unconditioned to be an internally constituting function of the object of knowledge, through which the metaphysical order would be open to knowledge, Kant holds to be impossible. The ideas, it is true, are affirmed as regulative principles of theoretical reason and postulates of practical reason, but practical reason here is too completely separated from theoretical reason.

This failure is also evident in the other shortcomings of the transcendental method as developed by Kant. He does not go far enough in his question concerning the conditions of possibility. Although transcendental analysis exists in order to apprehend the immanent object as the product of an immanent activity of the knowing subject, he does not completely evaluate this position (IV, p. 351). It is true that he often uses expressions of a dynamic and causal order (e.g., "operation of the understanding," "act of spontaneity," "synthesis," etc.), which, as fulfilling and active, precede the representation of what is unified, viz., the relation of "that which conditions *a priori*" to what is "conditioned" (V, pp. 62f.). But he fails to make use of this dynamic aspect. By so doing, he closes off the way for a further understanding of the relationships between the various levels of *a priori* conditions. Kant's analysis leads ultimately to an unclarified, strongly correlative duality of the elements of content and form in knowledge and, with regard to form, to the duality of the forms received in sensibility and the synthetic forms of the understanding. Thus the double derivation of the categories, first from the transcendental unity of apperception, which must be differentiated, and then from the schemata of sensibility, which require the corresponding forms of the understanding, leads to the question concerning the relationship of the "pure categories" discovered in the first way to the "schematized categories" attainable in the second way. It is true that the first derivation in itself offers absolute necessity, but the difficulty lies in the principle of differentiation. Kant tries to resolve this difficulty with the construction of the table of judgments. Ultimately, however, this differentiation can only occur in relation to experience. The second derivation presupposes experience and, to this extent, has it easier, but it also basically leads only to hypothetical necessity because a sensibility different from that found in human nature could lead to other categories. The dialectical correspondence of the two derivations can only be guaranteed "if transcendental deduction encounters an absolute principle of synthesis in the direction of its own development which, due to the same deductive necessity, regulates simultaneously the *a priori* concepts of the understandings and the *a priori* intuitions of sensibility" (IV, p. 92; cf. Wd. II, p. 93). Maréchal ennumerates other inconsistencies of this sort in Kant which we need not go into in detail here (Mel. I, p. 364). They all, however, have a common source. "The root of Kant's error lies in a too complete separation of the theoretical and practical orders, of the 'formal' and the 'dynamic.' This separation (which leads to a false antinomy of the 'formal' and from there either to ontologism or agnosticism) appeared at the very beginning of modern philosophy—Descartes was one of its first victims" (Mel. I, p. 364).

THE DYNAMIC POINT OF VIEW

That a development of the transcendental method which would try to avoid Kant's one-sidedness is not excluded from the very beginning is shown from the historical fact that Fichte, precisely in terms of his enthusiasm for Kant's approach, developed transcendental philosophy from precisely the dynamic point of view (V, p. 37).

Fichte's starting point is the same as Kant's—actual consciousness, the objective content of consciousness. Whatever is known, however, is not possible without something else. Thus our thinking is pushed to the unconditioned (IV, p. 346). Fichte, however, holds that the thing in itself is a contradictory concept, here introducing the fundamental idealist premiss into his thought. This means that he must introduce an absolute principle that comprehends simultaneously what is sensibly given, the forms of space and time and the forms of pure reflection. In order to be absolute, this principle must at one and the same time comprehend the speculative and practical self in a radical unity. This cannot be accomplished by means of conceptual knowledge, but only through an intuition which penetrates to the heart of the self, viz., the intuition of the very

activity through which the self is posited in its conscious ex-
ternalizations (IV, pp. 348f.). "The intuition of activity appears objectively as a fact of consciousness for the reflecting
self. For the deeper and fundamental self, the principle of the
reflecting self, it can only be an operation, a fact—the direct
coincidence of a fundamental activity with itself. This intuition
of active positing is the one firm fundament for every philosophy" (IV, p. 349). "Kant cannot speak of an 'intellectual
perception' because, in his terminology, this is always related
to a 'being,' to an already posited thing. On the other hand,
'intellectual perception,' which is treated in the *Scientific
Theory of Knowledge* (*Wissenschaftslehre*), does not have a
being for an object, but an activity, an operation. Although the
first is non-conceptual, the second is required, and although
Kant presupposes it, he in no way mentions it. Most probably,
it would be pure apperception (cf. IV, pp. 353–360). In the
Critique of Practical Reason, he accepts it, but without this
characterization; yet what is the awareness of the categorical
imperative if not an intellectual perception? —certainly not a
static reality, but an autonomous activity. According to Fichte,
Kant thus failed to unify the speculative with the moral realm
in the fundamental intuition into the pure operation of the self"
(IV, p. 350).

Maréchal feels that Fichte is correct here in accentuating the
dynamic point of view in opposition to Kant. Maréchal finds it
strange that Kant, although not denying the active function of
the subject of knowledge, nevertheless ignores it whenever dealing with the critical value of the formal effects of this activity.
"It would, however, appear evident that transcendental reflection, when it distinguishes a 'pure apperceptive form,' indicates
this to us necessarily as the 'form of an activity'" (IV, p. 351).
To this extent Fichte is in agreement with the Aristotelian-
scholastic theory of causality. "Every form is dynamic, so
if we apprehend the 'pure form of apperception' in us, we
thus apprehend 'the pure activity of apperception.' Nothing
prohibits us from calling this knowledge a 'perception of the
operation of the self,' although the scholastics prefer to speak
of a 'reflection of the subject upon his act.' The reservation

with which we approach Fichte is, therefore, connected less with the intuition of the operation of the self than with the nature of this activity and the self" (IV, p. 352).

Fichte thus completes Kant through the development of his transcendental approach. "Fichte's interpretation brings the static transcendentalism of Kant to a necessary completion insofar as it implies a radical finalism and restores activity, which signifies form, to its proper place" (V, p. 38). Maréchal feels that we should not deplore the fact that the framework of the *Critique* is thus filled in with a metaphysics which absorbs it, because "a 'critique' is not required to raise a veto against metaphysics. If it begins with deliberately limited premisses as given and then comes to the objective necessity of a metaphysics and sets down the conditions of its validity, why should it not turn in that direction as the provisional frame disappears? That would only clearly show that the methodological provisions which were imposed in the beginning in no way constitute a real incapacity of reason" (V, p. 38). "Kantian agnosticism must be overcome. This can occur only through the recognition of the speculative role of dynamic finality. Post-Kantian transcendental idealism, which initiated the move in this direction, did not succeed in jumping the rationalistic track. Although it undertook the boldest speculative program which philosophy has ever attempted, it stands powerless before the secrets of higher reason" (V, p. 39). "The great systems of pantheistic idealism actually arrive at metaphysics once again, but not . . . to the 'thing-in-itself' (which they consider to be unthinkable and contradictory)—rather only to the transcendental subject" (V, p. 38). "These brilliant rational constructions, unfortunately, center around an insufficient analysis of the conditions of 'knowing' " (V, p. 38), for the motivating force of rationalism is still operative here, "pretending to raise the understanding to the level of transcendental reason while actually dragging reason down to the relations of the understanding" (V, p. 39).

Maréchal criticizes Kant not because he has formulated the transcendental mode of inquiry and applied it to philosophy but because he has given it a slanted and static interpretation.

Fichte moves beyond Kant by taking the dynamic aspect into account, viz., the direct givenness of the effective activity of the subject without which the analysis of the forms of this activity becomes one-sided and loses its significance. Such idealism also suffers under the cloak of rationalism and thus does not succeed in analyzing this activity sufficiently. It does not seek "merely to posit a strict deduction of the *object,* as Kant had attempted, but rather an objective deduction which, in its principle and procedure, presents the absolute development of thought as such. This aim, which results in monistic idealism, issues into a presumptuous dogmatism and goes far beyond the demand for unity inherent in objectifying reason" (IV, p. 444).

Is there any escape? "There is room for a philosophy which retains the advantages of transcendental idealism without partaking of its essential weaknesses, i.e., for a rational, but not a rationalistic, finalism, viz., for a theory of knowledge which limits the deceptive presumptions of reason while actively justifying the priority of reason over the abstractive understanding" (V, p. 39).

"The Aristotelianism clarified and perfected (and, one might say, vindicated) by scholasticism, and above all by Thomas, fulfills these demands" (V, p. 39). "According to Thomism, our thinking reflects absolute thought without coinciding with it entirely, since whereas absolute thought is a creative power, ours is a self-assimilating striving" (IV, p. 443). "A theory of knowledge inspired by Thomism is motivated in a mediating sort of way equidistant from the uneasy dualism of Kant and the presumptuous monism of Fichte" (Prem., p. 293). This expresses Maréchal's fundamental viewpoint, which guides his investigations and attains systematic development in the fifth volume. In short, it is to lay bare the fundamental characteristics of a theory of knowledge in Thomistic metaphysics so as to gather the elements for the theory of knowledge which would satisfy the critical demands of modern philosophy (V, pp. 41f.). This theory of knowledge should not merely criticize modern theories of knowledge from the viewpoint of Thomistic metaphysics, but should proceed along the very methodological way which Kant has blazed. To attain this end, historical

75

studies of Kant should present his own development and the evolution of transcendental thought into idealism, showing "(1) that the Kantian method is not limited to formal transcendentalism, (2) that it permits (and perhaps even demands) a dialectical evaluation of the dynamism of mind, and (3) that the dialectical utilization of this dynamism *can* lead to a metaphysics, or not, without introducing an ontological premiss to the effect that the concepts of 'ought,' 'becoming,' 'act,' and 'faculty,' on the whole merely indicate analytical relations and logical elements which are knowable through reflection of the contents of consciousness. The inner dialectic of intellectual dynamism *can,* therefore, through methodological 'precision,' take place on a neutral plane and still find no use for the oppositions between 'phenomenal' and 'noumenal,' or 'logical' and 'ontological.' The logical consistency of the syllogistic process, which rests upon the transcendental dynamism of thought, is the same whether the content of consciousness inheres in a psychological subject, or not, or whether it represents a 'thing' in itself, or not. Only at the end of the 'dialectical journey' would the question about being merge in its full significance and perhaps find its solution" (Wd. II, pp. 124f.), and then the transcendental would merge with the metaphysical method (V, p. 567).

METAPHYSICAL AND TRANSCENDENTAL CRITIQUE

According to his program, the fifth volume is divided into three parts. The first book takes a quick look at the preceding historical investigations and makes a few general remarks about the transfer from the metaphysical to the transcendental method. The second and most comprehensive book works out the fundamental elements of the Thomistic metaphysics of knowledge in terms of the critical problem. The third book shows how this theory can be developed by means of the transcendental method without metaphysical presuppositions and then

76

how the possibility and necessity of a valid metaphysics can be proven.

The introductory summary and the general remarks about the transcendental method draw together what has already been worked out in the first four volumes, viz., the initiation with the givenness of the consciousness of object-oriented knowledge, the transcendental analysis of the object immanent to consciousness through the reductive reference to the *a priori* conditions for the possibility for the fact that a subject of knowledge can have such a consciousness of objects, the deductive derivation of the necessity of certain *a priori* structural elements for every mode of the consciousness of objects in discursive understanding, and the essential consideration not only of the static-formal, but also of the dynamic-active element of knowledge, because the determination of form presupposes actuation, because this points to the consideration of the act of knowledge present in consciousness and because later it will be shown that otherwise objectivation would be impossible for a non-intuitive understanding. Such an extension of the transcendental method by means of a stronger emphasis of the dynamic element does not thereby destroy the essence of the transcendental method, as the historical investigations have shown.

This leads to the essential difference between a metaphysical and a transcendental critique (V, pp. 68f.). In both, the object present in consciousness is brought under critical reflection, but the first, e.g., the "classical critique," views the object precisely in the fullness of its objectivity, as absolutely posited, as a thing which is the possible goal of effective action. A metaphysics of knowledge and a critique of knowledge can here be reached only through the systematic development of metaphysics. This, of course, is the longer way, but the one most suited to the natural activity of man. The modern transcendental critique, on the other hand, considers the consciousness of objects in the precisive sense as the form of consciousness only, and then, if it is carried completely to its end, finds that this is made possible through the absolute affirmation of ends and, from what is relative in consciousness, concludes to the ontological absolute. One result of this difference is that expressions which describe and explain knowledge have an ontological meaning in the metaphysical critique, rather as faculties of knowledge in the sense of metaphysical psychology, while they lose this far-reaching meaning in the transcendental critique, where they merely signify logical functions of the constitution of the object immanent to consciousness shown to be conditions of possibility of the structure of the object. Whether these functions could and must be conceived as psychological faculties, according to which the transcendental development of the proof is concluded and metaphysics grounded, is ignored for the time being (V, p. 125). The same is true for expressions which describe the structure of the object. Depending upon the methodological connection in which these expressions are used, we must be careful to distinguish between their precisive transcendental meaning and their fufilled metaphysical meaning. This distinction must be kept clearly in mind if we are to understand Maréchal's exposition properly.

4. THE METAPHYSICS OF KNOWLEDGE

The second book develops the Thomistic metaphysics of knowledge in terms of the critical vindication of the affirmation of being. The first section bears the title of a "critical preamble" and contains a general vindication of the affirmation of being and therefore an ontological theory of knowledge in the traditional sense (V, pp. 99, 491). Here the attempt to cast doubt on the ontological value of knowledge is reduced *ad absurdam*. This theory, according to Maréchal, actually constitutes an objective transcendental deduction of ontological affirmation (V, pp. 86, 98). What follows appears already in the metaphysical framework and is intended to advance the question raised concerning the possibility of this affirmation of being (V, p. 491). He carefully investigates here the elements which activate the affirmation of being necessarily contained in each objectivation (V, p. 99). The second section of the second book sketches the necessary relation of the consciousness of objects (as it has thus been rendered possible) to the absolute order of being. The final two sections correspond to the analytic-reductive and to the reductive phases of the transcendental mode of proof (V, p. 317).

THE ONTOLOGY OF CONSCIOUSNESS

The basic aim of the second section can be summed up by saying that if one wishes to understand the conscious act of knowledge of the object-oriented human understanding in terms of being, i.e., within the total network of metaphysics, then one should not look for the primary ontological condition of becoming conscious in the existential unity of subject and object, but in the inner unity of the immanent intellectual act itself, insofar as it is act (V, pp. 110f.). That is to say, an object is known insofar as the unity of the immanent intellectual (and therefore conscious) activity receives a new specification through a causal connection with the form of the object, which is subordinated to the natural form of the active potency of the immanent activity (V, pp. 121f.). The psychological aspect of the conscious givenness of knowledge thus appears as the direct effect of the ontological aspect of knowledge, viz., of the immanence of the object in the subject. The object, through its causal influence on the subject, confers final determination on the ontological link of the subject with the immanent intellectual act and thus specifies the conscious act—knowledge (V, pp. 111f.). This is the viewpoint from which logical truth, viz., the agreement of the subjective determination of thought with the absolute referential order, must be defined (V, pp. 105f.). Strictly speaking, logical truth is to be found only in judgment, not in sense knowledge or in concepts (V, p. 127). It is not a result of knowledge, insofar as it is conscious, but the other way around (V, pp. 115f.), i.e., the essence of truth is realized in the constitution of the subject which unites the self and the other in the identity of the immanent act. Objective knowledge is nothing but the awareness of such an actuated object (V, p. 126). Judgment is thus the conscious completion of objective knowledge, for in judgment the object is not haphazardly known, but known precisely as object (V, pp. 128f.). Since it is the case that the pre-conditions of objective knowledge become known precisely in judgment (and are known clearly only in judgment; cf., V, p. 131), Maréchal turns to an analysis of the pre-conditions of objective knowledge as they appear in the essential structure of judgment (V, pp. 131f.).

But for the moment, we shall interrupt our summary of Maréchal's line of thought in order to evaluate the meaning of what was just discussed.

Maréchal made it quite clear that he was not interested in formulating a complete and detailed theory of knowledge, nor in distinguishing the modes of evidence and the particular criteria for their validation, nor in distinguishing what is truly evident from what is only apparently evident, viz., truth from error, nor in specifying the degrees of certainty. He also does not wish merely to describe the intentionality of knowledge, nor to give rules on what we must do in order to attain certain knowledge in the consciously directed and controlled advance of knowledge. He presupposes all this insofar as he is concerned with giving an ontological explanation of knowledge (which strikes us as certain and sufficiently grounded and thus presumes the claim of being related to ontological objects) and with vindicating the fundamental ontological value of such knowledge. If, then, judgment is taken as the conscious process and result of a certain constitution of the subject, this would not necessarily seem to exclude the possibility that judgment, for purposes of a phenomenological description of knowing, appears as the result of insight into states of affairs and that thinking has its ultimate logical foundation only in such an insight. That is to say, Maréchal is not interested in how we ground the certainty of a judgment, but rather in how we explain the fact of the consciousness of an object as such (viz., the fact of a grounded and certain judgment as an appearance in the order of being), i.e., in how we are able to understand it metaphysically. One could perhaps look upon this manner of understanding as belonging chiefly to the psychology of knowledge, if one means by psychology not merely a description of the processes of the mind but also their metaphysical explanation. This investigation, however, essentially transcends psychology insofar as it is to serve as the clarification of the fundamental metaphysical value of knowledge. Later we shall see how extensive this possibility is, and then we shall also be able to determine the relationship of Maréchal's method to the method of a direct critique of knowledge.

Thus one cannot criticize Maréchal for having mixed the intentional with the ontological order. Knowledge, "it is said, is essentially intentional and not a natural form of the subject. That is entirely correct if what is meant is that it brings a formal element to the knowing subject which passes into consciousness. But does it then cease to be an ontological reality, a real state of a real subject? It would surely be an exaggeration if one wanted to assert not only the distinction but the complete separation between 'real' and 'intentional,' between being and idea. A representational form must have another relation to the real than the signification of the real. It sinks its roots into the real. . . . In opposition to the bias of nominalism, a metaphysics of knowledge which determines the real conditions of the intentional is not a hopeless science" (Abstr., 163f.). If in the course of such metaphysical-epistemological investigations the general structural elements of the act of the consciousness of objects are understood in terms of the formal and dynamic determinations of the active faculty ordered to such an act, this should not be taken as a disintegration of consciousness and of the receptive character of knowledge into a blind, non-conscious striving. "I do not explain consciousness through striving, but rather, much more modestly, I explain a peculiarity of discursive consciousness through the act of that 'inborn striving' which, according to Thomas (*Summ. theol.*, I, q. 80, a. 1 ad 3), is proportionate to each speculative faculty for the completion of its nature" (Abstr., p. 176).

It would seem, then, that no significant objection can actually be raised against the position of Maréchal's metaphysics of knowledge, which regards knowledge as the act of a knowing subject and then looks for the pre-conditions which must be given previous to the act in order that the subject can posit the act. The further question, whether this investigation is useful for the critical evaluation of knowledge, can be posed only in terms of the result. Moreover, it is legitimate to seek these conditions chiefly in the knowing subject itself, for the act of knowledge is, after all, an act immanent to the subject, produced and performed entirely by the subject. Maréchal does not exclude the fact that the subject, in order to be able to produce this act, must itself be determined by another being. Rather, he requires such an influence, because only in this way is the act of knowledge possible as the act of knowledge of this object. At the same time, it must be made clear that this influence is not the only determination upon which the act of knowledge is dependent. To demonstrate this fact briefly, we might ask why, despite the essentially same real influence of the object, this influence produces no knowledge at all in a stone, only sensible awareness in an animal, whereas in man it produces a knowledge of this object as object, which is represented as an object in the order of being and as the possible object of deliberate activity. How must such a faculty be really constituted so that its act is not only conscious but manifests the general properties of certain, objective knowledge? We return again to the fact that the metaphysical-epistemological ground of what concerns us here does not coincide with the logical ground of certainty, viz., with insight into states of affairs. It has to do with the ontological nature of a being for which it is possible that the influence of another being on it is not only received as an effect but is developed into a knowledge of this other being. "If all the conditions for objective assimilation are present, then the act of understanding essentially consists in the illuminative consciousness of this acquired richness, in this 'cognito,' which Thomas derives from the actuated truth (i.e., from the assimilation of an outside form) as a direct formal effect" (Abstr., p. 157). If, then, a knowing subject must have certain real, universal properties through which it can know objects as such, and if these properties must be involved in every knowledge of objects, then is it not to be expected that there will be certain universal results from this for every act of knowledge which will perhaps even affect the very nature of the value of acts of knowledge? Maréchal is convinced of this fact and it is on these terms that he works out his metaphysical-epistemological investigation. We shall now pick up his train of thought again.

The universal form of the complete human knowledge of objects, viz., judgment, possesses as an essential structure a *content* (through which various judgments are distinguished from each other) and a *form*. Form possesses a double function. As *synthetic form,* it unifies the subject and predicate as elements which determine content. As *objective form,* it transforms the judgment into a deliberate affirmation whereby it attains that through which judgment is the expression of complete human knowledge, viz., of the definite knowledge of an object, which can also function as the possible term of deliberated, free activity. If the form of judgment is ignored, the subject and predicate remain which, as *concepts,* are themselves composed of content and a form-giving element. If the differences in content are analyzed, one finally goes beyond all unifying forms subordinate to the concept to physical elements which cannot be reduced further, viz., sensible elements which, as it were, constitute the first matter of human knowledge (V, pp. 132f.). How, then, is it possible to show that the judgment of objects necessarily manifests this structure and which active faculties of the knowing subject (operating for the effect of the influences of the object) are present in this structure?

Consider the following. If we agree to a general structure appropriate to all the acts of a faculty which distinguishes the acts of this faculty from those of another faculty, this implies that the faculty is structured so as to produce such acts. The differences between acts of the same faculty according to content are not determined by linking the faculty with such acts, but through the concrete and variable conditions under which the faculty stands determining it to the production of concrete acts. Such a faculty must show itself to be determined by such concrete conditions if an act is to be actually produced. However, the concrete conditions, considered in themselves, cannot be the ground for the universal uniqueness of the acts of this faculty, otherwise it would not be possible for another faculty to produce another kind of act, viz., an act with a different universal structure, under the same conditions. In the case of a cognitive faculty, this means that all the specific, structural elements common to the concrete acts of a faculty cannot be explained through the action of the external object as known, but through the real constitution of the subject of knowledge and its faculties (in a sense, then, not *a posteriori,* but *a priori*). Only that through which similar acts are to be distinguished according to content, irrespective of the explanation of how such acts are at all possible, can be explained *a posteriori.*

The metaphysics of knowledge, therefore, must look upon human knowledge as the point of intersection of *a priori* and empirical conditions (V, p. 109). Insofar as the *a priori* element is not sufficient in itself to produce the actual act of knowledge, i.e., insofar as the cognitive faculty is also formed by the concrete, causal influences of other things, objects are not given *a priori,* rather only the conditions for their objective apprehension (V, p. 108). This distinguishes discursive from intuitive intelligence. "Every kind of objective knowledge below the level of intellectual intuition originates from the co-operation of *a priori* requirements (which determine certain characteristics *a priori*) and *a posteriori* empirical givenness (which fills them with content)" (V, p. 125). "In Thomism, the whole theory of human knowledge revolves around two focal points: the externality (contingency) of the sensibly given and the apriority (necessity) of cognitive determination, insofar as it is cognitive" (V, p. 147).

But how are the kinds of noetic acts distinguishable? Through the special mode of their relationships to their objects, or more precisely, through that aspect of objects by which they are at all objects of intentional acts, viz., through the formal object. That aspect of the object through which such acts are referred to their object is, on the one hand, absolutely necessary for all such intentional acts and is thus *logically a priori* to the extent that it must necessarily belong to all objects of such acts independent of the content of specific objects. On the other hand, the fact that all acts of this kind, as opposed to other acts, are directly related to this aspect of objects must, in terms of metaphysical epistemology, be referred back to a previous, real determination of the active faculty to produce such acts. The reference to acts with this formal object is thus *psychologically a priori.* Thus the formal object of a faculty of knowledge finds itself "already constituted by definition between two orders of relations: the relation to particular objects, whose universal unity it constitutes (the logical *a priori*) and the relation to the knowing subject, in which it constitutes the form of a natural striving (the psychological *a priori*). Is it not clear how the undividedness of the formal object forms a bridge between subject and object?" (V, pp. 155f.). "The formal object thus determines both the kind of a definite level of knowability with respect to the knowable object and the mode of knowing for the knowing subject" (V, p. 157).

It does not suffice to say that in knowledge the object is perceived (directly or indirectly) to have this aspect, through which the act of knowledge is made possible. This would confuse the viewpoints of describing the intentional occurrence of knowledge and of clarifying this occurrence, insofar as it is an immanent act of a subject. Likewise, it does not suffice simply to say that we have, as the facts show, the power to perceive objects, for what is to be explained is precisely how this power can produce an act in which objects are known. If, in the sense of a direct critique of knowledge, one refers to the direct evidence of consciousness, from which everything else can be discovered, this serves as a clarification of what is indirectly evident in our knowledge of the world. This clarification has critical significance, but it does not explain the natural activity of knowledge as directed toward being transcending consciousness. It also does not explain how the direct evidence of the given elements of consciousness and of the first principles and the capacity for this evidence are to be understood metaphysically, nor where they belong in the real process of the activities of the subject. Such explanation requires that what we *describe* as a grasping of objects or an insight into conditions must be *understood* from the point of view of a more precise, real determination of the subject of knowledge and its faculties as the immanent act of this subject. Such a metaphysico-epistemological explanation does not go against the findings of description, but clarifies them, for the immanent act of the knowledge of the object (which is experienced and which can be described as the intentional apprehension of the object) is made possible and is causally explained through the form, which determines the natural striving of the faculty of knowledge to produce an act of the knowledge of the object in terms of what is definitely and concretely given. "The natural precedence of a form of knowledge does not close off the view of an external object from the subject, for the *a priori* determination which bears this form is itself essentially referred to objects" (V, p. 166).

THE METAPHYSICAL ANALYSIS
OF JUDGMENTAL KNOWLEDGE

Now we must ask which faculties cooperate to make human knowledge (which is expressed in judgments or something equivalent to them) possible (Dyn., p. 98). Maréchal takes this question up while examining the essential structural elements already dealt with, beginning with the sensibly given and leading to the objective synthesis of judgment.

In order that a differentiation of the consciousness of objects be possible in terms of content, something must be *sensibly given*. This is where the causal influence which the object exercises on the subject and which places the subject in the concrete position to know a certain object attains its primal consciousness. But how can the actions of bodies on the senses (as concretely and spatially determined in every moment of time) be received through the activation of the corresponding sense faculties into the unity of a conscious act with the qualitative properties of their acts? This requires that the unity of this act be open to spatial determinations, i.e., that it be referred *a priori* to the realization of spatial determinations. However, since it is impossible to receive all spatial determinations at the same time (the sense organs can at any one time only receive a determinate selection of the spatial determinations of the bodies in the area), space, or the synthesis of extension, must be completed in terms of time (V, p. 171), which presupposes a kind of rudimentary, pre-conscious memory (V, p. 171). This means that "space and time constitute a law, the universal rule of sensibility" (V, p. 170). Since the active faculty for sense consciousness, previous to the synthesis of space, is determined through time, we can see:

(1) "How a *'sensibile in potentia'* (an external, sensible object), if it is to become a *'sensibile in actu,'* must receive a double transformation through space and time with respect to the materiality of the sensibly knowing subject.

(2) "How a *'sentiens in potentia'* (a sensibly knowing subject), in order to become a *'sentiens in actu,'* must, with re-

spect to its own materiality (which corresponds to that of the object), take in what is externally given under the double aspects of space and time" (V, pp. 172f.).

If the requirements of the sensible knower, as well as the requirements of that which is sensibly perceivable through the sense faculties, depend on an *a priori* law of activity, viz., on the determinability of the objects of possible acts of perception through space and time, this in no way contradicts the objectivity of the quantitative determination of what is perceived, rather it guarantees this objectivity, for it follows from this metaphysical explanation of sense knowledge and its *a priori* that anything which is neither extended nor temporal, viz., which does not belong to the realm which underlies quantitative instability, cannot in any way be a normal occasion for sense perception. In a faculty which brings to consciousness the concrete state of the sense organs as activated through the influences of the bodies in the area, viz., "in a material faculty, the spatial determinations of the 'actually known' dialectically depend on the spatiality of the subject and the spatiality of the object" (V, p. 180). The quantitative *a priori* of sensibility thus does not confuse, rather it logically and psychologically requires, the objectivity of the senses (although in terms of the knowledge of the understanding this objectivity is rather weak). "Under the simple condition that the *a priori* includes . . . a relation to the object, it ceases to be a hinderance to objective knowledge and becomes a proper means thereto" (V, pp. 177f.). The *a priori* does not have to be directly known as such. It suffices that it "is simply activated as a functional disposition and is knowable only insofar as it enters into a connection with some objective content (as do the forms of sensibility). . . . Later we shall show that objectivity increases in direct proportion to apriority as understood in this way" (V, p. 178).

Sensible knowledge, however, which is apprehended in the forms of space and time, does not produce the *concept*. "For the concept includes the form of a super-sensible and non-quantitative, universal and necessary unity which is not in the least open to such an involved association of sensible elements"

(V, p. 185). What, then, do we mean by the *a priori* determination of the faculty adequate to concepts and subordinate to sensibility? How do we explain the activity of the understanding ascribed to the formation of concepts and characterized as abstraction?

Abstraction can be considered from two points of view (V, p. 265). On the one hand, it is the analysis of the object to which it is related in that, through the concept, it brings forth and represents a special characteristic of the object, for the object merely grounds the universality of the concept, it does not contain it as such (V, p. 263). On the other hand, however, if it is considered in terms of the knowing subject it is a synthesis, either as an abstractive activity or as the end term of this activity (the abstract, the universal), such that abstraction is a higher unification of what is sensibly given. This latter point of view must be examined.

If the understanding essentially transcends the spatiality and temporality of the synthesis of perception as conditioned through the inner dependence of the faculties of sense on matter, then the understanding must be intrinsically independent of matter (cf. V, p. 226). Nevertheless, its activity retains a certain dependence on sensibility since it raises what is sensibly given to a higher unity. The concept is *a posteriori* with respect to its content (which differentiates objects) and *a priori* with respect to form (V, p. 191). How should this relationship be approached?

The interconnection of the faculties can be considered statically or dynamically. Considered statically, the faculties appear as different stages whose interrelationship is defined through matter-form causality. The subject, in terms of its lower faculty and its act, appears as matter, as a receptive element, while the higher faculty and its share in the act of knowledge appears as a form-giving and determining element. If the relation is considered dynamically and actively, a kind of external causality appears insofar as the faculties are reciprocally required and regulated. The lower faculty seems to be ultimately directed to the higher faculty, which it serves and which is the proximate cause and direct end of the lower faculty (V, p. 204). This puts us in the position to examine the explanation of *abstraction* which Maréchal gives with reference to Thomas. The understanding contains an active component (*intellectus agens*) which, as an *a priori* determination, does not intend the unification of the content of knowledge simply in terms of space and time, or simply in terms of quantitative being, but a unification in terms of the whole of what is knowable (V, p. 223). In itself, however, it cannot produce determinate, objective knowledge if the senses do not present the material. Because of the body-soul unity in man, the senses are ordered to the understanding such that the constructive perfection of the sense image occurs under the natural influence of the understanding and such that the sense image is opened to the higher unity of the understanding (V, p. 207). Along with the emergence of the sense image, there arises in the understanding a dynamic disposition in which the relation of the understanding to the objective unity of all that is knowable qualitatively determines what is given through the sense image (*phantasma*). This is the intellectual form of knowledge (*species intelligibilis*) (V, pp. 216–219). The intellectual form of knowledge does not itself enter into consciousness as something known, but is discovered only in the explanation of knowledge as the dynamic relation of the understanding to the sense image at hand (V, pp. 215, 219). This intellectual form of knowledge, the result of the influence of the active components of the understanding on the sense image, is itself intellectual and immaterial, as is the understanding itself, but it is completely related to the qualitative differences of what is sensibly given and is itself determined with respect to this relationship (V, p. 212). The intellectual form of knowledge, which is a means to the knowledge of the particular thing experienced, finds its ultimate determination through its real relation to the sense image (*conversio ad phantasma*), for here it becomes the form of a real activity of the understanding and yields conscious knowledge of an object (V, p. 218). Thus human knowledge, because of this necessity of turning to the sense image, considered of the multiple wholeness of the activities of the different faculties of knowledge, begins with the perception of the

90

particular object. This is the only point from which concepts can be derived which ignore particular determinations and are universal (V, p. 225). The intellectual form of knowledge thus stands at the point of intersection of the relation to the totality of what is knowable on the one hand and the relation to what is concretely given in the sense image on the other. Through the first relation, human knowledge is freed from the conditions of sensibility, viz., from intrinsic imprisonment within the quantitative and the limitation of knowledge to appearance. However, the reference to what is given in the sense image is necessary for the knowledge of a particular body. Thus concepts, arrived at in terms of the sense image, represent the material beings which appear in them, but not to the exclusion of the possibility that these concepts may signify still others (V, p. 235), because the intrinsic structure of the understanding (in terms of which the formation of concepts and the transcendence of the quantitative conditions necessary for this is at all possible) goes beyond the realm of things which underlie quantitative conditions and which can therefore appear in sensibility. This orientation, then, transcends all the objects which can be directly *represented* in concepts as directly taken from experience. This orientation of the understanding implies a super-empirical "anticipation" in consequence of which the objective receptive power of reason extends beyond all limited being (V, p. 259). The highest objective unity to which every object of thought relates (due to the orientation of the understanding) is in no category and can be referred to none. It is, rather, the unity of elements which, with respect to their very constitution, are related to their ultimate source and thus merge into an analogous unity, whose lower members are the finite beings as represented in concepts (V, pp. 250–253). It is, however, possible to *signify* this unity through reflection upon the orientation, which functions in the formation of every concept, toward the objective unity of all that is knowable and toward the absolute being incapable of representation in direct, abstractive concepts. Therefore, transcendental and analogous concepts can be attained which make an indirect determination of absolute being possible, viz., as the principle term of the unity of all that is knowable as grounded in the relation of analogy. The intellectual *a priori* thus makes possible an objective knowledge which is not, strictly speaking, representation (V, pp. 271f.).

The second relation of the intellectual form of knowledge, viz., to the sense image, explains how the natural orientation toward the activation of all that is knowable is concretized in the conscious knowledge of a definite, particular object. Insofar as the understanding makes sensibility operable in the knowledge of a particular object, "it experiences external coercion, as every intellectual *agens* experiences the coercion of the matter upon which it operates" (V, p. 239). The given, therefore, functions as a restrictive condition on the actuation of the understanding as oriented toward all that is knowable and thus explains why precisely this object, and not another, is known. That it is being and not merely its appearance that is known, however, is not explained by the sense image, but by the orientation of the understanding, and ultimately by its intellectuality. This can be better understood if the structural elements of knowledge in the form of judgment are identified and discussed.

By the *form of judgment* Maréchal understands the totality of the conditions which guarantee and complete in judgment the synthesis of concepts proper to it (V, p. 281), i.e., not merely what one thinks of when the copula is mentioned. This synthesis is basically a *material identity,* viz., the "essential confrontation of two forms in a single suppositum" (V, p. 284). This "concretizing mode," however, is of the "synthetic kind which is proper to each objective concept adequate to the representation of an object" (V, pp. 283f.). The "unity of a form and a *suppositum* (the unity of concretion)" proper to the direct concept "is expanded in judgment, where the logical subject is considered as *suppositum*" (as defined either indirectly or by direct concept) "and the predicate as a form related to this *suppositum*" (Mel., I, p. 315). "If the synthesis actually expresses the structure of direct concepts, reflected in judgments, through concretion, then the ground for all this must be sought in the external dependence which intellectual power requires as opposed to sensible and material powers. The intellectual form of knowledge is objectified only insofar as it is concretized in matter through the *phantasma,* and thus, at the heart of knowledge, we discover the imperfect and contingent manner of subsistence which is inherent to material objects, viz., the grounding in a *primum subjectum,* viz., in an infinitely diversifiable suppositum" (V, p. 290). If reason were not linked with receptive sensibility, its only alternative would be the creation of the content of knowledge. It would, then, not judge in the manner of "concretion," i.e., it would no longer be synthetic, but intuitive. Thus we must hold that a non-intuitive intelligence requires the co-operation of sensibility, i.e., of a receptive faculty which is physically passive with regard to its objects and is therefore material and quantitative, such that the cooperation of this faculty results in the necessity of the synthetic mode of concretization for the objectified actuation of intelligence (V, p. 290).

What has been said so far, however, only explains how the production of an act occurs in the knowing subject which possesses a quality which relates not only to a quantitative determination of a corporeal being, but to its own being. We have only explained the *immanence* of the object in the subject. That property of knowledge whereby a thing is considered an *object* of knowledge, viz., as something over and against the subject, has not yet been sufficiently considered. "What is given in subjectivity is assimilated only in terms of an appropriated form. In order to present an object known, what is given must free itself from the subject and become the focal point of a relation whose other focal point is the subject. In other words, immanence must at the same time be antithesis" (Mel. I, p. 315). "This 'objectifying relation,' however, is nothing other than the relation of 'logical truth' which links the representational form to the order of being, or to reality ('*ad rem*')" (V, p. 298). As we have already seen, however, logical truth is found in judgment. "If, then, objective apperception takes place in judgment, the objective unity of apperception cannot have a larger extension than the determining form of judgment" (V, p. 299). "Now we already know that the unity of apperception excedes the unity of concretion" (V, p. 299), for it was shown in the explanations of the formation of the concept and of the peculiarity of the intellectual form of knowledge that the objective unity to which reason is ordered is not limited to the realm of those objects which are properly represented in direct concepts derived from phantasms. Therefore, the unity of whatever is objective is more comprehensive than the realm of that which is attainable through *conversio ad phantasma,* but nevertheless the psychological function (which must be accommodated to concretive synthesis in order to raise the judgment to the level of objective apperception) can be nothing other than *affirmation.*

Judgment is thus more than a merely formal unity. It is a synthesis through affirmation (V, p. 300). Through affirmation judgment reaches in an indirect and imperfect way what intuition directly possesses through creation or inner production, viz., the knowledge of the object as object (V, pp. 303f.). This function of affirmation can be understood as the highest and determining form of judgment if we consider that it stands at the intersection of two intellectual orders of finality. On the one hand, it is the cornerstone of the appropriation of the form of the object *as form* of the object, which attains completion in judgment. On the other hand, it is the beginning of a spontaneous striving for being which sees the object over and against the subject as the possible value of action and poses it *as a goal.* The assimilation of what is given is posed within the framework of the active, inclusive projection of what is given against the perspective of the ultimate goal through which objectivation finds its completion. In such a dynamic relation, the given elements become middle terms which make possible the transfer from finite objects to infinite being. Affirmation is thus not the mere connection of subject and predicate, but a transcendent anticipation through which the transcendental relation of objects to absolute being, as inclusively posited in direct knowledge, can be unveiled without doubt for reflection (V, pp. 313f.). "The transcendent term of analogical relation which raises each object to the level of objects (to 'being') in the mind is, therefore, in one way or another, impressed on our actual consciousness. It is implied (*implicite*) and the whole problem revolves around making it explicit" (V, p. 314).

THE METAPHYSICO-EPISTEMOLOGICAL DEDUCTION OF ONTOLOGICAL AFFIRMATION

"But after all, is not this highest goal toward which the mysterious 'forward drive' of affirmation is directed merely a subjectively postulated ideal? Is it, on the contrary, as Thomas would have it, an objective, necessary, absolute reality?" (V, p. 315). The answer to this question is found in the subsequent third section which, from a different point of view, tries to present a deeper understanding of the logical structure of the object of knowledge. This third section bears the title "Deduction of Ontological Affirmation." Maréchal here seeks "to demonstrate *a priori,* 'through concepts' " (viz., concepts in terms of which the structure of the immanent object and its necessary conditions of possibility are described) "that for a non-intuitive intelligence, the means, and the only means, for the representation of what is contained in consciousness as objects is their strict metaphysical affirmation, i.e., their (at least implicitly so) determined relation to a transcendent reality, such that any reduction of this affirmation leads to the negation of the possibility of object-oriented thought" (V, p. 318). The metaphysical value of objects is thus connected with object-oriented thought as such, which is the minimal requirement for any critique. In this section, the transcendental deduction of ontological affirmation takes place against the background of the Thomistic metaphysics of knowledge, but it would be possible to free the deduction from all metaphysical trappings and to translate it (without, of course, its metaphysical depth, but in its full, demonstrative force) to the immediate domain of Kantian philosophy. "Such a polemical application will occupy us in the third book" (V, p. 318). The deduction worked out in the third section of the second book has essentially the same logical structure and thus prepares the reader who is chiefly

95

versed in the Thomistic metaphysics of knowledge for an understanding of the deduction in the third book.

The structure of this deduction is summarized by Maréchal in the following six points (V, pp. 458–460), which we shall expand upon in connection with some of the other positions of the third section.

(1) "For a non-intuitive intelligence which receives formal determinations (species) from an external cause, these formal determinations do not directly have the quality of an object unless the way in which they become immanent to the subject is itself the way in which they are posed over and against the subject" (V, p. 458). For a non-intuitive intelligence, not all of the objective elements of its cognitive activity are inborn, and therefore it must receive objective determinations from without (V, p. 351). It is a question of direct knowledge, not of reflection (which already presupposes direct knowledge). "The complete reflection of the intellectual subject upon his own activities is of the intuitive order" (V, p. 350). This activity, however, as direct knowledge, presupposes something externally given and thus the reaction proper to sensibility in direct dependence on this impression, which presupposes materiality. Otherwise, the abstractive, intellectual power, viz., the understanding as the power of the "universal," cannot by itself represent the specific material determinations of sensibility. This tension is resolved through the explanation of abstraction already presented, viz., due to the body-soul unity, the spontaneity of immaterial reason is intimately connected with the receptivity of material sensibility such that the material determinations presented in sensibility express a restrictive condition on the autonomous, spontaneous drive of the self-activity of immaterial reason, which, as independent of matter, essentially goes beyond sensibility (V, pp. 351f., 239). Conceptual thought thus stands in a dual relation to the concrete as well as the objective unity of all that is knowable, and ultimately to the pure act of being, which, although not necessarily expressly conscious, is nevertheless active. Only in this way is the intellectual appropriation of the form of a definite object possible (V, pp. 443f.). However, this does not explain how this

appropriation not only yields the immanence of the form of the object in the subject, but also the confrontation with this form as the form of an object.

(2) "This confrontation in immanence is possible only by means of a relation inherent in the subject, and this confrontation itself can have meaning for consciousness only if the relation inherent in the subject is either implicitly or explicitly knowable by the subject. However, in agreement with the ontological theory of consciousness, only that is knowable by a subject which is immanent to it according to the final actuality of this subject" (V, p. 458). "Which relation is capable of contrasting certain aspects of subjective activity which inhere in this activity?" (V, p. 440). Which relation can set something as an object over and against the subject on the basis of the conditions in the subject?

(3) "The only immanent relations which fulfill the conditions presented in point two are the relation of cause to effect and the relation of striving to a goal. Only these two offer an immanent principle of contrast in the productive and striving activity of a subject, for to know oneself as cause means to know oneself as distinguished ontologically from reality, and to know oneself, implicitly or explicitly, as striving means to know oneself, implicitly or explicitly, as really different from an objective goal. The first of the two relations, however, is the ground for creative intuition, which lies beyond our frame of reference, and thus the secret of objective knowledge lies in the dynamic relation to finality" (V, p. 458). Thus an inner finality of the act of knowledge appears as the foundation of the opposition of subject and object in consciousness (V, pp. 440f.), because only this provides an explanation of the function of objectivation in the art of the subject of knowledge (pp. 453f.). How, then, is this objectifying finality related to the activity by means of which the form of the object as appropriated in abstraction and becomes immanent to the subject as the condition for the positing of the act through which this object is known?

(4) "In order to pose a directly external object corresponding to immanent determinations over and against the under-

standing, the dynamic relation of finality must be included in the act itself through which these determinations were appropriated such that the act which appropriates is identical with the act which contrasts. Therefore, the appropriation itself must posit and receive the immanent form in the objective stance to the subject, viz., in the realm of ends. This, however, is possible only if the appropriation is completed under the initiating and continuing movement of a comprehensive goal in relation to which the assimilated form is grasped and retained as a subordinated goal—as the beginning of possession, of some kind of means or of a possible approach. This introduces the immanent form directly into the order of being since the ends are noumenal" (V, p. 459). "Strictly speaking, no one desires a form (which is a *quo* and not a *quod*) as a pure abstraction. That which is willed is properly a good, and the goal of this activity is necessarily either himself who acts as he who acquires the form (subjective goal), or an object fitted out with this form and is chosen because of this (objective goal). In any case, the real condition of a goal includes the absolute of an 'in itself,' and this is why the *goal,* as opposed to the *form,* is not allowed to be thought of as appearance. The goals, if there are any, are noumenal. . . . Thus if the assimilated form is apprehended as a goal, it is apprehended as the form of an 'in itself' " (Dyn., p. 96). This last notion thus not only explains objectivation, since need and good, striving and goal, are distinguished and contrasted with each other, but also the fact that objectified forms belong to the order of the in itself. They belong to the order in which goals are striven for and realized through real activity (V, p. 445). Grasped in terms of the natural striving of reason, the appropriated and objectified form, the form as form of another, takes on a dynamic character and poses this other as an intermediate goal as such (V, pp. 442–444).

Maréchal does not slip into a confusion of *knowing* and *striving,* understanding and will. They are both, it is true, closely connected with each other, since the form which makes the activity of willing objectively possible is not a mere reproduction of the form of the understanding, but that very form itself (V, p. 383), such that the activities of both powers are intimately linked together through their reciprocal influences on each other. Thus insofar as willing depends on objective goals, the understanding maintains a priority over and against the will, but insofar as the activity of the understanding is initiated through a subjective dynamism, the understanding is subordinate to the will (V, p. 392). The way in which we approach new things as given actually adepends upon complicated speculative, affective and volitional dispositions which cover what can be signified as a habitus of hard-earned knowledge and which are continually strengthened and modified through the process of concrete experience. A logical theory of the understanding, of course, can ignore these contingent factors, but a psychological treatment of the activity of the understanding must take such speculative and practical attitudes into account (V, p. 405). The close connection of these two activities, however, does not reduce their relationship to the mere relative opposition of formal determination (*specificatio*) and actuation (*exercitium*). "The understanding, and every faculty of knowledge as well, has its own act, which does not consist merely in presenting a form to speculative or practical striving. This proper act, in which striving no longer has an inner role . . . , is consciousness, '*cognitio in actu secundo.*' . . . If consciousness consists in a 'rest,' viz., in a partial fulfillment, at least, of a striving, it does not on that account coincide with it. Consciousness means neither striving nor rest, but rather a kind of transparency (*transparence*) of an 'immaterial' form and, following from this, a direct, even if limited, reflection of the form on itself—'*reditio ad seipsum*'—a reflection which is in no way a forceful 'bending back' on oneself, but to a degree a '*subsistere in seipso.*' . . . Consciousness is the peak of the order of formal causality, just as possession is the peak of the order of final causality. At the hearrt of objective consciousness, consciousness and possession coincide, since consciousness is the characteristic development of possession in a speculative power" (V, pp. 408f.). Maréchal is thus far from abolishing the independence of the understanding or debasing the direct givenness of consciousness, but he sees the necessary connection between the speculative and the dynamic and insists that a sufficient explanation of knowledge can be offered only if the peculiarities of the object known (which make it into an object as such) are pre-formed in the dynamic-assimilative phase beneath the threshold of consciousness because otherwise conscious knowing would not be understandable as an act immanent to the subject (V, pp. 409f.). His analysis also succeeds in showing that the radical natural dynamism which is spent in volitional activity is the same as the natural striving of the speculative activity of the understanding (V, p. 429). In this way he can explain the close connection between the understanding and the will, despite all their differences, and thus prevent a cleavage between theoretical and practical reason while at the same time making it clear why objective knowledge has its objects in the realm of real things existing in themselves as objects of activity. This is not a falsification of consciousness as directly describable but an explanation of consciousness in terms of its structure as pointing beyond itself.

The occurrence of an act in which the object is set over and against the subject is thus in terms of a striving. This does not concern merely the production of an immanent act, but the objects themselves. The special forms of objects are not simply assimilated, but contrasted with the subject as forms of the partial goals of this striving, set over and against the subject, so that the consciousness of objects as such is made possible. All this, however, raises the question about the goal under which these partial goals are subordinated, for the actuation of a faculty is possible only insofar as the faculty, because of its determination, is related to this actuation. Yet the goal is precisely that to which the determination of a faculty is ultimately ordered, so that whether a further actuation of the faculty is involved or not, the concern is with the final goal or with a partial goal subordinated to the final goal. There is thus an inter-correspondence between a faculty, the determination of a faculty, the form of actuation, the form of the effect and the goal. The goal to be realized at the end of an activity already constitutes the specific determination of striving in the activity. However, since the goal, as something to be realized, belongs in itself to the order of existence, it must be fully determined. It is because of our abstractive knowledge that we represent it to ourselves in our conscious activities only under a universal form.

The goal of immanent activity can either be a subjective state of a new activity, but an activity of striving can never be its own goal because that through which one wants something can never be identical with what is wanted. Therefore, the ultimate goal must be different from all the activities of striving. However, since goals, insofar as they really determine an actual striving (and as partial goals they can do this only on the strength of a real subordination under the ultimate goal), could never be a pure succession of appearances, the ultimate goal is the fundamental condition for the possibility of particular goals (V, pp. 363–372). The activity of the understanding, however, manifests itself as the actuation of a movement, and therefore it must strive after a goal which itself must be expressed in the form of a perfected activity (V, p. 373). This leads us to the question about the ultimate goal of the natural striving of the understanding underlying the real actuation of the understanding. That there must be such a goal follows from the fact that the natural striving would otherwise be internally impossible. "Natural finality—the fundamental law of becoming—uncovers at the very least the self-consistent possibility of the goal toward which it strives. Were it otherwise, then the 'will of nature' would have to be conceived as a willing of the impossible. Being would be striving after nothing. . . . It would be logically contradictory to accept that a *natural* impulse should move something moveable toward a goal impossible in itself." "We insist on the word 'natural,' for in man conscious acts of the will [*élicites*] are arbitrary in themselves and can twist toward impossible and imagined goals" (V, p. 421). Since, then, the goal and the form of activity correspond to each other, the goal of noetic activity must be determinable from an analysis of its goal.

The analysis of abstraction, however, indicated that the intellectual assimilation of the forms of objects is possible only through an orientation of reason to the objective unity of all that is knowable. The faculty of conception as well as the active orientation of the understanding are without inner limits (V, pp. 374f.). The vindication of this objective infinity of the understanding centers around what is given in inner experience, for the affirmation in judgment transcends the formal representation of corporeality and is regulated by the reality of objects (V, p. 376). Properly speaking, we can directly "represent" only something quantitative, but the power to "signify" and to affirm goes beyond representation. This is undeniable as a fact of inner experience, but whether it is true is not open for discussion here (V, p. 379). The natural, objective form of the understanding is thus expressed through the concept of "transcendental being" (V, pp. 380, 412). The only unsurpassable limit to thinking is therefore not some determinate limit within the order of being, but the "absolute limit," viz., non-being as such. "Reason's total, objective power of conception rejects every limit, with the exception of non-being, and extends itself as far as pure and simple being. Only an ultimate and absolutely completive goal—infinite being—can satisfy such a faculty for the reception of forms" (V, p. 380), because only "a reality which is free from every limited determination" is adequate to this form of noetic striving as the ultimate and completive goal, or, "in other words, it must be a transcendent object, a subsistent, infinite being" (V, p. 412). It follows, then, that God is the ultimate goal, not only in the sense that he is the goal for every creature (V, p. 414), but "objectively," in a manner proper to reason and to the will (V, p. 415). "The ultimate, complete subjective goal of noetic dynamism—perfect happiness, possession of the perfect good—consists in a satisfying 'appropriation' of the form of being, in other words, in the possession of God. This goal, although supernatural, must *in itself* be possible, otherwise the natural orientation of our intellectual nature would become a logical contradiction —the striving after nothing" (V, p. 448).

We must here discuss briefly the meaning of the supernatural goal in Maréchal's argument. First of all, it deals merely with a remote possibility of attaining this goal (V, pp. 423f.), and secondly, the working out of the relationship between the natural orientation of man and the supernatural goal fits in very well with Maréchal's interest in the mystics, but this does not disrupt his metaphysico-epistemological thought. He himself wrote a few years after the publication of the fifth volume: "I would especially like to note that as far as the foundation of my epistemological theory goes, it is necessary that I show merely that absolute being is naturally striven after in every noetic activity as the ultimate *objective* goal and that this remains true whether we transfer our ultimate subjective goal into a direct vision of God or into the analogical knowledge of him" (Mel., I, p. 336). He goes on to say here that in the third section of the second book he deliberately dealt with the deeper question of the supernatural goal because he wanted to investigate the ontological causes of knowledge with reference to Thomas in this section since in the third book he only used what was necessary in terms of strict, transcendental arguments to reject agnosticism. There the question is no longer one of supernatural goals. L. Malevez, in his preface to the new edition of the third volume, thus insists that it would be a false interpretation of Maréchal's thought to say that "it is the possibility of the supernatural goal which, from Maréchal's viewpoint, grounds the objective value of metaphysical knowledge" (V, p. 9).

Let us return to Maréchal's argument. Man's subjective goal is the possession of God through object-oriented acts. "The possibility of the subjective goal (*'finis quo'*) presupposes the reality of the 'objective goal' (*'finis cuius'* or *'finis qui'*; cf. V, p. 499), for in order that the appropriation of absolute being be possible, absolute being must first of all exist" (V, p. 448). With respect to a finite object, it is sufficient that the object of striving can exist at the time and under the conditions which regulate the state of affairs pertaining to the attainment of the object (V, p. 449), but because absolute being is identical with being which is necessary in itself, it follows, not only from the striving but from a consideration of the object of the striving, that "to affirm the possibility of God is nothing but to affirm that he exists, because his existence is the condition of every possibility" (V, p. 450). Since, then, the concern here is not merely with a real striving after a subjective goal leading to the actual affirmation of the (necessary) existence of the objective goal, but with a goal which is striven after on the basis of a natural inclination since it is the ultimate goal, providing the explicit or implicit possibility for every mode of striving, then the necessary existence of absolute being is affirmed not merely factually, but necessarily, *a priori* (V, pp. 450f.). "Our implicit affirmation of absolute being thus bears the stamp of *a priori* necessity, which was what was to be proved" (V, p. 451). The metaphysical analysis of noetic finality in this way results in the necessary existence of its ultimate goal. But what about the subordinated partial goals? Because of the finalism of the understanding, these are projected externally as just so many differentiated partial goals with respect to what is contingently and empirically given along with the corresponding appropriated forms posed over and against the subject. They do not possess pure necessity since they do not follow directly from a necessary relation to the ultimate, but are rather essentially dependent on contingently specified conditions. However, once they have merged with the orientation of the understanding toward the ultimate goal, they become related to the ultimate goal with *a priori* necessity as subordinated partial goals. Thus, as the scholastics held, limited objects manifest the "hypothetical necessity" which belongs to finite and contingently existing things (V, pp. 451f.).

"The special forms immanent to the understanding derive their objective character from a finalistic subordination under absolute necessity. . . . They enter the order of the strict network of metaphysics virtually, under the guidance of the absolute goal" (V, p. 459). These considerations open the possibility of presenting metaphysical affirmation in its *a priori* necessity.

(5) "If by 'affirmation' we mean, in the most universal sense of the word, the active relation of the content of a concept to reality ('*ad rem*'), we must then hold that immanent representations attain objective character in thought only on the strength of an *implicit affirmation,* not through an affirmation which relates the object to the absolute of being. Metaphysical

affirmation, as a dynamic process, is thus the condition of possibility for objects in thought, i.e., in discursive thought, which was to be demonstrated" (V, p. 459). This marks the attainment of the goal of this section. However, there still remains one point which is relevant to an understanding of what has come under discussion here.

(6) "It should not be overlooked (a) that affirmation is 'actuated' at the very first moment of objective knowledge, but is not yet known in all its properties and logical implications, and (b) that the ontological conditions required by objective affirmation are *really included* [*réellement implicites*], viz., they really constitute objects" (V, p. 460). To be implicitly (*exercite*) known, for Maréchal, means "everything which is to be found there," viz., in a conscious act of knowledge, "in the state of being intrinsically knowable, without, however, being actually perceived." "The 'implicitly known' must be able to enter into clear consciousness by the mere reflection of the subject upon his conscious act. In mental representation there are two kinds of implications, viz., that which is *implied purely analytically,* i.e, that which becomes evident through the analytical dissection of the representation, and that which is *subjectively implied* (true transcendental implication in Kant's sense), i.e., the totality of the transcendental conditions, or functional requirements, of the understanding as such, which are actuated in objective knowledge, being the subjective conditions of possibility for objective knowledge. They can be known through self-reflection and then set up in a rational deduction, giving them the character of objective necessity" (V, p. 460). In terms of Maréchal's complete argument and the function which deduction assumes in it, it seems proper to conclude that he does not want to hold that a full knowledge of the conditions of possibility, of what is "implicitly known," is the fruit of a *direct* reflection, viz., of a pure consideration of the immediate structure of the conscious act of the consciousness of objects. Such a consideration, rather, only offers the starting points which permit us to conclude to the conditions of possibility for real noetic activity, which can be of a thoroughly preconscious nature. This conclusion is necessary, since offense is

often taken at this mode of expression. Our meaning here is that Maréchal did not decide on the expressions *"connu implicitement,"* *"affirmé implicitement,"* because he was of the opinion that the implicit elements are in the conscious act of knowledge, or affirmation, in such a way that it could be demonstrated by a simple reflection, but because he conceives of the real actuation of knowledge, or affirmation, as a co-constitution. It is of fundamental importance, for a correct understanding of Maréchal, to keep his point of view in mind. He is not concerned with a description of knowledge as an intentional act, but with the metaphysico-epistemological explanation of knowledge. Maréchal thus views the whole of universal metaphysics, including the metaphysics of the transcendent, as open to development by means of such a reflection, viz., as a "system of absolute conditions which cannot deny object-oriented thought without incurring self-destruction through logical contradiction" (V, p. 461). This means, however, that "logical contradiction, which is here taken as the sanction of any sort of disregard for the absolute requirements of affirmation, is not directly a formal contradiction (*contradictio in terminis*), but a contradiction between what is *implicit* and what is *explicit* in judgment" (V, p. 496). Since, then, what is implicit is, at least in conclusion, shown to be necessarily presupposed by the conscious structure of the noetic act, fundamentally speaking it must be possible to demonstrate that the affirmation of being is the *a priori* condition for the possibility of knowledge, and from there to develop metaphysics. This, however, requires that right in the beginning, before the *a priori* necessity and constitutive function of metaphysical affirmation is demonstrated for all object-oriented thought, the full metaphysical interpretation of the conditions of possibility must be worked out. Maréchal does this in the third book.

5. TRANSCENDENTAL CRITIQUE

The second book is designed to show that the metaphysical affirmation of being is the condition of possibility for all object-oriented thought in a metaphysico-epistemological sense. The third book tries to translate this metaphysico-epistemological argument into a transcendental proof. The *key for the translation* consists in the fact that the conditions for the possibility of object-oriented thought, as it is directly known, are demonstrated through transcendental reflection. This implies, however, that, for the time being, an interpretation of these conditions of possibility against the background of a complete metaphysical point of view will be set aside. The faculties productive of the act of knowledge are considered only as functions of the determination of an act which lends certain structures to the object insofar as it is known and which are demanded precisely as conditions of possibility for these universal and necessary structures. "Transcendental reflection relates an object, which is thought, to various a priori determinations, which constitute it as an act in consciousness, or, if one would rather express himself in this way, to various faculties upon which it depends (under the condition that the various faculties are defined only through the very functions which they exercise in the object)" (V, p. 507). Such a "transcendental" critique must, according to Maréchal, conform to the following points.

(1) "The *method* of a critique of knowledge is essentially reflective. It consists in seeking the *value* of the truth of knowledge in the *immanent* essential characteristics of direct knowledge. Therefore, this method basically includes, first, the analysis of what is directly and necessarily given in consciousness,

and second, the quest for a principle of evaluating that which is given (in its proper unity) as well as the elements which make it up" (V, p. 516).

(2) "That which is truly *given directly* is, prior to any sort of analysis, the *objects,* insofar as they are intellectually known. These objects are, unquestionably, given to us as 'objects in themselves,' which have ontological value, but since it is the goal of the critique to examine the rational foundation of this claim to objective truth, it is agreed . . . , for the time being, to refrain from the absolute assent to the intrinsic reality of the objects thus represented. . . . Along with Kant, we refer to the direct, but precise givenness of consciousness as *the phenomenal object* (*realitas-phaenomenon*). As a phenomenal, or phenomenological, object, it is only an object insofar as it affects consciousness, and therefore it is also called *the immanent object* (to the subject)" (V, pp. 516ff.). This limitation to the phenomenal object, as the "classical critique" shows, is, in fact, not absolutely necessary, but certainly possible. Moreover, it stands as the sole basis of discussion within a certain historico-philosophical tradition and, beyond this polemical significance, has a distinct methodological advantage, for it brings the essential characteristics and insurmountable limits of metaphysics to light before metaphysics is actually developed. Of course, it also possesses a distinct disadvantage, viz., the danger of becoming lost in purely critical ventures under the guise of metaphysical pursuit, which, although necessary, is in itself fruitless" (V, p. 517).

(3) "Therefore, our procedure will be the following. (a) Our prime aim shall be the exposure of the elements, and their interrelationships, which make up the 'object as such,' through a reflective *analysis,* without taking into account the ontological value of the object. Only then shall we begin to examine the logical value of the implications of this position. (b) The first result of the examination of the analytic elements of the object as such is the absolute value of the necessary object of affirmation as a *practical postulate.* Although absolute, the value of the affirmed object is, basically, still indirect and subjective, grounded in the *a priori* necessity of a volitional act by an

active subject. Kantianism does not go beyond this position. The Kantian metaphysics of 'postulates' is a moral dogmatism. (c) In order to free ourselves from Kant at this point, we must go on to posit the absolute objective value of the affrmed object, from which we derive ontological ('noumenal') affirmation as a *theoretical* or *speculative necessity*. It must be shown that the practical and external necessity of a 'transcendent order,' which is admitted by Kant, is itself grounded in an absolute necessity which extends intrinsically to every immanent object in its very constitution in consciousness. Then, according to the admission of the critical philosophers, a necessary and 'constitutive' condition of each immanent object has a part in the necessary theoretical value of the object which serves as its basis, for a denial of this condition leads to the denial of the very possibility of the object in thought, that is, to the denial of that which is given at the starting point of every critique—actual thought. If, therefore, this condition logically contains the affirmation of a transcendent object, such an affirmation does not merely possess the practical necessity of a 'postulate,' but the theoretical necessity of what is speculatively evident, at least in the speculative sense of being indirectly (i.e., 'analogously') evident. Our proof, drawn out to its conclusion in this way, corresponds to what Kant would have called, had he held it to be feasible, 'the transcendental deduction' of ontological affirmation" (V, pp. 518f.). Maréchal insists that the heart of the proof, prepared by the other two points, lies in point (c) (V, p. 516), and he works this plan out in the following three sections. We must fix our attention especially on sections one and three, dealing with the reflective analysis of the object as such and the deduction of affirmation respectively, since they are essential for the theoretical proof.

For a clearer understanding of the following remarks, it should be noted that the analysis of the immanent object, according to Maréchal, leads to *subjective* as well as *objective conditions of possibility*.[19] "The object in consciousness has two aspects, being, at one and the same time, subject and ob-

[19] Cf. Kant's distinction between subjective and objective deduction discussed above (pages 67ff.).

ject, knowledge of an essence and the essence known (*'cogno-scens in actu'* and *'cognoscibile in actu'*). The transcendental can be considered under both points of view, either as subjective possibility or as objective possibility of knowledge" (V, p. 507). The subjective conditions of possibility thus constitute the transcendental self as the totality of the conditions which logically form the basis for the possibility of the intellectual act of the content of consciousness, whereas the objective conditions of possibility constitute the totality of conditions which logically form the basis for the content of consciousness, such that it may be intellectually actuated (V, pp. 507f.). Of course, the conditions of possibility of both orders basically have only a precisive character as a result of transcendental analysis. They are, properly speaking, only what they have been discovered to be as what the immanent object necessarily presupposes, independent of any later, though possible, metaphysical depth of meaning. This could only be possible if the restrictively interpreted conditions of possibility should lead to the deduction of the absolute affirmation of being, such that it would contain a metaphysical "co-efficient" (Prem., p. 296). This is where critical deduction blends into the metaphysical (Prem., p. 296; V, pp. 567f.).

REDUCTIVE ANALYSIS OF THE CONSCIOUSNESS OF OBJECTS

The implications of the *analysis* of the object as such are summarized in the following four theses (V, pp. 519–528).

(1) A content of consciousness is an object and thus requires logical truth only in *judgment,* viz., in the affirmation of judging. Final objective apperception is therefore the formal effect of an affirmation, not a mere sensible or conceptual representation.

(2) The power of affirmation, however, is not restricted to "representable" objects, viz., to objects which can be directly represented in terms of their own form. Furthermore, the immanent object, insofar as it is thought as object, is determined

110

as the product of the affirmation of judging. The power to think objects, therefore, surpasses the power of directly representing an object through its proper form. The realm of knowable objects thus does not necessarily coincide with the realm of directly representable objects. In knowledge, more can be *meant* than can be *represented* through the structure of a concept directly related to an object.

(3) Because the object is the product of affirmation, it comprehends essentially: (a) something sensibly given. The differences between concepts are possible only through a differentiation of the empirical material produced from without. They are not explainable through an *a priori,* necessary law. What is sensibly given is subject to quantitative conditions, those of space and time. This is not contradicted because of the possibility of producing further differentiations among concepts through reflection. Reflection, after all, is not possible without direct knowledge, and direct knowledge is itself directed toward what is empirically given, even though it is made up of concepts which are entirely *distinguishable* from each other and represents *definite* objects. This indicates that knowledge does not coincide entirely with sensible representation.

(b) *Concretive synthesis.* That which is receptively given can lead to a concept which represents objects only if intellectual representation is conceptually related to undetermined subject. A subject, or *suppositum,* of the represented form is necessary because the intellectual content cannot otherwise be related to something present in itself. The subject must be undetermined because sensible representation is possible only by means of the transcendence of the conditions of sensibility in conjunction with the relation to a definite experienced thing given sensibly. However, since in judgment the concept is once again inserted into the order of reality, the indeterminacy of the subject must be rescinded, which gains expression in the relation of the predicate to the logical subject.[20]

(c) *Objective synthesis.* Since the function of affirmation goes beyond the function of the representation of a differentiated conceptualization corresponding to what is sensibly given,

[20] Cf. the explanation of abstraction above (pp. 84f.).

111

the relation of what is given to the objective unity of all that is knowable in affirmation cannot simply coincide with the relation to the realm of sensibly distinguishable particular things. However, this does constitute an extension of the concretive synthesis of the form and the quantitatively distinguishable suppositum, viz., of form and matter, to an objective synthesis with being as such. This objective synthesis contains a *formal aspect,* viz., the content of consciousness is brought under the form of being by being related to transcendental (i.e., that which is self-related to all that is knowable) and analogical (i.e., that which can no longer be directly and conceptually represented, but can be signified) being. This relation, however, cannot be brought about by a direct representation, but only by an orientation to being actuated in affirmation and presupposing the representation. This, as the ultimate goal of dynamic orientation, is absolute being. Thus the analogical relation of finite beings to absolute being is actuated in knowledge before it can be reflectively developed. Along with this formal aspect, objective synthesis also possesses the aspect of *positing.* The relation of the subject to a being over and against the subject is not merely a particularly complicated representation possessing its highest form of unity through its relation to the absolute. What is judged is just as much conceived as the possible object of activity, viz., as the objective means to a goal.

(4) The constitutive conditions of the immanent object, as demonstrated through reflection and analysis, logically imply a number of suppositions which concern the nature of the subjectivity of knowledge (subjective conditions of possibility) and the object known (objective conditions of possibility). (a) The first of these is the relativity of what is sensibly given and the quantitative character of the faculty which is designed to receive that which is given. The relativity results from the fact that what is given, because of its contingency, cannot be referred to an *a priori* structure. It therefore refers to something else which is operative in the subject, since the content of objective consciousness is determined in this way. This unification of object and receptive faculty for what is external yields the phenome-

non at its first level. In terms of the state of inner experience, it occurs as a "concrete quantity" and thus presupposes a quantitative element in both co-operative factors.

(b) The power of concretive synthesis lacks every inner quantitative determination. It is therefore to be taken as intellectual, even though it is, at the same time, dependent on quantitative conditions. This power is called the abstracting understanding and it produces an intellectual representative structure from what is sensibly given which requires an essential transcendence of and a reflective relation to what is sensibly given in order to be related to a determinate object of experience. If the understanding, as is sensibility, were intrinsically dependent on matter, then its product, as well as the product of sensibility, would have to serve as a basis for the quantitative determinations of sensibility. It would then be impossible to abstract from them. It would also no longer be necessary to be related to them again in order to represent a definite object. On the other hand, it would not be possible, without some kind of dependence by the understanding, for it to give to its product the unity of a synthesis of form and matter, i.e., for it to order the differences of what is qualitatively given under the unity of the object of experience under "numerical unity" (unity of objects determined through quantity).

(c) Objective synthesis, or affirmation, contains the positing of analogical relation. This means that, corresponding to the logical hierarchy, first of all, the implied absolute positing of infinite being as the upper, only and necessary datum point of the whole analogical relation, and secondly, the absolute positing of what is given, viz., of the content of the representation, as the subordinate, multiple and contingent datum point of the analogical relation, i.e., the necessary existence of God and the essential contingency of directly represented objects. What is given is objectified only through its introduction into the orientation of knowing as characterized by this analogical relation.

This is the indispensable premiss of every object as such. Whatever value belongs to the explicit affirmation of the object also belongs to the implicit affirmation of the premisses of the

113

object. This means that the question of value must be gone into more deeply. It can be answered only through the demonstration of the *a priori* necessity of ontological affirmation. Up until now, only the presuppositions of affirmation have been analyzed, but it has not been shown that this affirmation is not merely an optional presumption. Only when this latter possibility has been excluded, through the demonstration of its *a priori* necessity, is the fundamental value of ontological affirmation protected, because then the very attempt to cast it into doubt would already presuppose it.

TRANSCENDENTAL DEDUCTION OF ONTOLOGICAL AFFIRMATION

The proof of the *a priori* necessity of the affirmation of being follows chiefly from the demonstration that the *a priori* necessity of volitional activity already includes the necessity of an absolute, objective affirmation. The existence of a noumenal reality thus takes on the value of a practical postulate (V, p. 530). The demonstration essentially consists in the fact that it can be shown that volitional activity consists in a conscious pursuit of a goal. Contained implicitly in this demonstration, however, is the absolute affirmation of the fundamental possibility of the realization of goals, i.e., the existence of the objective conditions for their possible realization. However, this implies the affirmation of the presuppositions of the absolute conditions of objective existence as such, and thus of ontological reality (V, p. 530).

True theoretical necessity, however, requires the following (V, p. 532), that according to the definition of the object, the immanent object contains a content of representation posited over and against the subject in the subject under such conditions that this immanent objectivation at least implicitly affects the consciousness of the subject.

In discursive understanding, viz., understanding in which direct intuition is denied, these properties can belong only to

114

the successive phases of an active process of assimilation from what is externally given.

Such an assimilation, however, fulfills directly the necessary and sufficient conditions for ontological affirmation.

Therefore, ontological affirmation, with all its logical presuppositions, is the inner condition of possibility for each object of discursive understanding, irrespective of the validity of the affirmation of the object.

Maréchal summarizes the proof of the two sub-propositions which require a process of assimilation for the constitution of the immanent object in discursive understanding, and which represent the conditions of ontological affirmation as such, in the following eight points.

(1) Direct reflection, as well as the analysis of the structure of judgment, shows that the understanding is discursive and that its noetic activity is a dynamic progression, viz., a *movement* from potentiality to actuality. Therefore, the *a priori* determinations of the object must be grasped not only as static forms, but as the expression of the spontaneity of the transcendental subject, viz., as the proper determination of a power which is actuated through what is given, actuates what is given itself and subordinates it to the final determination of this power. Thus discursive intelligence presupposes an *a priori,* a determination logically prior to particular knowledge, which bears, virtually inscribed within, the goal toward which it strives and under which it subordinates each particular appropriation.

(2) In the concept of movement, i.e., of the transition from determinable to determined not of the sort of a merely new, unconnected beginning, the fact is that each movement strives toward an *ultimate goal* in accordance with a law governing this specific movement, which is expressive of the dynamic orientation of each phase of movement toward the final goal. This final goal, moreover, does not necessarily have to be a temporally final moment of the movement itself.

(3) The specifying form which guides the dynamic progression of noetic activity *a priori* (the adequate formal object) can only be the universal and unlimited form of being. Likewise,

no limiting determination can belong to the "objective final goal." which is the term at which the movement of the understanding might come to rest and which, as goal, must be possible in the order of subsistent reality. This goal, therefore, must be unlimited in the order of act, the *absolute being*—God. For wherever a limit is set up, knowledge, at least problematically, reaches beyond it. The limit, moreover, is seen only because the virtual apprehension of the understanding transcends it.

(4) Since discursive noetic activity does not bring forth its contents from within itself, it is forced, in its step by step striving toward its final goal, to actuate this progression as an assimilation of what is externally given. Noetic activity, therefore, requires *sensibility* subordinate to itself.

(5) A universal analysis of movement further requires that the assimilation of new determinations through sensibility display the following two aspects in the sphere of active noetic activity. First, the new determination is received under the *a priori* form of active activity, under the form oi being, and thus enrichens the subject. Second, the determination is received precisely in such a way that it is related to the final goal of noetic activity and thus assumes the role of means, or *subordinate partial goal.*

(6) The first of the above mentioned points, viz., the purely static consideration of the assimilation of what is given as an enrichment, does not yet possess the requirements of the immanent contrast of object with subject, as required for objectivation and objective consciousness. On the other hand, the second point, viz., the dynamic relating of what is given to the final goal of the understanding, implicitly contains the elements of such an *opposition of the object.* Thus the active relating of what is given to the ultimate goal of noetic activity, i.e., to absolute being, directly constitutes that which was given and assimilated as an object of consciousness. This means that the immanent object is constituted as an object only by being inclusively related to the metaphysical order.

(7) The assimilation of what is given, however, which in-

separably accompanies the introduction of what is given into the absolute order of finality, is nothing but affirmation—the "transcendental act" or the objective form of judgment. At this point, the affirmation of judgment takes on metaphysical value. Thus it is that with the transcendental deduction of finality, which is here shown to be the necessary condition of possibility for objective consciousness, we complete the transcendental deduction of affirmation. If the word "affirmation" should be objected to, one could also say that it has been determined that "the introduction of what is externally given under the absolute finality of the intellectual subject, if this introduction fulfills the necessary and sufficient conditions of objective apperception (in the precise and phenomenal sense), also fulfills the necessary and sufficient conditions of *metaphysical apperception*" (V, p. 554).

(8) If the relation of what is given to the final goal of the understanding belongs to the *a priori* conditions of possibility for the "constitution" of every object of the understanding, then the analogous knowledge of absolute being as the highest and, according to the concepts which are taken from what is given, not directly representable member of this relation is "implicitly" contained in the knowledge of each object as object. Kant and his disciples also hold that the proof that something necessarily belongs to the object of thought as a constitutive condition offers the highest speculative guarantee for the value of this condition. Likewise, for Aristotle and Thomas the proof of the inevitable necessity of affirmation is the surest way to oppose the radical doubt of the legitimacy of affirmation. Maréchal therefore concludes that the affirmation of transcendent being as the final goal and first cause, and the character of ontological absoluteness (noumenon) which whatever is contingently given receives from this absolute being, consist in an objective, theoretical necessity for reason. "In every object of thought, whatever it may be, we affirm absolute being implicitly and contingent being explicitly. Outside of this simultaneous dual affirmation, there is no possibility of objective thought" (V, pp. 554f.), which is what was to be proved.

THE TRANSCENDENTAL METHOD
ACCORDING TO KANT AND MARÉCHAL

If we look back now, we can see how Maréchal's argument fulfills the essential conditions of Kant's transcendental method on the one hand and eliminates its deficiencies on the other, as the further development of transcendental philosophy (as it was conceived by Kant or as it might be conceived by others) requires.

With regard to Maréchal, the *essential aspects* of this development would be, first of all, the reference of objective consciousness to the conditions in the subject which make this consciousness possible, where this reference is imposed by means of a structure directly manifested in consciousness (V, pp. 507f.). Both in Kant and in Maréchal, the power to perceive this reference as directly known is never questioned and is accepted as a fact (V, pp. 61, 65, 533; Abstr., pp. 116, 173). Further, the power of analytic-noetic manipulation of what is given is presupposed by both (Abstr., p. 108), but no attention is given to whether being is in fact apprehended and absolutely affirmed by means of a direct givenness because the absolute affirmation of being, although in fact included in it, should not be grounded in a mere reference to insight (that is excluded by this historical dimension of the philosophical situation) but should be vindicated through the *a priori* necessity of the affirmation of being (V, p. 514).

This leads to the *deficiencies* of the transcendental method as conceived by Kant. It is true that he was able to discover some of the conditions of possibility, but he did not succeed in a sufficient analysis of them. This shows up, first, in certain unsolved problems, some of which have been worked out in the continuing historical development of the transcendental method, and, second, in his conclusions.

Kant did not succeed in solving the *problem* of the relation of the *a priori* of sense knowledge and the *a priori* of the understanding, nor the relations of reason (which transcends phenomena) to the understanding and of theoretical to prac-

118

tical reason. This is clear in his own problematic of the "thing-in-itself" as the problematic reality which limits the phenomenon (V, pp. 476, 551f.). Kant does not at all succeed in an analysis of the transcendental act of affirmation, which is not merely a specific category opposed to negation, but a super-category, unlimited by the schemata of sensibility, from which alone the "thing-in-itself" could have gained an acceptable meaning and its vindication (V, p. 513; Abstr., p. 147). The basic reason for the fact that Kant did not go further, according to Maréchal, lies in Kant's inconsistency. When he introduces transcendental analysis, he conceives knowledge dynamically, but he does not take this dynamic aspect into account in what follows (V, pp. 37, 476, 604). Fichte went further by making full use of the dynamic viewpoint for transcendental philosophy and by attempting to render Kant's dualisms meaningful through this viewpoint, but in a way which itself is still weighed down with rationalistic trappings, to which Kant owes his extremely static outlook and Fichte his ideal of deductive understanding.

Maréchal was convinced that this conclusion was not a necessary one. He therefore tries to solve the problems left by Kant in consistent fashion through his transcendental deduction of the absolute affirmation of being. As a condition of possibility for the consciousness of objects in discursive understanding, such as we possess, he arrives at noetic finality, which lends necessary unity to sensibility and understanding, to understanding and the affirmation of absolute being and to theoretical and practical reason. He does not try to show the direct actuality of the discursive activity of the understanding as a necessary result of the absolute, but Maréchal's disciples tend to approach noetic finality in terms of being, viz., being as manifested in the self-activity of finite intellectual being within the act of object-relatedness.

Kant also did not succeed in a comprehensive clarification of the *a priori* conditions of possibility for the consciousness of objects in his *conclusion* to the transcendental analysis (V, p. 567; Abstr., pp. 147f.). His conclusion involves the reduction of the value of theoretical knowledge to the realm of experience. Pure rational knowledge is a "synthesis *a priori*" in the pejorative sense, viz., without objective validity, i.e., where the constitutive *a priori* forms do not reach reality. The transcendent is attainable only as a postulate of practical reason, which in itself is not seen in its inner connection with theoretical reason. Theoretical reason remains limited to the phenomenal object. Maréchal, on the other hand, develops transcendental analysis to a consistent proof of the impossibility of a phenomenal object, in the exclusive sense, and to the necessity of the knowability of the transcendent (V, pp. 517, 554; Abstr., p, 149; Prem., p. 291).

This concludes the extensive basis of Maréchal's historico-critical and theoretico-systematic investigations. He has shown how the problems which come to the fore in the history of philosophy can be brought to their solution. This solution is basically grounded in the Aristotelian-Thomistic metaphysics of knowledge but can be vindicated with the method which is identified with modern criticism. Moreover, the differentiation required by the modern way of putting the question has yielded fruitful insights into the structure of metaphysics and its position in human intellectual life.

With regard to the goal of our work, viz., an investigation of the structure of the transcendental method in neo-scholasticism, we must yet work out the elements of the essential sructure of the transcendental method as conceived by Maréchal in order to be able to follow the development of Maréchal's thought in other neo-scholastic thinkers.

The Structure of the Transcendental Method according to Maréchal

What are the essential elements of the transcendental method which Maréchal employs in his transcendental critique (V, book 3) and which he believes to be in essential agreement with the basic elements of Kant's method in his critical period and also with the method of the post-Kantian transcendental philosophers? For an answer to this question we must turn first to a *formal determination* of those elements upon which these several thinkers agree, even though they differ in the ways in which they give concrete expression to these elements. This formal determination, therefore, will contain whatever is essential to the transcendental method. Let us now briefly review the concrete expression, or *content-structure,* given by Maréchal to these elements, i.e., let us consider the starting point, the development through transcendental reflection and deduction and their result as elements of the transcendental method.

6. STRUCTURAL ELEMENTS

The *starting point* is the knowledge of objects, viz., the consciousness of objects insofar as it is immediate. Although this consciousness requires that real objects be represented and that we apprehend this as the act of a substantial self, this requirement and its apprehension will be determined as things given to consciousness, but their validity will be ignored. Thus the starting point is the phenomenal object in the precisive sense, viz., the immanent object, or the object in consciousness.

The consciousness of objects thus becomes a starting point which expands beyond itself, since it is taken as a unity, incomprehensible in itself, in the manifold, but which is constituted as such through understanding. Although this characterization is somewhat abstract, what is thus characterized is actually proper to the starting point of the transcendental method. Therefore, Kant's question, "How are synthetic judgments *a priori* possible?" entails: (a) the (at least for Kant) evident fact of the consciousness of objects, which (b) is itself made up of a double unification, viz., on the one hand, of subject and predicate, and on the other, of the knowledge of this unification and the objective existence of this unification (the demand for objectivity), a unification (c) which is not understandable through the mere conscious possession of synthetic judgments *a priori* (as opposed to analytic judgments) and (d) which always asserts itself if the understandability of this unity is denied, since the result otherwise would be a suspension of judgment.

This also shows why the transcendental method is not concerned with whether analytic thought or knowledge is at all basically possible and why this is presupposed without discus-

122

sion, for they are non-problematical facts of a self-understanding consciousness. The transcendental method is concerned more with how these facts are to be interpreted and understood uniformly. All transcendental philosophers admit that there is knowledge. But what it is, viz., knowledge and the relation to objects which it requires, they try to explain by demonstrating the necessary conditions under which alone they can solve the aporetic of the starting point. Maréchal also takes the phenomenal object, in the precisive sense, as the starting point in his transcendental critique. This starting point clearly distinguishes it from the metaphysical critique,[21] which accepts the fundamental justification of the demand for the consciousness of objects in order to reach the absolute order of being. In the transcendental critique only the act of knowledge directly given to consciousness is taken as a result, and with regard to the affirmation of what is demonstrated in this act, no stand is taken from the viewpoint of what is directly given in consciousness as to whether the claim that this affirmation is to be related to the absolute order of being is a valid interpretation of this act of knowledge and of its foundation. Even though Maréchal does not express this concept directly, it appears to us to be a necessary premiss of his procedure, which does not deny what is evident but would rather ground the fundamental validation of what is evident, and the requirements of knowledge contained in it, through the deduction of ontological affirmation.

Maréchal underscores the aporetic of the starting point differently than Kant insofar as he, following Fichte, takes the dynamic character of the consciousness of objects into account more than Kant. The unity of the two different aspects of the directly conscious act of the consciousness of objects is taken seriously, viz., as representational and active, or as passively speculative and actively practical. Thus the object is meant not as a mere something which opposes, but as the focal point of a possible activity, and knowledge can be taken actively, as dependent on a volitional influence. Transcendental *reflection* then turns its attention to the structural elements of the con-

[21] Van Riet, *L'Epistémologie thomiste*, pp. 274–276.

sciousness of objects and works out the necessary conditions for the possibility of the unity, incomprehensible in itself as such, of the different elements. It seeks the conditions under which what is given in consciousness can be demonstrated with those characterizing determinations which it actually possesses. Therefore, these conditions must be worked out in two directions: first, as the "objective" conditions of the fact that the *object* can be presented as it is actually known, with the characteristics proper to it as the determinate unity of the manifold, and secondly, as the "subjective" conditions of the fact that the present *consciousness* of an object is made possible. The relation of both orders of conditions to each other depends on the result of transcendental analysis. The distinction between the two orders is itself the fruit of transcendental reflection since the unity of the manifold in the object, as well as the unity of the immanent subject-object opposition, which is given with the intentionality of the consciousness of objects, require its conditions.

In order to have a correct understanding of transcendental reflection, it must be kept in mind that it is neither a purely empirical not a purely logical analysis of direct consciousness. A purely *empirical* reflective analysis would limit itself to the description of the various given elements and conrast them with each other. A purely *logical* reflection would only determine the necessary and *a priori* elements and forms of unity. *Transcendental* reflection, however, yields the conditions which must necessarily be accepted as determinate for objective consciousness so that it can demonstrate the characteristics which would determine an empirical and logical reflection. This leads to the *a priori* conditions of possibility as understood by the transcendental method, which consist in the conditions which precede the actual act of consciousness, not temporally, but essentially, and determine it in its existence and essence. Then it must be determined how the conscious act is understood as posited, viz., in the knowing subject. Of course, intentionality, and the elements of the consciousness of objects which are not understandable in the subject alone, e.g., the elements of the

124

contingently given manifold, require a further extension of the search for conditions of possibility.

But how can we gain a conceptual grasp of the conditions of possibility at all and say of them that they are to be found in the subject, or somewhere else?

The conditions of possibility, insofar as they are demonstrated through transcendental reflection, are determinable only as that which exercises a determining influence on the real act of the consciousness of objects and thus gives a definite elemental structure to this act. These conditions become distinguishable through the characteristics which they condition in the consciousness of objects. The conditions of possibility are basically conditioning functions which, in terms of what they condition, become knowable, distinguishable and thus nameable. The transcendental subject, therefore, is that condition of possibility for consciousness through which, despite its organic structure, it is shown as the all-encompassing characteristic of self-relatedness. The connectedness of the conditions of possibility are then determined. Thus the totality of the elements necessary for the consciousness of objects, which necessarily coincides with the consciousness of an object, and therefore with the relationship of an object to a self, is identified as the transcendental self, viz., as the *a priori* structure of the knowing subject. It is also possible to rely on common significations in the determination of the conditions of possibility, as used in psychology, to explain that which requires a definite condition of possibility in transcendental reflection. Thus the conditions of possibility for the fact that the manifold of what is contingently given is related to a higher unity of true objectivity, is called "understanding," the condition for the differentiation of the given manifold is called "sensibility," and, more generally, the chief (subjective) conditions of possibility for definite forms of unity are called "faculties." In connection with transcendental procedure, however, nothing more is meant by these words than precisely the conditions determining the conscious act. In terms of properties and the relation to others, only that should be considered which results from the transcendental analysis of the conscious act. Thus significations derived from other areas receive a completely determined and demonstrable meaning in connection with transcendental procedure. All other properties not transcendentally derived, which are nevertheless connected with these significations, are ignored. This means that we must distinguish the meanings of these words in the *limited* sense demanded by transcendental reflection from the *full* sense proper to their normal use.

According to Maréchal, transcendental reflection is, strictly speaking, an *analysis of judgment,* since full objective consciousness occurs in judgment. As a transcendental analysis, it is after the *a priori* conditions of possibility for the sort of consciousness that bears the essential traits of an explicit or virtual judgment, and consequently it does not dwell on the mere investigation of the expressly conscious meaning of the elements of judgment. An investigation such as the latter could not lead to the results which Maréchal achieves. In the reductive phase of the transcendental analysis of judgment, Maréchal singles out the conditions of possibility for whatever is contained in the determination of judgment, for the affirmative form of judgment and for the relation of these conditions to each other, and he ultimately concludes that the affirmation of being is a constitutive condition for the possibility of judgment.

The transcendental *deduction* completes the transcendental analysis which is begun in transcendental reflection. The latter had shown that the actual consciousness of objects is determined by a string of conditions of possibilty. Transcendental deduction moves in the opposite direction. It shows the necessary connections between these conditions of possibility (V, p. 59), and therefore that certain conditions of possibility must necessarily determine the consciousness of objects, whereupon it follows that every phenomenal object whatsoever is determined through these conditions, which necessarily demonstrates the corresponding structural elements.

The result of all this is that the necessary structural elements, free from any psychological contingency, must belong to the object, such that their denial includes the denial of objectified subjectivity, which would be the very negation of denial. This means that these structural elements of the object must necessarily be recognized, viz., that they possess objective value. It is not enough merely to concede that this necessity might be a necessity of thought, undeniable for our way of thinking, but which might nevertheless be relative, in the sense of a purely subjective necessity, because such relativization is nothing but a disguised form of denial, and thus it negates itself. It cannot lay claim to value and attention while conceding that there is yet another value which casts doubt upon itself. This makes it clear that the transcendental deduction of a structural element of every consciousness of an object frees its value from the logical possibility of doubt, which, in effect, means that it guarantees its absolute value.

We must also distinguish, corresponding to the distinction between subjective and objective conditions of possibility, between a subjective and an objective deduction. Transcendental deduction in the *subjective* sense derives a necessary connection of subjective conditions of possibility (III, p. 119). Therefore, it is not *a priori* excluded that subjective conditions of possibility may be shown to be required which determine the act of knowledge, but which do not affect the inner structure of the object of knowledge as such. In this case one would have a *purely* subjective deduction, similar to the one which Kant attempted with the ideas of pure reason. However, insofar as the subjective deduction recognizes subjective conditions of possibility which enter constitutively into the determination of the structure of the conscious object as such, it arrives at the same conclusion as a transcendental deduction in the *objective* sense. This shows the necessity of definite objective conditions of possibility for every immanent object. Thus the transcendental deduction of the categories by Kant is an objective deduction, although certain elements enter into it which also belong to the subjective deduction. Only the results of an objective transcendental deduction can serve as a guarantee of the value of knowledge.

Since Kant ignores the dynamic aspect of the consciousness of objects and the conditions of possibility connected with it, his objective deduction suceeded only for the categories in the

127

realm of experiential knowledge. Subjective deduction was unable to prove fully the necessary correlation of the subjective conditions of possibility which constitute human knowledge. Ideas, for Kant, can only have a regulative function.

Maréchal, in his deduction comes to the dynamic orientation of discursive understanding toward the absolute of being. The subjective deduction leads to a proof of the necessary correlation of the *a priori* of sensibility (with its forms of space and time) and of the understanding (with its function of representing experiential objectivity) with the orientation of the understanding toward non-representable and unexperienceable absolute being (which constitutes the intrinsic possibility of representation) and further with the will, which is oriented toward the good. It follows that objective deduction demonstrates the constitutive function which is proper to the relation to absolute being which is the ground of any particular object and to the ordination of the object into the absolute order of being and into the order of nature. As opposed to Kant, this result permits the establishment of a metaphysics which determines the exact place proper to a particular object in the absolute order of being, and also the understanding of the act of knowledge itself and its conditions of possibility no longer merely in a limited sense, but in terms of its place in the order of being, viz., metaphysically, in the full sense of a metaphysical psychology or anthropology.

In order fully to understand these structural elements of the transcendental method, we must still consider a few more topics, viz., the relation of the grounding of validity through transcendental deduction to retorsion (in the sense of the metaphysical "classical critique"), the understanding of the structural elements of the transcendental method in terms of its result (beginning with the metaphysics of knowledge which it entails), the consequences of some of the properties of the transcendental method, above all their effect on the role and the complete character of the evident and the *a priori*, and finally the relation of the transcendental method to Maréchal's historico-comparative method.

RETORSION

First, we must decide how two statements by Maréchal can be unified with each other, viz., the claim that retorsion contains in itself the essential elements of an objective deduction (I, pp. 86, 88, 254; V, pp. 98, 496, 503), and the claim that the transcendental method, as opposed to the method of the metaphysical critique, begins with the phenomenal object (III, p. 109; IV, pp. 15f., 341f., 346; V, pp. 59, 502, 507, 516, 554, 567ff.). The key to the joint understanding of these statements is given by Maréchal himself when he explains why he did not simply use retorsion instead of the transcendental method (Prem., pp. 291f.). Retorsion, in the sense of a *reductio ad absurdam,* as used in the "classical critique," compels assent to the universal necessity of the affirmation of being and the impossibility of doubting its fundamental validity, but it does not explain the why and the how of this necessity nor the steps which our mind must naturally complete in order to attain objective knowledge. Because it demonstrates the universal necessity of affirmation, it indicates the affirmation of being as the inner *a priori* condition of every object of consciousness. As such, it contains an objective transcendental deduction of ontological affirmation, although in hidden form (V, p. 98). On the other hand, historical developments have led to further demands. The modern critique of knowledge begins with reflection on the act of knowledge and seeks to understand it in terms of the conditions of its production and then to determine what we have to hold with regard to this act and the object contained in it. We must first examine how it happens that we confer being on an object and then determine what this conferral actually means (not what it presumes to mean, but what it really signifies), viz., whether this being has an absolute meaning or only expresses its belonging to the realm of experience (Prem., pp. 292f.). So we must take a look at two characteristics which are decisive for the transcendental method, of which retorsion is included in only one, although it is the one which is most decisive for the foundation of validity.

129

(1) The transcendental method expresses that which is necessarily included in knowledge. Therefore, whatever has been shown to be the necessary and intrinsic ground of every object of thought cannot have its very value called into question. This shows up in retorsion, which demonstrates the actual (*contradictio exercita*) although not conceptually formulated (*contradictio in terminis*) contradiction between that which is included in judgment and that through which it is expressed, which is presupposed in the attempt to deny the validity of the affirmation of being, i.e., the principle of contradiction, or the possibility of the knowledge of truth (V, pp. 496–501).

(2) The transcendental method considers the act of knowledge and the analysis of the conditions of this act in order to derive explanations of the properties of this act. The key to the discovery of the conditons, therefore, is the very structure of the act, which also refers to the conditions, as we have seen in the presentation of the three fundamental elements of this method. The self-cognitive apprehension of an object cannot apprehend itself in its own structure without apprehending itself as conditioned. The analysis of these conditions leads to the express knowledge of what occurs in the apprehension of an object, because these conditions are necessarily included in it.

We may call the first of these two elements the *retorsive* element, and the second (which indicates the concrete means of determining the connection between the expressly known structure of the object and the constitutive conditions of the intentional act of the object), the act-analytical, or *operative,* moment of the transcendental method. Therefore, that which distinguishes the transcendental method from retorsion is that it is opertive whereas retorsion is not. We must now determine exactly what this term "operative" means.

OPERATIVE ANALYSIS

"Operative" does not characterize simply any sort of reflection on the act of knowing or the investigation of any sort of activity, because then retorsion would also be operative. "Operative" means rather the determination of the structure of meaning through an act. One would thus speak of an "operative definition"[22] if a concept is determined by means of its connection with an activity, viz., in some way as its result. For example, hydrogen is the gas which is freed at the cathode when an electric current is passed through acidified water. The operative definition, in its essentials, had already been employed in metaphysics by Aristotle, e.g., when he distinguishes the categories in terms of the functions and kinds of propositions.[23] It is, in fact, in metaphysics, where one is concerned with all-embracing concepts which cannot be defined through a super-imposed genus and the distinction between kinds, that operative definitions can be put to good use in the determination of concepts. Thus, according to Hoenen,[24] the concept of being can be defined operatively as "that which affirmation bestows upon the apprehended state of affairs" ("*id quod affirmato tribuit dispositioni rei apprehensae*").

It should be clear by now that the transcendental method is operative, for it tries to determine the meaning of the object of noetic activity through an analysis of this activity and fixes a tight correlation between the conditions of this act (subjective conditions of possibility) and the structural elements of the object (objective conditions of possibility). It then establishes the orientation toward an activity which corresponds to an absolute, non-relative object which is the ground of all other objects as the constitutive condition of every particular act of knowledge as related to particular objects. The analysis of the conditions of noetic activity shows that this activity must be such that its object, in order to be knowable, must be related to the object of the knowledge of all that is knowable. If this analysis is followed out exactly, it means that an analysis of the activity of knowledge shows that its object is related to the object of an all-encompassing and absolute knowledge in such a way as to justify the assertion of the relation of every object

[22] P. Hoenen, "De definitione operativa," *Gregorianum,* vol. 35 (1954), pp. 371–405.
[23] P. Hoenen, *op. cit.,* p. 402.
[24] P. Hoenen, *op. cit.,* p. 403.

of knowledge to the absolute order of being. All this implies, however, that an analysis of the activity has determined the meaning of the object of this activity, viz., in the sense of a necessary relationship to the absolute, self-sufficient and self-knowable order of being (a procedure which is characteristic of the operative method) which at the same time expresses the necessary affirmation of being as contained in the act of knowledge. However, this procedure, which we have just identified as the operative explication of objective knowledge, is nothing but the transcendental deduction of ontological affirmation as it is carried out by Maréchal. Consequently, we can justifiably say of the transcendental method that it offers an operative explication. The transcendental method is distinguished from the method of retorsion, then, precisely by means of this operative aspect, which does not presuppose from the very beginning the meaning of that which is to be proven by leading the doubter to absurdity, in which it is shown that his doubt contains *exercite* that which he claims to doubt, but rather determines the exact meaning solely in terms of the analysis of the conditions of the activity of knowledge. (Later on, we shall return to the method of retorsion and its role with respect to the transcendental method.)

METAPHYSICO–EPISTEMOLOGICAL SIGNIFICANCE

Our examination has concentrated chiefly on the logical structure of the transcendental method. Now let us consider this method in terms of its ramifications, beginning with the metaphysics of knowledge. We begin with a review of the results of Maréchal's metaphysical critique (V, book 2). The transcendental method begins with the object-oriented act of man, which is self-knowing. This act cannot be understood unless it is understood as dependent on various conditions. The analysis of these conditions yields a reflective knowledge of the contingencies of subjective and objective reality, the effects of which permeate the act in different ways, pointing to absolute reality as the ultimate efficient and final causes. This procedure corresponds to the metaphysical constitution of the human mind, since the mind can know only through intellectual acts and since such knowledge is explicable in its real differentiation only if there is a corresponding real differentiation of the act itself, which then must be referred to the nature of man and the influences of the environment. The nature of the subject of knowledge (the psychological *a priori*) is responsible for the universal form of the noetic act and the universal and necessary determinations (logical *a priori*) under which it apprehends its object, and the concrete influences of the environment are responsible for particular actualizations of content, and thus for the determination of the knowledge of objects. The intellectual apprehension and objectivization of the object in knowledge are possible only insofar as the mind is open for and related to the final ground of all being and projects its own activities to their ultimate goal with reference to it. Thus human knowledge, despite its many dependencies, stands fundamentally in the realm of absolute and non-relative truth. The transcendental method determines the necessary properties of knowledge through the analysis of self-knowing human knowledge, and by this means attains the *a priori* determinations of objects and the existential validity of these determinations. In this way, the structure of the subject and of knowable reality, which support knowledge and are contained in it, are developed through transcendental analysis.

7. DEDUCTION AND THE EVIDENT

Transcendental analysis can derive the necessary structural elements and real validity of objects, e.g., the contingency of objects of experience and the absolute validity of the metaphysical principle of causality, through the operative explication of knowledge. But does not the principle of causality, at least at its most decisive point, owe its validity to a direct insight into essence?[25] How can it then be the consequence of a derivation? This is, as a matter of fact, a question of great importance for the clarification of the logical structure of the transcendental method. The starting point for the answer to this question is to be found by viewing the relationship between the *a priori* and what is evident (already discussed above) against the properties of operative analysis. This indicates that the principles which give expression to insights into essences can be transcendentally derived because they are directly open to insight, although their openness to insight is not the logical ground of their derivation. Besides, this answer cannot be universalized, nor is its converse true, since not everything which is directly open to insight can be transcendentally derived. Thus the determinations of what is contingently given cannot be transcendentally deduced precisely because of their contingency, and not everything which can be transcendentally derived is directly evident, e.g., the existence of God. How can this axiom be explained?

The division of judgments according to the way in which they are evident considers the conscious relationship of the affirmation of judgment in terms of its noetic ground. We can distinguish between being directly or indirectly evident according to

[25] J. de Vries, *Critica,* n. 102.

whether the insight which vindicates judgment is possible in the circumstances without the logical mediation of another judgment, or not. With indirect insight, further distinctions according to the kinds of mediation are possible.[26] This division is to be distinguished from another division of knowledge into the direct and indirect, which is focused on a phenomenological description of noetic intention. That is to say, we distinguish between direct and indirect knowledge according to whether direct knowledge is related to something which our fundamental concepts intend, or to something that is first determined by means of a relation to objects which are directly intended through concepts derived from a spontaneous confrontation with experience. Thus knowledge of a particular concrete object of experience over and against us appears first of all to be grounded in what is only indirectly evident, and on the other hand to be a direct knowledge, since the intention of concepts goes to the objects consisting in themselves, although this is not directly evident. Otherwise, deception would be impossible. But however this may be, such divisions in any case center on a characterization of the *conscious* relations of our express knowledge.

This division does not exclude the possibility that what is directly and indirectly evident, along with problematical knowledge, is cast under operative analysis. The latter investigates the act of knowledge in terms of its conditions and then seeks to infer the relations of the structure of knowledge. One possible result (we know of Maréchal's attempt to demonstrate this method through transcendental deduction) that every object of knowledge which is not itself the absolute and unlimited being ultimately is entirely dependent in its being on the absolute. The principle of causality is a consequence of this dependence.

This conclusion can be given formal characterization by saying that the operative analysis brought about through transcendental deduction shows not only that thought is being-oriented, but that this being-oriented thought cannot affirm a contingent being unless the affirmability of its fundamental dependence

[26] J. de Vries, *op. cit.*, nn. 136, 180, 243.

also follows from this. If it should be asked in what way this notion is evident, the answer would have to be indirectly, because it is related to a conclusion. The direct evidence, to which this conclusion refers, is centered on what is directly given in the act of knowledge, which is the starting point for the transcendental method. But how is it possible that a direct insight into essence can be the result of an indirect foundation?

Strictly speaking, these two facts do not relate to the same judgment. The judgment that a contingent being is necessarily caused is directly evident. The judgment that the affirmability of a contingent being necessarily includes the affirmability of its being caused is basically the conclusion of a deduction. The second judgment, of course, can be derived from the first, and vice versa, but can it be shown to be logically impossible for the second judgment to be derived from other judgments, say from a general theory of the objects of affirmation, since it follows from the operative analysis of knowledge? Since the first judgment follows from the second, then the judgment which is directly evident is demonstrable as the result of what is indirectly evident—not, of course, *insofar* as it is evident (viz., insofar as the direct insight into essence is demanded for its foundation); rather, insofar as it is a judgment which can be grounded in a direct insight, but which can *also* be grounded in a demonstration. The characterization of a judgment as directly or indirectly evident does not affect the affirmed structure of the proposition as such, but rather its relation to a logical ground from which its affirmability follows. However, since the act of knowledge does not merely stand in the context of the intentional relation to its object, but also in the context of the conditions of the actuation of the act of knowing definite objects, basically it is possible to derive the affirmability of the structure of a proposition from the one as well as from the other context since it is not previously determined that both derivations must coincide with each other with regard to directness or indirectness. What is directly evident can be involved in the foundation of the intentional order, and what is indirectly evident in the foundation of the conditions of the act of knowledge.

136

Furthermore, because it is proper to the mode of procedure of transcendental analysis to derive the necessary unifying forms of objects of knowledge from the conditions of possibility for object-oriented thought, and because universal judgments referable to what is directly evident in the intentional order signify necessary unifications in the object of knowledge, it is not surprising at all that such judgments can be transcendentally derived. The metaphysics of knowledge following from the transcendental method, e.g., the metaphysics of knowledge developed by Maréchal from Thomas (V, book 2), therefore must require that every logically *a priori* structure, viz., every essential unity, is a result of *a priori* conditions of possibility in the subject of knowldege and must therefore be derivable from the conditions of the act of knowledge. However, implicit in this requirement is that every directly evident universal judgment which expresses an insight into essence be transcendentally deducible.

The evidence of an insight into essence, which is grasped with an objectivity directly intended through concepts, can be designated as what is *internally* evident and contrasted with what is *externally* evident, which is external because the grasp is by means of a cognitive relation to objects. They can also be distinguished as what is "directly" or "objectively" evident as opposed to what is "reflectively" or "transcendentally" evident. Only we must take care that "objective" stands opposed to "transcendental" and not to "subjective" evidence. If what is "objectively" evident is opposed to what is "subjectively" evident, the opposition between what is "objectively" and "transcendentally" evident would cause a division of what is objectively evident (which is possible in relation to a definite judgment of necessity).

The advantages of the proof by means of what is externally evident consists in the following:

(1) It can be shown, apart from the internal evidence of the judgment in question, that it is affirmable.

(2) Since the inner and direct evidence, on which the external and indirect evidence of judgment in question depends, has an epistemological character other than the inner evidence

of the judgment, it is possible to prove the truth of a universal judgment and its real validity for something else, which such judgments are incapable of doing on the basis of an insight into essence. With regard to transcendental analysis, then, it is proper to use internal evidence in its procedure not as something which gives us an insight into reality, viz., into self-subsistent being, but only as something which exercises a definite function in our noetic activity. What is to be retained from a knowledge which "functions" in this way is what is itself a derived result of the transcendental procedure. Thus the epistemological characters of the evidence used in transcendental deduction and of the "internal" evidence which is referred to for the critical vindication of knowledge are different. We can also derive the truth of essential judgments without having to refer to insight as the ultimate criterion of its conformity with being, because the fact that this evidence is the ultimate criterion is itself a derivable conclusion. The foundation of the truth of a definite universal judgment in its openness to insight is replacable through a transcendental deduction.

(3) It also becomes clear how the foundation of necessary judgments, such as the principle of causality, is to be found in a reduction to a contradiction, because the decisive part of transcendental deduction, that which grounds its validity, is the retorsive aspect, as expressed in the *reductio ad absurdam*. It should be noted that the reduction to contradiction is such only in the sense of an analytical reduction, since the reference to what is evident as a proof for the validity of being never occurs by means of a synthetic judgment, and that the contradiction itself is not a contradiction between concepts, but a contradiction in fact, viz., between what was proven to be the condition for the possibility of an assertion and what was actually asserted.

(4) A further ramification of the transcendental deduction of principles is that the concepts which are employed in a principle, because of the operative aspect of the deduction, receive a reflective explanation and at the same time become operatively definable.

It should be clear by now that the (internal) evidence of

knowledge and transcendental deduction in no way exclude each other, but rather they expand each other insofar as what is externally evident can clarify the structure of what is directly evident. This clarification can bring about the elaboration of the universal characteristics of all objects of knowledge, or of certain realms of objects, more clearly than is possible through a reflection on what is directly evident. This is a property of the transcendental method which we shall refer to as "all-pervasiveness."

THE CHARACTERISTIC
OF ALL-PERVASIVENESS

As we have seen, Maréchal is not interested in presenting a detailed theory of knowledge, or with guaranteeing the possibility of certain kinds of specialized knowledge. His aim is to determine the fundamental orientation and power of knowledge and to demonstrate a necessary property of all objects of knowledge, viz., their relation to the absolute order of being, a relation which is capable of a multiple differentiation. Maréchal accomplishes this in his transcendental critique (V, book 3). Whoever is wont to begin with what is directly evident, in the sense of a direct critique of knowledge, which focuses on internal experience in order to demonstrate the metaphysical validity of knowledge, and to derive all other knowledge by means of inference from direct judgments of this kind and to construct knowledge from these elementary insights, will look upon Maréchal's procedure as a curious enterprise. How, they might say, is it possible to say something about all objects of knowledge if I have not once known particulars in a critically vindicated way? How can I come to the whole if I do not yet possess the parts? It might be asked in rebuttal, how is it possible to reach the whole through a connection of the parts?

Such a knowledge of the essential characteristics of the whole is made possible through transcendental analysis. Insofar as it derives the necessary structure of every object of knowledge, along with the necessary existential validity of these fundamental structures, in terms of the conditions of possibility of knowledge, a universal knowledge of the whole realm of objects is offered independent of the determination of particular objects. In terms of this framework, further knowledge leads to a differentiation of this realm. The knowledge of particular objects plays an essential role in the general determination of all objects and in the regulation of the modes of belonging to this realm. Insofar as the transcendental method permits the derivation of the necessary and universal structures of the whole order of being, or of a particular realm, a totality is known within which particular objects have their place and attain cognoscibility. This property of the transcendental method, by means of which it offers directly the whole, although not yet fully differentiated, realm of objects of knowledge and also the essential properties of particular objects, insofar as they belong to this realm, is called the *all-pervasive* mode.

This characteristic corresponds to the generation of knowledge, as Maréchal has already explained it from the psychological point of view in his work on the givenness of reality (Sent.). Our knowledge develops by means of a differentiation of the orientation (which is immediately directed to things as experienced) to the totality of being. This differentiation occurs in relation to what is given in particular experience and in accordance with the orientation of knowledge as expressed in the first principles. The result of this differentiation, viz., particular knowledge, necessarily goes beyond the mere reception of what is given in experience, in the sense of a determination of the reflection on what is directly and evidently given in immediate knowledge. Thus our basic concepts and knowledge itself mean more than what is directly evident. They directly intend something that is not directly evident. Therefore, the object of knowledge proper to man, it would appear to us, is experienceable reality in itself (*quidditas rei sensibilis,* not only as the directly evident differentiation of the content of representation, but as the ontological reflection on the very things of experience) and the sort of evidence proper to man, viz., indirect evidence. This should be clear from a phenomenological analysis of everyday words.[27] This fact has ramifications for the application of the transcendental method in the theory of knowledge and in metaphysics.

THE CONTRIBUTION
TO THE CRITIQUE OF KNOWLEDGE

Since the transcendental method consists in a reflection and an analysis of knowledge in order to determine the meaning and validity of its object, it is not its task to replace the activity of knowledge, which occurs on the everyday level or in the special sciences, or to carry out a reflective differentiation of this knowledge according to criteria of the intentional order, e.g., according to the sorts of evidence, which would be the undertaking of a direct critique and would refer to direct, inner evidence. The result of noetic activity is presupposed, with its own claim to validity and grade of certainty, while the fundamental justification of such a result of the activity of knowledge and its limits and relation to being are determined through transcendental analysis. The question of how this knowledge, insofar as it is justified, could be conclusively derived from direct insights, is ignored. The transcendental method thus leads to a determination of the universal regulations of the objective realms of human knowledge, of their relations to each other and of the universal principles which regulate the manner of being and the knowledge of objects of knowledge. It does not show in particular the criteria according to which the act of knowledge consciously engages with what is given in the ways in which it is given. The determination of the various grades of certainty and the indication of the conscious conditions, examined in reflective consciousness, as to when and to what degree a par-

[27] E.g., J. Geyser, *Einige Hauptprobleme der Metaphysik mit besonderer Bezugnahme auf die Kritik Kants,* Freiburg i. Br., 1923, pp. 9f. Cf. J. de Vries, *Critica,* n. 20, pp. 164ff., where it is shown that in the proof for the existence of the things of the world of experience the natural belief in what is given as limited is valid as a sufficient ground of the totality of our conscious knowing and striving since it is directly evident.

ticular, concrete mode of knowledge reaches certainty would appear to be the task of criteriology. It investigates how particular knowledge can fundamentally be referred to what is directly evident, a task which we contend cannot be accomplished by the transcendental method alone.

A reflection on an act of knowledge expressing the claim of certainty cannot determine when and if, in a particular case, the knowledge of a concrete object can claim certainty (at most, it can determine the universal rule of such an act of knowledge directed to the determination of a mode of certainty). The universal standards of criteriological activity, in the sense indicated, can themselves be transcendentally founded, but it cannot be substituted for this activity itself. However, the transcendental method can determine the character of the validity of a mode of knowledge (which satisfies these criteria in a way other than the already mentioned foundation of criteriology) and the validity of universal synthetic-necessary principles, by means of which knowledge can be referred to directly evident facts. These tasks are proper to the transcendental method.

All this points to the necessity for the cooperation of both procedures for the needs of a theory of knowledge. If the transcendental critique is absolutized, then the critique becomes useless as a source of norms for the evaluation of concrete knowledge. If this method is disregarded, then we are deprived of an appropriate means of developing a foundation for universal principles which can cover the current demands of scientific philosophy and of explaining what is meant by saying that our (evident) knowledge is true and conforms to being. The relationship between both methods, viz., the transcendental method and, if we may express it in this way, the intentional method of direct critique, in the theory of knowledge can be summarized by saying that the transcendental method is at least implicitly dependent on the intentional method in order to be able to distinguish the content of the knowledge whose validity is to be investigated. This also clarifies the significance of the relation of the phenomenological method to the transcendental method, viz., it conveys the structures, whose relations and position in knowledge can be mediated through transcendental analysis, to what is given. This does not presuppose that the meaning or validity of its claim to evident truth is guaranteed and vindicated through the intentional method, for this is done through the transcendental method. Thus the intentional method depends, at least implicitly, on the application of the transcendental method insofar as this indicates what the validity of knowledge, corresponding to the criteria supplied by the transcendental method, means.

It is, therefore clear that any attempt to demonstrate the meaning of truth and its logical foundations through what is evident, e.g., in terms of what is directly evident in a conscious judgment, as do J. Geyser[28] and J. de Vries,[29] is not possible unless a reflective analysis is used from the start, which leads to and implies the development of the transcendental method. If the structure of judgment is limited to what is directly evident, excluding whatever is only indirectly evident, and it is then shown that what is expressed in judgment is simply what is directly found in consciousness, then either it has only been explained when to call a judgment directly evident or it has been shown that a directly evident judgment is true, viz., that it corresponds with reality, and that enough is known about this truth to exclude falsity and vindicate assertion. In the first case, the question of the validity of judgment has not been answered. To be able to do that, as in the second case, judgment, as well as the direct consciousness of something, must be understood as activities which are related to objects and which underlie certain demonstrable conditions which ground the necessary interrelationships of these activities.

In other words, the direct consciousness of something is an act which is related to a certain object in such a way that the actual existence of this object is immediately present. This distinguishes the confrontation with a concrete object from the representation of a concrete object where the object can exist

---

[28] J. Geyser, *Erkenntnistheorie*, Münster, 1922, pp. 143, 147, 159ff., 198f., 225. Also his *Das Prinzip vom zureichenden Grunde*, Regensburg, 1929, pp. 35f.

[29] J. de Vries, *Critica*, nn. 24ff.

but is not represented conceptually as existing (viz., a concept) and from the representation of a concrete object which expresses the object in the representation precisely as existing (viz., a judgment). Thus there are two different ways of relating to an object, so that a judgment presupposes the determination of an object, upon which existence is bestowed, through conceptual representation. Furthermore, the exact determination of the content of a concept presupposes the relation of confrontation, at least in cases where the content is determined precisely by the fact that it attempts to represent exactly what was confronted. It follows, however, that a judgment, whose propositional form is determined by the conceptual representation of the directly conscious object and which is connected with the act of this direct consciousness, must necessarily attain its intention. This can be expressed linguistically by saying that judgment asserts what actually is, that it bestows being on a state of affairs that actually exists, that judgment is true in the sense of an intentional conformity of thinking and being.

But what does this mean? Is it merely shown that there is truth in the realistic sense and that we can confirm it? Does this mean that the concern with the confronted "existence" of the state of affairs, which precedes judgment, is with the in-itself, viz., with something not at all relative? Does it suffice to answer this question be referring simply to that which is directly present in consciousness, or is it the case that a reflective analysis is required which can clarify reflectively, by means of at least a simple operative analysis and retorsive vindication, that a true judgment, in the sense taken here, is not relatively valid but is related to an absolute order, so that no one can deny that it is grounded? It would seem to be necessary to show that the relation to objects which appears in judgment is so fundamental for knowledge that every attempt to provide a more transcendent relation to objects is excluded, viz., a relation which would relativize judging, and therefore truth and its logical foundation, which in the case of a conscious judgment appears through the relation to what is directly given. In other words, being, to which judgment as such is related, grounds the most comprehensive order of objectivity. An indication for the necessity of such reflections is that exponents of a more intentional method of critique, who start with a theory of conscious judgments, use a method of retorsion to reject skepticism, relativism and epistemological idealism by demonstrating internal self-contradictions[30] and further insist that the concept of being, insofar as it can be abstracted from what is directly given to consciousness and what is judged in the conscious judgment, is not known as transcendental and absolutely excluding non-being, but that it has need of a further reflection and a synthetic knowledge of necessity.[31]

The demonstration of the direct evidence of conscious judgments thus does not itself give the full, reflective explanation of the truth of knowledge as absolute and non-relative. This explanation is supplied by the demonstration of the impossibility of transcending the order of being to which judgment, as grounded in what is directly evident, is related by means of universal, synthetic *a priori* insights. A confrontation with opposing epistemological opinions is also still considered to be useful, where the denial of the character of the absolute is shown to be an actual contradiction. If we accept transcendental analysis as the appropriate means of demonstrating the validity of judgments which express synthetic insights, then it follows that transcendental analysis serves as the explanation of evident judgments. Why not, then, make the question of validity in general an object of the transcendental method and assign the field of operation to each of the two methods for which it is appropriately suited? In this way, both methods, and a critique of knowledge worked out with them, would stand to gain. Besides, a direct critique must accept elements of the indirect critique whenever it comes up against complicated circumstances, such as the knowability of the material world.[32]

Obviously, the transcendental method is deeply significant

[30] J. de Vries, *op. cit.*, nn. 111f., 119, 127f.
[31] J. de Vries, *op. cit.*, nn. 75, 293f.
[32] For example, J. de Vries' proof (in *Critica,* nn. 164ff.) does not demonstrate the inner evidence of our knowledge of the external world, but only the outer evidence. This is valid, but it also clearly shows that the method of the direct critique is open, and must be open, to other methods.

for the communication of philosophical insights and a discussion of them, either in relation to the historical systems of philosophy or the kind of discussion which is necessary for the cooperation of individual thinkers so characteristic of contemporary science. If communication with others is to be fruitful, it is above all else necessary that one be understood. To a certain extent, such understanding is possible independent of theoretical contexts. But would it not be most fruitful if, through an operative analysis of the act of communication and the noetic activity contained in it without which no discussion is possible, one would succeed, through the transcendental method, in determining the meaning of the basic philosophical concepts on a common basis, viz., the very act of discussing them, and in demonstrating the validity of the assertions under discussion as included in the very act of mutual discussion? The transcendental method thus demonstrates its significance as a reflective explanation of concepts and as a foundation for the propositions of philosophy, which satisfies the contemporary demand to be scientific and the requirements of communication. It also indicates the fundamental significance of language and of the views of others communicated through language with respect to the development of true knowledge. Can a critique of human knowledge ignore this method? We shall return to this point in our treatment of the disciples and critics of Maréchal, who have developed the method more extensively. Now, however, perhaps we are in a position to ask whether Maréchal's historico-comparative method is relevant to his transcendental method.

THE TRANSCENDENTAL AND HISTORICO-COMPARATIVE METHODS

The historical method serves Maréchal chiefly as a preparation for his systematic investigations. The development of views which have appeared in the history of philosophy, their confrontation with each other, their premisses and dialectic, should indicate, first of all, in which systems the recurrent philosophical problems tend to crop up and in which systems they find their most comprehensive solutions, and secondly, should produce a familiarity with these problems and with the limitations of various attempts at solving them, which should yield important clues for the systematic development of an attempt at a satisfying solution. What should this method be in order to fulfill this function? It must obviously presuppose that the thought of a particular philosopher is, first of all, directed at the solution of the outstanding problems in a way which promises success, and secondly, that in the actual attainment of this end it is dependent on conditions which determine the thought of the philosopher in question. Without the second premiss we could not explain why a certain thinker may have a solution for certain problems but no adequate solution for others, or why he is contradicted by other thinkers. Furthermore, the unique positions of particular philosophers can be understood as influenced by the views of other thinkers, or as developed in opposition to them, so that the personal conditions in the starting point of a particular philosopher also includes his understanding of, and his position with respect to, the viewpoints of others. An investigation into the psychological, biographical and sociological conditions of a philosophy can explain its one-sidedness, distorted generalizations and misinterpretations conditioned by such factors, and can contrast them with the valid, but distorted, insights which are operative in them. Without the first premiss, it cannot be explained why philosophers communicate with each other at all and why there is a demonstrable dialectic between extreme solutions. It is only because of a common goal and because of the possibility of knowing when one has come close to it that it can be explained why a particular philosopher rejects opinions which he considers to be opposed to his own, and that in the history of philosophy, which is so varied and dependent on such diverse conditions, a general stability of problems seems to prevail, viz., particular viewpoints can be explained as more or less one-sided or comprehensive solutions to these problems, their one-sidedness can be explained in terms of the personal conditions within which each philosopher operates, and the conflict among philosophers can be led back to their one-sided and insufficient answers to these problems. Is it, then, not the case that an all-comprehensive solution to these problems is possible, which would avoid the one-sidedness of other viewpoints and would correspond most precisely to the goal which particular philosophers strive after and which supports their philosophizing? It should be made clear that the problem of the validity of the true point of view is itself a philosophical problem! If this is correct, then the historico-comparative method of demonstration is fundamentally vindicated as a method. It is, then, a legitimate philosophical method to adopt a philosophical position because and insofar as it is demonstrated to be the basic point of convergence with respect to philosophical activity. This is precisely what Maréchal tried to do with the Aristotelian-Thomistic theory of knowledge (I, II) and with his own theory of knowledge within the context of modern philosophy (II–V), whereby his own theory of knowledge is shown to be nothing but an extension of the Aristotelian-Thomistic system. Consequently, his investigation into the history of modern philosophy is not simply a psychological and heuristic preparation for his own systematic solution, but rather an historical argument for it.

Taking this historico-comparative method in this sense, what is its essential relation to the transcendental method? In their logical structures, as well as in their epistemological significance, both methods exhibit great similarity. The cognitive development of the salient results of philosophical knowing are referred to the presuppositions of their actual occurrence and compared with each other. The modes and limits of their value are determined along these lines. In an at least logically distinguishable first step of the historico-comparative method the conditions are drawn out under which alone the philosophical propositions under discussion, which claim to be real knowledge, can be cognitively actuated and understood.

These conditions, however, are not only what explain the relativity of particular points of view, but such that include (although limited by the first conditions) the approach of these points of view to the absolute goal of all knowledge, viz., to the absolute order of being through absolutely true knowledge. Therefore, as a second step, we have the relations of particular points of view to this goal, wherefrom the extent and measure of their validity and their claim to truth can be derived.

In terms of the metaphysics of knowledge, this method can be taken to mean that the orientation of the understanding, according to which what is given is worked out to lead to a knowledge of reality, is operative in each individual philosopher. Included in what is given to be worked on are the expressions of others who claim to express true knowledge. Because of the reciprocal dependence of knowing and willing, there is a dependence of concrete knowledge on free and unfree attitudes toward value, which not only direct attention to but also determine the personal evaluation of knowledge. This means that the points of view of philosophers, on the one hand, are conditioned by the premises of their concrete philosophizing, and that, on the other hand, they are supported by the absolute orientation which belongs to every philosopher, as to every man, in essentially the same way. Thus a deviation from this orientation creates the demand for a critique, whereas approximation to the goal of orientation shows up in the convergence of the various points of view. There is, then, a similarity between the self-correcting process[33] whereby the knowledge of experience is appropriated and the self-correcting dialectic of philosophical systems. Consequently, it is not surprising if, from a reflection on history, inferences can be drawn with respect to the validity of the proposed points of view (this, of course, cannot be a simple inventory, although that too is required). This reflection must, on its own strength, include a transcendental reflection. This historico-comparative method is a development of the transcendental method. One can, of course, dispense with such a development for many systematic questions, but not if we are concerned with a fully structured philosophy, because the transcendental method itself can refer the concrete thought of man, in everyday life and in science, to

[33] B. J. F. Longergan, *Insight,* New York, 1957, pp. 174. (Cf. the index under "learning process.")

the results of the thoughts of others and thus demand expansion through the historico-comparative method.

The above certainly indicates that the proper relation of the historico-comparative method to the systematic methods in Maréchal's work is not a mere accidental relationship, but is grounded in the necessities of the situation. The same is true of the dialectical characteristics of these two methods.

THE TRANSCENDENTAL METHOD
AND DIALECTIC

Maréchal claims that transcendental analysis "is easily referred to the logical schema of rational synthesis, which unifies the opposed terms" (IV, p. 343) viz., "to the triadic form of a synthesis which reconciles thesis with antithesis" (IV, p. 343), because in the search for the conditions of possibility, that whose conditions of possibility are being sought does not yet fully realize the rational harmony without which, however, it would be negated. Consequently, a higher point of view is sought in the conditions of possibility, in terms of which the disharmony is negated (IV, p. 343). He views the interrelationships of philosophical systems in their historical connectedness as a dialectic (II, p. 8) of insufficient solutions. They suffer under hidden contradictions (I, p. 256) and yet also contain justified insights (I, p. 15), since every error contains a partial truth (II, p. 245). They overcome each other with proofs of contradictions (I, p. 13) and seek an harmonious adjustment of the various validated elements (I, pp. 14f.; V, p. 34). The realization of this harmony, however, does not grow in simple proportion to the progress of history, since conditions in the history of thought can be imagined, and actually demonstrated, which constitute regressions.

The ground for this dialectic is precisely the connection between actually attained knowledge and that toward which the striving of knowledge is oriented, in terms of which the striving of the understanding, which tends toward all that is knowable, easily leads to an improper generalization of partial knowledge which places it in contradiction to some other not yet considered mode of knowledge. The contradiction impels thought, which is oriented to the whole, to transcend the absolutized partial viewpoints at a higher point of view where the partial insights can be restricted to their valid core and systematically ordered, so that the contradiction of thesis and antithesis is raised to a higher synthesis. We can approach the examples of dialectical thought under discussion,[34] which is proper to common, everyday[35] and also to scientific thought,[36] if we consider that one begins with a certain formulation, contrasts it with another formulation which, in terms of the premises under which the first formulation takes on meaning, is shown to be ununifiable with the first formulation. This forces one to give up the absolutizing of the first complex of premises, whose retention would lead to a contradiction, and to introduce a new set of premises, in terms of which both formulations are meaningful and toward which the dialectical formulation is tending. The "contradiction" thus points to the understanding of the new, comprehensive unity, viz., the understanding of the new set of premises, in terms of which the contradiction is negated. This structure is also signified in the transfer of the starting point of the transcendental method to the conditions of possibility, as well as in the relation of historically demonstrable philosophical systems to a harmonious solution of their problems. This dialectic, however, at least with Maréchal, is not a requirement present from the beginning, but is the form with which the structure of the development of the transcendental procedure, which is conditioned by the self-imposing and essential inner laws of thought, can be described.

[34] For instance, examples such as these are used by R. Heiss in *Wesen und Formen der Dialektik,* Köln, 1959, chapter three.

[35] One need only point to the forms of paradoxes, jokes and aphorisms. Cf. R. Heiss, *op. cit.*

[36] The classic examples can be found in the history of the natural sciences, above all physics and mathematics, especially as studied by the Zurich Circle under F. Gonseth, whose organ is the journal, *Dialectica.*

THE TRANSCENDENTAL METHOD
AND METAPHYSICS

Since we have explained how the all-pervasive characteristic of the transcendental method works out into a theory of knowledge and how this method is related to the methodological evaluation of the dialectic of the history of philosophy, we shall now examine its meaning for metaphysics. This can be shown by considering that, according to the circumstances, metaphysics is concerned with investigating things in terms of their positions in the totality of reality, viz., to investigate their relations to the ultimate ground of reality. The transcendental method, moreover, sketches the fundamental relation of all objects of knowledge to the ultimate goal of noetic striving, viz., to absolute being, and distinguishes and orders together the different modes of relation proper to the different realms of noetic objects. The transcendental method, therefore, leads directly to that which is the concern of metaphysics.

As a matter of fact, we have seen how Maréchal, who was not interested in constructing a detailed metaphysics but simply in the fundamental justification of the affirmation of being, nevertheless arrives at some basic theses of metaphysics (Prem., p. 297) from which further theses follow. However, if we may anticipate ourselves somewhat, a glance at the fundamental theses of metaphysics shows that the interpretations of them, oddly enough, conflict with one another. Thus those which pertain to the transcendental method usually mean something else than those which ground metaphysical propositions in what is directly and internally evident. The first takes ultimate being as grounded in really distinguishable constitutive elements[37] while the other denies this possibility and only permits conceptually distinguishable constitutive elements.[38] This difference points to a difference in the conception of being. How does one explain the fact that the exponents of the transcendental method

[37] E.g., B. J. F. Lonergan, *Insight*, p. 501.
[38] E.g., J. de Vries, "Zur Lehre von den inneren Prinzipien des Seienden," *Zeitschrift für katholische Theologie*, vol. 76 (1954), pp. 343–348.

incline more toward a conception of being connected with Thomism in the strict sense of the word, while the exponents of a method which seeks to ground the concepts and propositions of ontology in terms of what is directly and evidently given, incline toward a conception of being reminiscent of Suarez? Perhaps an explanation can be found in an evaluation of the methods.

In both methods, it is fundamentally possible and also actually necessary[39] to relate the being of an object to judgment. However, the concept of being, as it is concretely explained and employed in ontology, without affecting certain mutual fundamental formal determinations (e.g., transcendentality, analogy, etc.), consists in a somewhat different meaning, which helps to clarify the differences in the ontologies in terms of content.

The transcendental method, through its analysis, reaches the conditions of possibility of knowledge, viz., that something corresponds to the assertion expressed through the "is" of the copula of an actuated judgment[40] in the intended object,

[39] In the transcendental method this results directly from its fundamental function, which often takes the form of an analysis of judgment. But this also appears in the other method. J. Geyser, in *Erkenntnistheorie*, p. 4, states: "As 'being,' the object stands over against judgment as such, but not particularly to the judgment of this or that subject; rather to judgment pure and simple, and therefore to the judgment of any subject." The concept of being is closely connected with judgment, "because if we were only capable of perception and representation the concept of being would never be known. However, as soon as we judge and have even the slightest awareness of the nature of judgment, what we experience as being is unavoidably caught up in a relation to consciousness" (*Allgemeine Philosophie des Seins und der Natur*, 1915, p. 4). Thus "the answer to the question concerning universal being is essentially achieved through a reflection on the judgmental apprehension of what is. . . . The consideration of the source of the representation of being lies in this judgmental apprehension" ("Zur Grundlegung der Ontologie," *Philosophisches Jahrbuch der Görres-Gesellschaft*, vol. 49 [1936], p. 297). These quotes clearly show how the analysis of reflection, as used by the transcendental method, has been accepted, but without further development. J. de Vries also holds that judgment loses its meaning if what it asserts is not ultimately grounded in real being (*Critica*, n. 285).

[40] The judgment "This is a table" must be fundamentally distinguished from the context of judgment, the *enuntiabile*, viz., the problematical representation of a state of affairs "that this is a table." It is only through

whereby it is not only the absolute norm of the judgment, but through which the object is grounded in its existence and related to the absolute and all-encompassing order of being, which includes the ultimate grounding in the absolute being as the ultimate ground of the order of being. This yields a concept of being which views being not merely as the factuality of the existence of a being, but as the ground of existence and knowability. Every being is thus inclusively related to the ultimate ground of all being, in terms of which particular being receives its position in the order of being.

The other method, however, determines the concept of being in terms of the factuality of the existence of the adjudged state of affairs directly evident. This factual existence, whose engagement grounds the validation of judgment, is that which is meant by being. This concept of being includes a relation to the ground of finite being insofar as a comparison of beings indicates their limitation and contingency and a comparison of what is meant by contingent being and caused being makes evident their necessary essential identity. In terms of this different notion of being, a different understanding of the relation of finite being to being as such follows, viz., if being as such is conceived as the ground, then finite being cannot be understood if it is conceived as the pure effect of being as such, which is essentially ground; in other words, it needs a different ground than being as such as ground, one which causes the

---

assertion that this context of judgment becomes a judgment, i.e., "I assert that this is a table," or "It is true that this is a table." If "judgment" is made the object of a reflection in which the question is posed, "Is it true that this is a table?," we see that the object of reflection is, properly speaking, the context of judgment in which we want to know whether a judgment affirmed and concretely determined through it is true, viz., whether this context of judgment is validly affirmable. Thus because of its close relationship to the judgment concretely determined through it, we speak of the context of judgment as being true if the judgment is true. However, this does not validate the derivation of the meaning of the linguistic expression of judgment as given with the copula in a categorical judgment through a mere consideration of the context of judgment in abstraction from affirmation. For the distinction between statement and *enuntiabile* as different syntactical categories, cf. J. M. Bochenski, "On Syntactical Categories," *New Scholasticism,* vol. 23 (1949), pp. 257–280.

uniqueness of what is finite and which cannot fulfill this function if it coincides, as ground, with being as such. This means, however, that both of these inner grounds, which are incapable of existence independent of each other, are, like physical things which we confront in concrete situations, and which they are supposed to ground, distinguished from each other, i.e., they are, metaphysically, really distinct. However, if being as such is conceived as the factuality of existence, then finite being is signified directly in the fact that its existence is contingently related to what is contained in its determination, viz., they are only conceptually distinct from each other. The true conflict between the exponents of a real, and those of only a conceptual, distinction between essence and being, therefore, lies in the conception of being, which is presupposed according to the exact determination of the constructural elements of finite being. With that taken into consideration, both conceptions are unified and ordered together.[41] The true conflict consists in the question of the conception of being, which is decisive for ontology, but also in the method which is required for the foundation of ontology.

If we compare both methods in terms of their adaptability for ontology, the transcendental method, because of its all-pervasive character, seems to correspond better to the given end of ontology. First of all, it corresponds more to the logical character of the universal and necessary proposition of ontology, which gives expression to the universal and essential relations of real being. If what was said in the discussion of the significance of the transcendental method for the critique of knowledge is correct, then it is definitely a task of this method to demonstrate reflectively the meaning and validity of such propositions.

Second, ontology is concerned with demonstrating the universal structure of the order to which something belongs because it is a being. This makes the ground for the correspondence of the transcendental method to the task of metaphysics, as discussed above, of special value for ontology, because the

[41] J. B. Lotz, "Die Unterscheidung von Wesenheit und Sein," *Der beständige Aufbruch* (Przywara-Festschrift), 1959, pp. 161–171.

transcendental analysis of knowledge leads principally to an understanding of the proximate object of human knowledge with respect to the absolute order of being and the essential structural elements of this order.

Third, the conception of being at which transcendental analysis arrives is in better correspondence to the understanding of being which is necessarily and legitimately at work in all human knowledge, both scientific and common, everyday knowledge, including the thought of each theoretician who works on the conception of being, even if the conception of being resulting from his theory does not coincide with the understanding of being which supports his thought (which cannot be considered as a complement to his theory, although it is not rendered entirely false on that account, but certainly inadequate). This is precisely the meaning of operative analysis and the demonstration of necessity through retorsion, as elements of the transcendental method, viz., to determine and show the necessary structure of every object of knowledge and that this is impossible if it is not constituted as a being in a definite realm of being through a relationship to the ultimate ground of the analogous order of being itself. Thus not only is this assertion grounded in a way which satisfies the demands of critical scientific thought, but its meaning is also determined in correspondence with these demands, viz., by means of the operative determination of the concept. Of course, this by no means explains what we actually think when we use the word "being" (this can only be determined through an intentional, descriptive and phenomenological method), but it at least explains what we must think and what is connected with what is intended if we want to use the word "being" and its different variations in a meaningful sense, viz., as it corresponds to reality and to the thought signified through the orientation to the knowledge of reality, without which an actual use of this word and a connection with a definite meaning are not possible.

The metaphysics of knowledge makes this point even clearer. Judgment, the acknowledgment of being, is as such supported essentially by an orientation to absolute being and by the relation of each individually affirmed being to absolute being. This orientation supports and characterizes all knowledge and is the source of the insights into essence which flow necessarily into actual knowledge and which receive their express formulation in first principles and in other necessary judgments. Must not an ontology interpret this actualized knowledge of being instead of merely directing itself, in the fundamental conception of being, to particular effects of this understanding of being (viz., to a determination of what is directly given in the existence of beings and some insights into essential relations), an interpretation which would seek the inclusion of these particular effects into the whole? The propositions derived from these limited points of view are true, but they do not move into the focus of the science of being as such and are, therefore, not a sufficient foundation for metaphysics since they lack the scientific guarantee which the transcendental determination of concepts and demonstrations can offer.

If the transcendental method is conceived in the way we have come to know it, viz., through an analysis of Maréchal's procedure, it may be said that if the transcendental method is actually possible, then it contains a fundamental meaning for the theory of knowledge, for metaphysics and for the critical foundation of metaphysics. It does not, however, exclude cooperation with other methods. Yet if one is of the opinion that the transcendental method is not possible as a means to the philosophical knowledge of reality, then one must show why the grounds introduced into the historical and systematic demonstrations are insufficient.

In the following sections, we shall investigate how this method was later developed and what objections were brought against it. On both sides, we shall primarily consider those works which will best lead to an understanding of the structure of the transcendental method. What we have had to say about Maréchal had this end partly in view.

PART TWO

REACTIONS TO MARÉCHAL

8. TRANSCENDENTAL DYNAMISM AS THE FOUNDATION OF THE KNOWLEDGE OF GOD

Auguste Grégoire and Josef Defever have interpreted Maréchal's transcendental mode of demonstration as a critical foundation of the natural, philosophical knowledge of God. Following Maréchal, they begin with a reflection on noetic activity, show that the finalistic dynamism of knowledge is operative in this activity, and then demonstrate that this finalistic dynamism is the condition for the possibility of noetic activity in such a way that without the existence and knowability of absolute and infinite being, noetic activity, as we find it, would be impossible. The concepts in which the dynamism of knowledge is formulated, as in Maréchal's transcendental critique, refer only to moments of the directly conscious and given act of knowledge and whatever proves to be a condition of possibility of this act. Thus despite the metaphysico-epistemological means of expression, this is a transcendental foundation, since the expressions are taken only in the limited sense of being demonstrable through transcendental reflection, not yet in the full sense which they would acquire against the background of metaphysics.

The work in which the methodological position of Auguste Grégoire (1890–1949) gains its clearest expression is *Immanence et Transcendance*,[1] which covers a series of questions on theodicy. In the first and by far the most comprehensive chapter, he examines the five classical modes of proving the

[1] A. Grégoire, *Immanence et Transcendance, Questions de Théodicée*, Paris, 1939.

161

existence of God according to Thomas and shows how they are made possible through the metaphysical principle of causality. He employs the principle in a formulation modelled after P. De Backer: "L'être par participation dépend de [une cause d'être, qui est] l'être par essence" (IT, pp. 90, 125) ["being by participation depends on (a cause of being which is) being by essence"], whereby "*être par essence*" means basically a being which exists through its own essence, while "*être par participation*" signifies a being whose essence is outside of existence, viz., which is contingent (IT, p. 90).

The validity of the five ways, therefore, depends on the principle of causality, but according to Grégoire this is not to be taken in a purely analytical sense. At this point he separates himself from P. De Backer. How, then, can it be grounded in order to guarantee the foundation of the philosophical study of God? In answering this question, Grégoire proves himself to be a true disciple of Maréchal and Scheuer (IT, p. 7) and as clear a thinker as he was a mathematician.[2] He takes from Maréchal's transcendental critique the elements essential for a transcendental deduction of the principle of causality under the tight support of the critical steps and develops them free from all philosophico-historical accessories.

Josef Defever[3] was also concerned with clarifying the foundations of the traditional proof of the existence of God through a reflection on the spontaneous activity of knowing (Pr., p. 7), and with vindicating the procedure which they employ (Pr., p. 8; *ibid.,* p. 5).[4] His thought is not only influenced by Maréchal, but he also endeavors to present Maréchal's ideas to the reader despite a mode of presentation that differs from Maréchal's (Pr., p. 11). The crucial point lies in the demonstration that the argument moves entirely in the realm of the real and

[2] A. Grégoire, *Leçons de philosophie des sciences expérimentales,* Paris, 1950 (Avant-propos des éditeurs, p. 5).

[3] J. Defever, *La preuve réelle de Dieu: Etude critique,* Paris, 1953.

[4] J. Defever, "Idée de Dieu et existence de Dieu," *Revue philosophique de Louvain,* vol. 55 (1957), pp. 5–57. This article is an answer to a review by F. Grégoire (*Revue philosophique de Louvain,* vol. 54 [1956], pp. 112–129) and includes a methodical discussion of the mode of proof in *La preuve réelle de Dieu.*

is not derived from the mere idea of the existence of God. "By a real proof of the existence of God we mean a proof which begins with what is real, does not leave the real in the course of its procedure and leads to the existence of the real God" (Pr., p. 7). The proof, therefore, is sympathetic with the concerns of existential philosophy, viz., it is not an abstract game which ignores man, but grows out of the development of the true human situation (Pr., p. 8).

Whereas Grégoire and Defever emphasize the analysis of noetic activity as end-oriented in order to demonstrate the necessary structure of what is affirmable, George Isaye evaluates the necessary structure of what is affirmable by showing that the attempt to deny it negates itself. In both cases, there is an investigation of the necessary structure of noetic activity in hopes of discovering the necessary characteristics of the object known. This is worked out in such a way that there is an express reference in the demonstration, as conceived by Grégoire and Defever, to the structural elements of the activity, whereas with Isaye the structural elements are taken in terms of their precise effect on the properties of the object.

We shall present Isaye's method in some detail, relying chiefly on two articles dealing respectively with the finality of the understanding[5] and the method of retorsion.[6] Now and then we shall consult other articles, which apply this method to the foundation of the special sciences and to metaphysics, and which seek to explain their mutual relationship.

INTUITION AND RETORSION

It is essential to see what position Isaye's method occupies in the whole scheme of human knowledge. When Isaye refers to the knowledge of principles, he openly admits: "The adherence to a first principle is a matter of intuition, not deduction, and

[5] G. Isaye, "La finalité de l'intelligence et l'objection kantienne," *Revue philosophique de Louvain,* vol. 51 (1953), pp. 42–100.

[6] G. Isaye, "La justification critique par retorsion," *Revue philosophique de Louvain,* vol. 52 (1954), pp. 204–233.

this adherence is completely vindicated from the very moment of intuition" (Fin., p. 43). There are, however, super-critical thinkers, in the twentieth century more than in the time of the Greek sophists, against whom Aristotle arrived at a vindication of the principles grounded in intuition (in the sense of what is directly *evident*) not by means of a proof of intuition, but through the process of *retorsion,* the *"redarguitio elenchica,"* which Thomas also employed. Contemporary critics can, of course, point to many more "intuitions" which are open to differences of opinion, e.g., the postulate which distinguishes Euclidean geometry from other geometries and the postulate of absolute simultaneity. They seem to be evident, and yet they are contradicted by relativity physics, calling forth a doubt which slowly extends to anything that claims to be evident (Fin., pp. 43f.). The principles must be defended against their critics, but this does not mean that they do not possess valid determination, although of a pre-scientific sort, before this vindication (Fin., p. 44). The meanings of concepts are also made explicit through this vindication, even though the sensible structures are known previously. Thus Isaye's method includes a necessary application even to contemporary science, vindicating knowledge by showing that it has its source elsewhere, viz., in intuition (Ret., p. 216).

ANALYSIS OF JUDGMENT

According to Isaye, the critique of knowledge does not begin with an abstract principle, but with a fact, viz., with the concrete activity of judgment. There are three moments involved here, which can be demonstrated through retorsion (Ret., pp. 210f.).

First of all, knowledge makes a claim on *truth*. When one denies, or doubts, he negates the claim that it is true that this claim is not negated, or at least, that it is not certain. Knowledge of the fundamental and undefinable concept of truth is given simultaneously with the undeniable experience of this

164

claim. Such an internal process, which implies the claim of truth, Isaye calls *judgment.*

Second, in judgment we must distinguish *affirmation* as such from the content which constitutes the difference between various judgments. If one denies this fact, this denial occurs in a judgment different from the original judgment, and that by which it is distinguished from the original judgment is precisely the content.

Third, in the content of judgment there is that about which someone thinks something and that which someone thinks about it. These two moments are called *"subject"* and *"predicate."* If this is denied, then what is denied, i.e., whatever is false, must be mentioned, viz., the original determination, so we have a subject. If something is attributed to this subject, viz., that it is false, or not certain, then we have a predicate. This rule, however, demonstrates that the act which negates the claim to truth itself relates to a synthesis of subject and predicate; it does not, of course, prove that judgment must be structured in this way, but that is not necessary.

VINDICATION OF THE PRINCIPLES

Each judgment making a claim to truth is a judgment of someone judging. If this statement is denied, the denial is unjustified because it makes its own claim to truth. This presupposes that the *self* enters into judgment and into its claim to truth. Is the concern, however, only with my truth, such that knowledge would be subjective, and hence relative? The answer to this question involves the first principles, of which Isaye deals chiefly with the principles of objectivity, contradiction, the universal predicate and the universal subject.

The *principle of objectivity* asserts that there is truth and that the claim to truth can be fundamentally satisfied. If this possibility is denied, thinking negates itself. *"Veritatem esse est per se notum, quia qui negat veritatem esse, concedit veritatem non esse. Si enim veritas non est, verum est, veritatem non esse,*

si autem aliquid est verum, oportet quod veritas sit.[7] ["Moreover, it is evident that truth exists, for whosoever denies the
existence of truth concedes that truth does not exist. If, however, truth does not exist, it is true that truth does not exist;
and if anything is true, then truth must exist."]

Second, the *principle of contradiction* holds that: "There
exists a pair of judgments such that both judgments are not
true (the principle of incompatibility) and such that both are
not false (the principle of the excluded middle)" (Ret., p.
212). The relationship between these two judgments is signified by referring to one of the pair of judgments as the "*negation*" of the other. "If an objection is raised against this principle, it is *ipso facto* the case that both of us cannot be right
at the same time, and that one of us is correct" (Priv., p. 32).[8]

The third *principle* is that of the *universal predicate,* which
holds that: "There exist true judgments whose subjects are
singular but whose predicates are universal" (Ret., p. 213).
The very objection which would deny this principle negates the
claim that the proposition with the universal predicate "false"
is true of the singular subject "this principle." It follows from
this principle that there are objectively valid universal concepts
which relate to the order of what is affirmable, while the universality of the predicate (the *modus universalitatis*) is posited
as incompatible with the singular subject and with concrete
reality.

The *principle of the universal subject* holds that: "There are
true judgments whose subjects are universal, viz., universal in
the distributive sense, i.e., such that the judgments can be
applied to particular cases" (Ret., p. 213). This, in fact, is
the principle of the syllogism, "Barbara," whose middle proposition is singular. If this principle is denied by saying that all
judgments whose subjects are universal are false, or uncertain,
then a universal judgment would be proposed, with the claim to
truth, but in such a way that it would follow that this particular universal judgment is false.

[7] *Summa theol.,* p. 1, q. 2, a. 1, ad 3.
[8] G. Isaye, "Le Privilège de la métaphysique," *Dialectica,* vol. 6
(1952), pp. 30–52.

RETORSION

What does retorsion (examples of which we have already come across) consist in? Retorsion is not a deduction in the sense of being a conclusion that leads to the first knowledge of something that is not directly evident. Rather, Isaye is concerned with the reflective explanation and critical vindication of those modes of knowledge which already possess their foundation in "intuition" (Ret., pp. 215f.), although retorsion can also be employed for other modes of knowledge which are not directly evident (Ret., p. 218). Retorsion does not replace *insight;* rather, it is a clarification of what is contained in insight. The critical vindication of what is contained in insight has two tasks: it should *defend* such insight against criticism (Fin., pp. 43f.) and should *filter out unjustified universalizations,* which should protect us from confusing customary modes of thought with evident and justified truth (Ret., p. 217).[9] Both tasks conform to the requirements which scientific procedure has imposed upon philosophy.

Retorsion fulfills these tasks by showing which insights must be included in the act of thinking because they are operative in it. It does this by indicating (not by proving, since, according to what we have seen above, we are concerned with the vindication of first principles; cf. Ret., pp. 215f.) that the insight in question is so fundamental and evident that the very act which would deny it is impossible unless it acknowledges it (Fin., p. 44). Again the crucial starting point of the procedure is the act of thought, because retorsion gains its strength from the indication that what is denied by the *actus signatus* of the objection is present in its *actus exercitus* (Ret., pp. 205, 220). Retorsion, therefore, is not necessarily applied only *ad hunc hominem,* but *ad objicientem qua talem* (Ret., p. 209), which, however, certainly applies with equal force to the critically reflecting philosophers themselves. According to which act is taken as the starting point, viz., judgment or dialogue, Isaye

[9] G. Isaye, "La logique scolastique devant ses récents adversaires," *Bijdragen,* vol. 13 (1952), pp. 1–30.

distinguishes between *fundamental* (retorsion *primitive*) and *derived* (retorsion *seconde*) retorsion (Ret., pp. 205, 224f.).

Retorsion, therefore, draws out the insights which are implied in the act of knowledge and make it possible, but are not directly observed, and demonstrates the necessity of acknowledging them. The determination of the *fundamental concepts* and the indication of the necessity of acknowledging the *principles* are possible because of their connections with the act of knowledge. Retorsion, therefore, has an *operative character* and unites within itself the *reflective* and *deductive* elements of the transcendental method, because it demonstrates the conditions without which the very act of knowledge is negated (including the act which absolutely denies the very objectivity of judgment) and derives from these conditions (negating the absolutely binding claim that it is so that the objection has its justification) the necessary structure of its relation to objects (viz., the vindication that the act of knowledge is oriented toward being and capable of truth), which is expressed in a now vindicated judgment (the principle of objectivity).

COMPARISON WITH MARÉCHAL

Although this method in its essential points is similar in structure to Maréchal's, considerable differences can be detected. The tight *connection between reflection and deduction* is more marked than, e.g., would be the case even with someone like Defever. The steps of the demonstration are, comparatively speaking, brief, each leading directly to the indication of the validity of the assertion demonstrated in the step. This leads to a multitude of steps, each conclusive in itself and developed from the previous steps, in order to reach the conclusions which Maréchal attained in a single, large-scale demonstration. This lends a great flexibility to Isaye's method, making it more comprehensible and simplified, especially if one is interested in demonstrating only a part of the conclusions.

This implies a different consideration of the metaphysico-epistemological ramifications of the transcendental method.

168

Naturally, Isaye follows Maréchal in the metaphysico-epistemological explanation of the knowledge of being vindicated through the transcendental analysis of the act of knowledge. As are analytic judgments, in their broadest sense, for Maréchal and Grégoire, so are synthetic judgments *a priori* for Isaye the judgments whose negation involves a contradiction in act (Fin., p. 45), which is the heart of the method of retorsion. Also for him, the necessary determinations of the contents of knowledge, which are expressed in judgment and affirmed in the act of knowledge as implied and affirmable, are present *a priori* not only in the logical sense, but in the psychological or metaphysico-epistemological sense of the word, viz., the necessary element of knowledge stems from the very nature of the power to know (Fin., p. 45), the nature of the understanding is expressed in the first principles while the nature of the many-layered totality of understanding and sensibility finds expression in other, less universal principles (Fin., p. 46). Thus critical reflection involves a reference to whatever is metaphysically evident in function of its necessary character, which is *a priori* in the sense that it is necessary for the acts of the power in question which, like any power, determines its acts in terms of its nature previous to the actual act. This necessary character is what gives a retorsive response its force in a critical discussion. The *a priori* here is the guarantee of objectivity.[10]

Nevertheless, where it is not necessary for the vindication of knowledge in critical discussion, there is no reference to metaphysico-epistemological elements (corresponding to the nature of the transcendental method taken in its limited sense), viz., to the subjective conditions of possibility. Of course, he relies on this procedure whenever it is necessary, e.g., in order to complete the proof for the existence of God on the basis of natural striving. In this case he considers the "nature" of the act and of the corresponding faculty only according to determinations directly accessible to reflection and to the indicated formal object, not according to ontological determinations not yet accessible to the demonstration at this point, since this

[10] G. Isaye, "Principes éternels et faits imprévus," *Sapientia Aquinatis,* 1955, pp. 69–77.

would require a full understanding of the metaphysico-epistemological elements (Fin., p. 58). There are, however, instances of retorsion, such as in the examples mentioned above, where it is not necessary to allow the subjective conditions of possibility to become fully thematic. This, it would seem to us, is the result of the division of his demonstration into a plurality of individual steps relatively complete in themselves.

Certainly one reason for the de-emphasis of the subjective conditions of possibility in his demonstration is that Isaye is primarily concerned with the application of critical vindication to discussion. If one is looking for the right answer to a proposed objection, one needs only those conditions of possibility which it requires. Other conditions of possibility, which would have to be brought in to answer other objections or for a comprehensive understanding of the apriority of knowledge, can be ignored. This leads to the diffraction into many brief, individual steps, corresponding to possible objections, and the refusal to give an answer directly against the background of a comprehensive view of the conditions of possibility. Consequently, the *adaptability* to discussion is purchased at the price of a renunciation of a sufficient *understanding* of transcendental necessity, which can be attained only after many retorsive steps. Accordingly, Isaye's procedure stands more on the basis of Aristotelian retorsion which, as Maréchal points out, demonstrates the fact of necessarily valid knowledge, but does not make this understandable in terms of its conditions and hence does not provide the retorsive response with a sufficient understanding in terms of the historically evolved condition of the problem in modern philosophy. However, as we pointed out above, this is not meant to deny that, through retorsion, the propositions of an epistemological theory can be finally attained, since retorsion is capable of such attainment.

There is, as we shall see, a *mutual relation* between the *connection between reflection and deduction,* on the one hand, and the *connection of the indication of validity with the understanding of validity* on the other. From Maréchal's point of view, reflection and deduction are rather widely separated from each other, but with Isaye they are closely related to each other at

170

every step. Consequently, whereas Maréchal attains an understanding of the necessary validity of knowledge, in terms of the transcendental structure of the subject and its orientation toward being, with the demonstration of the validity of knowledge, Isaye can only arrive at such a comprehensive understanding after many steps, which, however, has the advantage of demonstrating the necessary validity of definite kinds of knowledge. Thus the purpose at hand must be the basis for a choice between one of these two modes of procedure, viz., whether the concern is primarily with an answer from a comprehensive understanding of the context of the problem, or with an immediate answer to a definite objection.

Since the method of retorsion is more concerned with answers to particular objections, and not with the understanding of the context of the problem from which these objections stem, the comprehensive consideration of the subjective conditions of possibility, which are necessary for the solution to the whole problem, becomes less significant. In order to answer an objection it is necessary to consider only the objective conditions of possibility, viz., the conditions of the act of a definite objective content in thought insofar as they result in definite, necessary structures of the object. Retorsion consists precisely in showing that the very structure of the objection to the object contradicts the structure necessarily attributed to the object in the act of possible objection, which entails the necessity of this attribution.

In connection with this, it should be noted that Isaye does not derive the necessity of affirmation and its implications (including the value of knowledge with respect to being) from an analysis of the subjective conditions of possibility of the consciousness of objects, as does Maréchal, but by showing, through the retorsion of the judgment which raises the objection, that the objection does not hold true. Maréchal shows that the act of affirmation is necessary and, therefore, that the consciousness of objects is possible, for which reason every object which bears the traits of affirmation must, because of the absolute necessity of these objective traits, be related to the absolute and transcendent order of real being. Isaye does not demonstrate this necessity *a priori,* but evaluates the effect which this necessity has for knowledge, viz., that these necessary traits of the object cannot be denied without negating the very act of denial. However, the transcendental proof of the validity of knowledge with respect to being is grounded in the supposition that the necessary traits of the object are not merely shown to be the premises of a definite mode of knowledge already accepted as valid (which would result in only hypothetical necessity in the context of transcendental reflection), but that they are derived as necessary for every mode of the cognitive relation to objects (which is the task of transcendental deduction). We have already seen this to be the case with Maréchal, but is the same true for Isaye?

RETORSION AS TRANSCENDENTAL DEDUCTION

First of all, we must distinguish retorsion as Isaye uses it, viz., transcendental retorsion, from other similar arguments. Transcendental retorsion is not the retorsion of an assertion which begins with an optional statement, which can be contradicted by indicating other equally justified statements. A good example would be the classical dilemma in which Protagoras was to have demanded payment from his student, Euathlos, at the completion of his rhetoric course, under the threat of legal action. However, they had agreed earlier that Euathlos would have to make payment only if he should win his first case after having finished the course. Protagoras argues: I shall sue you for payment, and either you will win the case, whereupon you must make payment according to our agreement, or you will lose the case, whereupon you will be forced to pay as the result of the legal decision. Euathlos retorted by rearranging the elements of the disjunction: Either I win the case and do not have to pay because of the decision, or I lose it and do not have to pay because of our contract. This kind of retorsion only shows that the premises of the proof have not been clarified and require careful examination. As a result the proof is weakened and neither of the two conflicting claims is vindicated. Transcendental retorsion, however, does not refer to optional premisses of an opponent's argument in order to refute it, but refers to premisses whose justification the opponent must recognize in order to raise his objection and from which results that against which the objection is raised.

Second, transcendental retorsion is also not simply an *argumentum ad hominem,* which refutes a statement by showing that it contradicts another statement accepted by the opponent. Transcendental retorsion tries to show that the very statement against which the objection is raised must, at least implicitly, be recognized in order to be able to raise the objection.

Third, transcendental retorsion must be distinguished from the abstract reduction to contradiction. If retorsion were only this, as Wolfgang Stegmüller has pointed out, it could not lead to the justification of the statement against which the retorted objection is raised. Stegmüller[11] offers as an example an analysis of the objection which is directed against the thesis of objectivity. The objection is: "Not every proposition is true." Letting "s" stand for this statement, "$S(x)$" for the sentential function "x is a statement" and "$T(x)$" for "x is true," Stegmüller then works out the demonstration of the contradiction as follows (using the Hilbert-Ackermann notation) :[12]

$$(1) \qquad (x) < S(x) \rightarrow \overline{W(x)} >$$

This is the formulation of the objection through the statement s. Whatever holds for x, holds for s. Using the basic tautological rule

$$(2) \qquad (x)\, F(x) \rightarrow F(a)$$

if we replace "$F(x)$" by "$S(x) \rightarrow \overline{W(x)}$" and "a" by "s" according to the rule of substitution, then from

$$(3) \qquad (x) < S(x) \rightarrow \overline{W(x)} > \rightarrow < S(s) \rightarrow \overline{W(s)} >$$

11 Wolfgang Stegmüller, *Metaphysik–Wissenschaft–Skepsis,* 1954, pp. 318–323.
12 Hilbert-Ackermann, *Grundzüge der theoretischen Logik,* 1938.

and from the substitution of formulas (1) and (3) for A and and $A \to B$ respectively in the syllogistic schema (modus ponens)

(4) $A, A \to B / B$

we derive the formula

(5) $S(s) \to \overline{W(s)}$.

(5), together with the empirical stipulation

(6) $S(s)$

results, according to the syllogistic schema (4), in

(7) $\overline{W(s)}$.

This means that the objection against the thesis of objectivity is not true. But does this prove the thesis of objectivity? According to Stegmüller, it does so only under two premisses. First, the logical operations which permit the transition from formula (1) to formula (7) must be recognized by whomever raises the objection, and second, the validity of the principle of the excluded middle for any finite manifold. Only then is it valid to conclude from

(1) $(x) < S(x) \to \overline{W(x)} >$

that the thesis of objectivity

(8) $(Ex) < S(x) \& W(x) >$

is true. However, the validity of the principle of the excluded middle (*tertium non datur*) has been disputed. Even if the logical operations are accepted as admissible and the validity of the *tertium non datur* is proven, one could not possibly hold that a proof for the thesis of objectivity, based on such a complicated logico-epistemological investigation, constitutes a foundation for the thesis through a mere *reductio ad absurdam*. It is clear that such a notion of retorsion cannot attain what Isaye claims for it. It is precisely on this point that E. W. Beth[13] has

[13] E. W. Beth, "Logique scolastique et logique mathématique," *Algemeen Nederlands Tijdschrift voor Wijsbegeerte en Psychologie,* vol. 45 (1953), pp. 115–130.

challenged Isaye with reference to the discussion of the *tertium non datur* and has given him the chance[14] to clarify the earlier position[15] to which Beth refers.

Retorsion, as Isaye understands it, does not operate on a purely conceptual level, where a *reductio ad absurdam* consists in the analytical demonstration of a contradiction (*contradictio in terminis*). Such a procedure, of course, is useless for the vindication of synthetic judgments *a priori,* whether they be existential propositions, or necessary propositions which give expression to an insight into essence.

Transcendental retorsion directs itself to the true validity of the act of knowledge and the necessary acknowledgement of determinate structures of knowledge which it implies, which operate with such a necessity in thought that they are there irrespective of particular content, and consequently are operative in the very act of thought which would deny them. Because they operate in this way, they can be demonstrated in the very act of the objection. Because they are necessary determinations of the act of knowledge, insofar as it is directed to objects, they are explicable in the form of the necessary knowledge of objects, viz., in synthetic judgments of necessity. Because they belong to the act with necessity, independent of whatever is actually affirmed as content, the proof does not depend on the justification of the concepts used in the objection. The concepts of the judgment to be vindicated are themselves fundamentally demonstrable only insofar as they explain a necessary moment of the act of knowledge, such as the case actually is with retorsively grounded judgments. This operative determination of concepts does not replace the direct meaning of concepts as found in intuition, but it makes it possible to determine the concepts so far as the posed critical question requires in order to vindicate judgment retorsively, without having to refer to intuition for proof, although intuition constitutes the first source of the knowledge of this principle. Retorsion shows that

[14] G. Isaye, "Logique scolastique et logique moderne," *Bijdragen,* vol. 14 (1953), pp. 349–362.

[15] G. Isaye, "La logique scolastique devant ses récents adversaires," *Bijdragen,* vol. 13 (1952), pp. 1–30.

valid intuition operates necessarily in every act of knowledge, even the very act which would deny judgment grounded through intuition.

Primarily, then, transcendental retorsion is actually concerned with demonstrating the necessity from which the validity of a judgment which has been called into question can be vindicated, viz., a necessity which is not dependent on the validity of the particular affirmation of the objection, or the concepts used in it, but rather which is independent in the very sense of the necessity which is required for transcendental deduction. The differences between Maréchal and Isaye with respect to the evaluation and demonstration of this necessity can be explained by pointing to their different aims and their different modes of applying and coordinating the essential elements of the transcendental method.

Second, we can now see how transcendental retorsion can supply that which the purely analytical *reductio ad absurdam* cannot, because if Isaye vindicates the principle of objectivity and the principle of excluded contradiction through retorsion, then he cannot have previously guaranteed the validity of logic or the applicability of the *tertium non datur* to the finite manifold, nor can he have defined the concept of truth nor have determined the meaning of negation for propositions related to indefinite realms of objects. Retorsion is not an analytically deductive procedure which must presuppose the truth and certainty of its premises, but a demonstrative procedure which, in reference to the theme specified by the opposition of assertions and objection, shows how the act of thought must necessarily be understood and, as a result of this, how the opposition should be resolved.

It seems to us that the retorsion for the thesis of objectivity gains its strength from the fact that it makes us aware of the activity which we cannot possibly avoid, viz., thought, which is related to objects in such a way that it is determined in its content by these objects in an absolute manner represented in every performance of this activity. The very thing which has been called into question, viz., whether there is truth, is precisely this question of whether the content of the activity of

176

thought can be determined in this absolute manner by objects. Consequently, there is truth. The source of retorsion, therefore, is not the description which we have just given, but that which is described, viz., that which is thought in retorsion with reference to the *actus exercitus,* the sensible content which constitutes it and its relation to its expression in the *actus signatus.*

Truth is here that to which judgment lays a claim and which is determined through the activity. Correspondingly, the existence of truth is determined as the realization of this claim through the structure of the activity, which is a contradiction if it is bound by anything but judgment as absolute, whose claim to truth is known to be valid, and, therefore, which is impossible without judgments, as demonstrated with necessity. It is true that there is a mode of thought in which I do not relate myself, as judging, to a determinate object, viz., if I ask a question; however, every question presupposes a relation to other objects, or else it would negate itself, which bears the traits of judgment even though this relation is not expressly pronounced as judgment, but only as that which is operative in making this conscious and express act of questioning possible. As a matter of fact, Isaye works out an analysis of noetic dynamism on the basis of an analysis of the question (Fin., p. 71), in terms of which the question of error in particular cases can be answered through the fundamental capacity for truth of judgmental knowledge.

The retorsive demonstration of the validity of the principle of incompatibility and the excluded third is similar to the procedure of the above analysis. It is shown that in the activity of knowledge the relation to determinate and conflicting pairs of judgments is such that both cannot be affirmed at the same time and that one of the two must be affirmable. This relation leads to the operative determination of the concept of the negation of a proposition, viz., every judgment is the negation of the other judgment in such pairs of judgments. Consequently, for all such judgments contradictorily related to each other, both cannot at the same time be true, and one of them must be true.

In the use of this principle, it should be noted that there can be cases (and precisely in connection with an operative analysis) where the operative definition of contradictory oppositions (and thus the principle of the excluded middle) is directly applicable. Where this does not prove to be the case, it should be checked to see if there actually is a contradictory opposition. "The principle of the excluded middle does not make it superfluous to show in each case that a contradictory opposition is involved (or that it is not),"[16] i.e., whether the negation, in some determinate manner of speaking, actually intends the contradictory denial of a judgment. For example, if by "existence" is understood the constructive demonstrability of an object under specific conditions, it may be the case that the propositions (x) F(x), "all objects of a certain unspecified realm possess the property F," and (Ex) $\overline{F(x)}$, "there is an object in this realm which does not possess this property F," despite linguistic appearances, do not constitute a contradictory opposition, so that the *tertium non datur* is not applicable. However, the very occupation with such questions and the construction of a logic in which the *tertium non datur* is not valid, i.e., in which the negation of propositions has a different meaning than the contradictory negation of the judgments expressed by these propositions, presupposes an activity of knowing in which the principle of the excluded middle must be recognized as valid, which is retorsively demonstrated without having to work out a solution of the problem of the *tertium non datur*.

The case is quite similar with the problem of the semantical concept of truth in relation to the thesis of objectivity. Isaye defines the concept of truth operatively. Therefore, in his definition he does not depend on a special meta-language of the language in which the activity of judgment is expressed. The impossibility of defining an absolutely universal formal concept of truth only shows that the means employed by the point of view which deals with knowledge merely in terms of its linguistic expression is incapable of replacing a universal theory of truth, which includes that knowledge without which the pursuit of semantics would not be possible.

[16] *Ibid.,* p. 30.

THE DOMAIN OF APPLICABILITY
FOR RETORSION

This discussion of retorsion, as employed by Isaye, should make it clear how we can distinguish it, as transcendental retorsion, from other modes of reduction to a contradiction, viz., it includes the essential elements of transcendental operative analysis, through which it retains the methodological value which Isaye claims for it and through which it offers a suitable adaption of transcendental deduction for the purposes of dialogue.

This is especially true of retorsion insofar as it is capable of explaining what is necessarily implied in judgment, which, according to Isaye, is not only the critique of knowledge in its essential points, but metaphysics, for he defines metaphysics as that which "is itself contained in the objection which is raised against it, viz., formally, with respect to first principles, and virtually, with respect to the rest" (Priv., p. 32). Metaphysics cannot begin with nothing. "What it deals with begins with an inner necessity. What the answer to an objection deals with begins with what the objector sincerely offers it, viz., it begins with the objection itself" (Priv., p. 32). This conception is consistent with the Aristotelian conception insofar as a thesis arrived at in this way is shown to be necessary for each act of affirmation, "which means that it is included in every judgment, in *judgment as judgment*. According to the thesis of objectivity, judgment is necessarily posited in relation to being. Therefore, the thesis in question is ultimately related to *being as being*" (Priv., p. 33).

However, Isaye applies retorsion more extensively in that he also demonstrates those insights without which discussion as such is not possible, and which, therefore, must be acknowledged by both sides in a discussion. This has to do with the necessities which are implied insofar as the activity of thinking is expressed in sensible signs in order to be able to be communicated to others. Examples are the retorsive vindications of the acceptance of the existence of more than one person and of

179

the fundamental possibility of induction (Ret., pp. 225–227). Since the procedure focusses on the necessities of conversation, and not on those of judgment *as judgment,* Isaye does not consider this a transcendental proof in the Kantian sense (Fin., p. 60). The necessity for the recognition of these necessities beyond the one for the having of a discussion can be attained only if either the universal necessity of discussion, or at least of language, is demonstrated for human thought (Ret., p. 224) or if, independent of the necessity of discussion, one can explain the truth of this conviction necessarily presupposed by language (Ret., p. 231), as, for example, Isaye does for induction.[17] Here he shows the necessity of human activity as introduced through insight and indicates the validity of inductive conclusions as the condition of possibility for such activity.

In such cases, retorsion is actually only a technique for demonstrating the justification of certain assertions. Isaye does not demand more. In order to gain a sufficient understanding of this necessary acknowledgement by partners in communication, several other steps are required to show how this necessity is connected with the structure of the subject of knowledge as necessarily oriented toward being.

[17] G. Isaye, "Nécessité de la science: sa légitimité," in A. Grégoire, *Leçons de philosophie des sciences expérimentales,* pp. 196–228, 208–211.

180

9. IN DIALOGUE WITH HEIDEGGER

In this chapter we shall discuss two thinkers, Johannes B. Lotz and Karl Rahner, who have benefited from associations with Heidegger, in order to examine the function of the phenomenological moment in the transcendental method. First, we shall briefly consider Lotz. He is mainly concerned with deepening the knowledge of being. Referring to Heidegger, he insists that the question about being cannot be solved unless the analysis of the act of human being is pushed to the extent that being is understood in terms of subsistent being. This, however, means that the transcendental method must be extended beyond the limits which Kant set for it, not by abandoning the essentials of the method, but by fulfilling them.

Maréchal, as we have seen, begins his transcendental critique with the dynamism of our capacity to know, then fixes the goal of this dynamism through an analysis of judgment and thus arrives at the necessary relationship between all modes of knowing and the absolute of being. Lotz, however, begins directly with the act of judgment, examines its structural elements phenomenologically and then points to absolute being as the condition of possibility for judgment. Only then is a more extensive elaboration of the conditions of possibility attempted, with the aim of fixing the "prehension" (Vorgriff) of the absolute as the expression, or result, of a striving toward the absolute. Lotz, in a reflection on this distinction (MO, pp. 111f.), refers to his way of explaining the necessary relationship between knowledge and the absolute as a proof of the absolute through exemplary causality, whereas Maréchal's proof is through final causality. If anything, however, these two modes of causality include, rather than exclude, each other.

Lotz's procedure would seem to have two advantages. First, since he begins directly with the intention of judgment, and then, on this basis, demonstrates that the absolute is the condition of possibility for this act, while the striving character of the knower is developed later, the relationship between the direct intention of concepts and the reflective development of the conditions of possibility for this activity are clarified to a much greater degree of satisfaction. This is the advantage of the greater use of *phenomenological analysis* in the transcendental method, for when Lotz shows how being is grasped in judgment as the ground of being (*als Grund des Seienden*), it is much easier for him to use this concept with respect to direct knowledge if he has already given its validation and drawn out the implications of this grasp. The reciprocol notions of positing and seeing in the conception of knowledge thus grow closer together. If, however, the relation to the ground is introduced as the relation of the intermediate goals of noetic striving to the final goal, it would appear to be much more difficult to make use of this concept of "ground" for direct, object-oriented knowledge. It would then require proper mediation to show the immediate object of judgmental knowledge as an intermediate goal, and thus as grounded. This procedure is possible, of course, but perhaps somewhat more involved.

Second, by connecting the *a priori* with what is phenomenologically demonstrable, Lotz avoids the possible misconception that the formally constitutive *a priori* has to do only with something of a purely formal nature from which no *content* could be derived. When Lotz refers to the *a priori* as formal, in order to distinguish it from an inborn idea, he simply means that the constitution of knowledge requires another element, viz., the content components of experience. This, however, does not exclude the possibility that hyper-empirical content, necessarily determined *a priori,* which really constitutes the possibility of experiential judgment, may be included in experiential knowledge. Taken in this way, the formal *a priori* of knowledge, which it constitutes, regulates the content component. As a matter of fact, Lotz's analysis of judgment seeks to indicate the content which is necessarily contained in the *a priori* of

182

being which can be developed from the understanding of being that makes knowledge possible.

This aspect of the *a priori,* viz., that which grounds a necessary *a priori* content in the object of knowledge, is less evident if it is held that the content of human knowledge stems from experience. This latter point is true if it refers to the differentiation of content which distinguishes finite beings from each other, but not if it refers to the mode of content which belongs to each being as a being, which can in no way be grounded experientially and which makes all subsequent experiential differentiation of content possible. This, and the resultant rejection of Kant's formalistic conception of the *a priori,* is not quite so clear in Maréchal. This is, no doubt, because Maréchal distinguishes himself from Kant more in terms of emphasizing the dynamism of knowing and, as a result, the absolute object-relatedness of human knowledge, while Lotz begins with the phenomenological awareness of being insofar as it is the ground of the objectivity of whatever is included in judgment, and then moves to the vindication of the correspondence between the judgment and what is judged as the condition of possibility for the act of judgment and to the deeper explanation of its foundation in the dynamism of knowing (which, for both Lotz and Maréchal, is to be understood as the self-development of knowledge and not as the subsumption of the activity of knowing under an externally introduced principle of finality).

With respect to logical structure, we can distinguish the respective procedues of Lotz and Maréchal by drawing attention to the fact that Maréchal concludes to the relation to the absolute, the dynamism of the act of knowing and the fundamental value of knowledge in a single step, whereas Lotz insists that these *three stages* must be distinguished from each other. Maréchal's aim is to prove the fundamental possibility of vindicated judgment, which can be accomplished by an intentional critique or through retorsion, while Lotz's aim is to demonstrate the vindicated co-positing of the absolute as the condition of possibility for the act of judgment. Consequently, Lotz must derive the meanings of the act of judgment and of

183

the moments of being, which are present in this act, phenomenologically, and only then is this being disclosed as made possible through subsistent being. Since this discourse traces being, as it appears in its function of making knowledge possible, back to its ultimate roots, from which it can exercise this function, subsistent being is co-posited in knowledge as a condition of possibility, although only as prehension (*Vorgriff*), because it requires discursive mediation before, as such, it can gain expression. Only in a later step is knowledge, as made possible through being, developed more extensively in terms of its conditions of possibility in the subject and object.

We have already seen, with Defever and Isaye, that such a division of the transcendental method into a series of steps does not work against the method but is actually advantageous with respect to comprehensiveness. Whereas with Isaye the development of what is included in the act of knowledge is mainly by means of retorsion, Lotz employs the analysis of the expression of the understanding of being in the structure of judgment. This structure lends itself to a phenomenological derivation. It guarantees access to the understanding of being, which grounds the act of knowledge as its condition of possibility. The chief advantage of a phenomenological foundation lies in the easier connection between transcendental analysis and the content of the direct act of knowing. It should also be noted that this transcendental-phenomenological demonstration of the starting point for the deduction of conditions of possibility is completely open to a development possessing the logical sharpness of retorsion.

KARL RAHNER

Like Lotz (US, p. viii), Rahner is strongly influenced by Martin Heidegger and is also committed to Maréchal's interpretation of Thomas (GW, p. 9).[18] Rahner is careful to sep-

[18] Karl Rahner, *Geist in Welt: Zur Metaphysik der endlichen Erkenntnis bei Thomas von Aquin*, Innsbruck, 1939. References in the text are to the second edition as revised by J. B. Metz. ET *Spirit in the World*, New York, 1968.

arate himself from "what is usually called neo-scholasticism and to return to Thomas himself in order to approach more closely the problems posed by contemporary philosophy" (GW, p. 9). This necessitates "a complete re-thinking of the primary, but often neglected, foundations of his philosophy. . . . However, this is possible only to the extent that the dynamics of the matter are considered from a definite point of view so that the thrust of this development can be joined with the explicit statements of the philosopher whose system is under study" (GW, p. 11). We shall above all else be interested in what Rahner considers the starting point and the direction of the internal development of philosophy to be.

THE METAPHYSICAL CONDITIONS OF POSSIBILITY FOR EXPERIENCE

The problem which Rahner takes up in *Geist in Welt* is the question: "How can human knowledge, as interpreted by Thomas, be spirit in matter [*Geist in Welt*]?" (GW, pp. 14f.). Thomas explains the fact that human knowledge takes place in the world of experience and that the meta-physical is known only in, and in terms of, the world in his theory of the relation (and continuing relatedness) of the intellect to what appears, i.e., in his theory of "*conversio intellectus ad phantasma*" (GW, p. 15). Through the investigation of how, despite the necessity of this "*conversio,*" there is still room for the metaphysical, Rahner attempts to give a concrete answer to the current "question about the possibility of metaphysics on the basis of perception, which appears within the horizon of space and time" (GW, p. 42). This brings us immediately to Kant's question about the possibility of metaphysics and establishes a position with respect to his limitation of theoretical reason to the objects of possible spatio-temporal experience. Rahner adopts Heidegger's fundamental-ontological approach, but he insists that temporality and historicity deal with the relation of man to being (*dem Sein*), not to being as such (*dem Sein als solchem*), only insofar as it is made possible through a trans-

185

temporal and trans-historical realization of the human act of being (*des menschlichen Seinvollzugs*).

The question about the possibility of metaphysics is answered ultimately by showing that experiential knowledge implies a metaphysical understanding of being, which makes experience as such possible and which at the same time contains a metaphysical understanding of man and his historical relationship to the trans-temporal absolute. Thus "metaphysics is the conceptually constructed understanding of that very pre-conceptual understanding which man as man *is*" (GW. p. 47). It is "nothing but the reflective elaboration of the true ground of human knowledge, which pervades it thoroughly from the very beginning" (GW, p. 390). The explicit realization of this state of affairs is already metaphysics, since "the reflection upon that which makes metaphysics possible is itself metaphysics" and "fundamentally the whole of what pertains to human metaphysics" (GW, p. 398). "Metaphysics is not, as is the case with the special sciences, the discovery of something which was hitherto unknown, but rather a knowledge of that with which we are already familiar" (HW, p. 40).[19] "Metaphysics, as a science, is possible only if, through patient and meticulous toil, the already known is developed systematically and conceptually, viz., only if man seeks to re-create conceptually the metaphysics with which he is already familiar in his being and activity" (HW, pp. 43f.).

In *Hörer des Wortes* (*Hearers of the Word*), the value of this metaphysics is extended to the philosophy of religion and fundamental-theology. The metaphysics radically actuated in man is developed in this work to the extent that man is conceived as a being who is open to God and who must listen for the possible appearance of the word of God in history. The metaphysics of knowledge in *Geist in Welt* is restructured into an anthropology of man before God which represents man as someone who, because of an openness with respect to being,

[19] Karl Rahner, *Hörer des Wortes: Zur Grundlegung einer Religionsphilosophie*, Munchen, 1941. References in the text are to the first edition since the second edition, as revised by J. B. Metz, was unavailable before publication of the German edition of this book. ET *Hearers of the Word*, New York, 1968.

through which his knowledge and the experience of his intellectual life is made possible, is radically related to God, whether God speaks to him or not. This is the reflective explicitation of that which "we think and, as deeply as possible, live in the concrete metaphysics of our very existence, viz., a human existence which is basically nothing but attentiveness to what God has to communicate—eternal light and eternal life in the depths of the living God opened to us through grace" (HW, p. 41). *Hörer des Wortes,* which takes up the conclusions of *Geist in Welt* in their most austere form, without the apparatus of Thomistic interpretation, gives clearer expression to the systematic character of these ideas, although they must be seen against the background of their foundation in *Geist in Welt.* We shall have to make use of both works if we want to get at the uniqueness of Rahner's transcendental procedure.

METAPHYSICS OF KNOWLEDGE

Rahner's concern is not with a critique of knowledge as a presupposition for metaphysics, but with the metaphysics of knowledge internal to metaphysics itself (GW, p. 14). This is clear if metaphysics is viewed as the elaboration of an understanding of being essential to man, because then the demonstration of this understanding of being is not something which merely precedes this elaboration, but which is itself a part of it. This metaphysics of knowledge is not simply a description of knowledge, but a conception of it in terms of the fundamental understanding of being which makes description possible. This understanding of being includes not only the very being of being in general, but, necessarily, also the being of that which is essential to an understanding of the very being of being. The question about "what the very being of being is, which necessarily constitutes the being of man in human existence, is the starting point of all metaphysical questions and answers. Insofar as this starting point of all metaphysical questioning is conceived *a priori* as a characteristic of human being, it is clear how the metaphysical question about being as such

187

is at the same time a question about the being of that being who must necessarily pose this question, viz., it is a question about man" (HW, p. 48). The ultimate ground of knowledge must view knowing as a trait of being, and human knowledge as a consequence of human being, i.e., it must be a metaphysics of knowledge. This carries ramifications for the problem of knowledge as well as for the *foundations of ontology*.

"If knowing and knowability are internal traits of being, then a particular act of knowledge, in its metaphysical essence, cannot be conceived if it is regarded as an internalization by a knower of something objectively different from him, as 'intentionality.' At the very least, this cannot be the initial starting point for the metaphysical conception of the essence of the act of knowledge. The fundamentally primary starting point for a metaphysical conception of what knowledge is must rather be sought in the fact that being, in itself, is knowing and being known, viz., that being is self-presence [*dass Sein Beisichsein ist*]. . . . Species, according to Thomas, does not signify an 'intentional image,' or anything of the sort, but rather the existential fulfillment of spirit [*des Geistes*] as a being. Consequently, the problem of knowing something which is different from the knower cannot be solved by referring to the species as an intentional image, rather this word ["species"] includes, for Thomas, the very problem of how an existential determination can produce a knowledge of an object which differs from the species and the knower" (HW, pp. 55f.). "Therefore, the problem for the Thomistic metaphysics of knowledge is not how the gulf between knowledge and the object can be spanned by some sort of 'bridge.' This 'gulf' is nothing but a pseudoproblem. The real problem rather is how what is known, although identical with the knower, can be posited as something other than the knower, viz., how there could be knowledge which receives something radically other. There is no gulf to be 'bridged-over;' rather, we must determine how there could be a gulf at all" (GW, p. 88). "Man has a necessary, universal knowledge of individual, existing things. We must get hold of the inner possibility of such knowledge" (GW, p. 34).

As with Maréchal, the problem of knowledge is not viewed

here as the problem of a "bridge," but the problem of objecti-vication in the question of how the immanent activity of a being can be knowledge of something, and, as a result, how the true structure of human knowledge is to be understood. How-ever, as with Lotz, and as distinguished from Maréchal, being is not attained at the end of the transcendental analysis of the process of knowing, as its condition of possibility, but is given a phenomenological demonstration with respect to its function in knowledge quite early, although further analysis leads to a deeper development of what being, as well as what the knower, is. However, the tight link which Rahner sees between the anal-ysis of the knower and the transcendental analysis of being brings him closer again to Maréchal, since Lotz places the ac-cent on the development of the understanding of being while postponing the investigation of the conditions of possibility in the knowing subject. This is the conclusion that emerges from the fundamental function of the understanding of being which lies at the base of the problem of knowledge. With respect to the foundations of ontology, this means that every basic con-cept that is capable of grasping being in its very being, which makes knowledge possible and which includes a self-under-standing of the knower, must be capable of reduction. Every formal, ontological observation can really be "ontologically realized only if it is transformed into an epistemologico-meta-physical problem. Actually, ontological concepts can only be attained in conjunction with corresponding epistemologico-metaphysical concepts" (GW, p. 332). For example, "an ontology of matter . . . can be formulated only as an ontolog-ical application of an epistemologico-metaphysical problematic" (GW, pp. 332f.).

With regard to terminology, "ontic" refers to a formal ontological or metaphysical statement which ignores the epistemologico-metaphysical context, and "onto-logic" to an epistemologico-metaphysical statement. "If it is said of a spiritual substance that it is 'simple,' then we have an ontical statement. If we say that it is capable of *reditio completa in se,* then we have an epistemologico-metaphysical, ontological or existential-philosophical statement. The factual connection between these

THE TRANSCENDENTAL METHOD

two statements is . . . that they complement each other. The same factual situation is, first, explained through a property of self-consciousness (and consequently explained through a concept which pertains only to the realm of spiritual being), and second, through a concept of being which, negatively or positively, pertains to all being. Whoever conceived the scholastic metaphysical axioms, '*ens et verum convertuntur*' or '*ens est intelligibile et intelligens, inquantum est ens actu,*' was aware, at least rudimentally, that every ontical statement (positive or negative) can be translated into an ontological statement, no matter how difficult or impossible that may seem *quoad nos.*[20]

Although these statements refer but to the conclusions of his philosophical investigations, which are to be ultimately directed to a theological problem, they do make clear how this "reduction" of metaphysical concepts to the metaphysics of knowledge is to be understood. Here again we find the aim of the transcendental method to be to give an *operative* definition of the basic concepts of metaphysics, with the *fundamental-ontological* claim that being is to be conceived in terms of its "transparency" (*Gelichtetheit*) in man. What the very being of being is can be worked out only in terms of man's fundamental understanding of being. This understanding of being is, at the same time, man's own self-understanding. Thus the essence of man, whose act discloses the very being of being as such, can be approached only in terms of this act. "It is primarily in activity that the essence of man is itself. Consequently, it is primarily in activity that it is made known who man is, viz., that his essence (which is, basically, what is being questioned) is dis-closed" (GW, p. 30).

THE QUESTION ABOUT BEING
AS AN INITIAL STANCE

The *question* emerges as the act which grants access to the fundamental understanding of being. To question is an irrepressible human act, and it leads us to the understanding of

[20] Karl Rahner, "Probleme der Christologie heute," *Schriften zur Theologie,* I, 1954, pp. 169–222, 189. ET "Current Problems in Christology," *Theological Investigations,* Baltimore, 1961, pp. 149–200.

man as the being who must question. Thus everything which is co-posited with the act of questioning as a condition of possibility necessarily belongs to man's understanding of himself.

This question, however, is not an arbitrary, particular question about a unique object, but the "reflective articulation of that question which quickens, in the very ground of human existence, the question about being" (GW, p. 72), viz., the "metaphysical question." Every particular question is nothing but a unique instance of this question to the extent that it poses a question about the being of a determinate, particular being, viz., whether, what and how it is. Every judgment, to one degree or another, is an answer to this question. The very point of view adopted in conscious activity presupposes such an answer. Taken in this way, the question about being lies at the base of the whole of human life with irrepressible necessity. "The question about being necessarily belongs . . . to human existence because it is contained in every statement that a man thinks or speaks, and without thinking and speaking man would be totally incapable of being human. Every statement is a statement about a particular being and is performed against the background of a previous, though unexpressed, knowledge about being as such. Every true statement, every judgment and every deliberate action is not merely the synthesis of two concepts with the claim of validity for this synthesis, but extra-reference of such a mental synthesis to something 'in itself,' in terms of which it has value and whose objective synthesis it effects. This openness of the realm of the 'in itself,' in which the synthesis of the subject and the predicate of the statement is relationally regulated, is nothing but the previous knowledge about being as such" (HW, pp. 46f.). "The metaphysical question about the very being of being as such is the only possible starting point for the whole of metaphysics. Therefore, the analysis of this question must indicate, in general and in particular, what the essence is of that being who necessarily poses this question about being in his very existence" (HW, p. 48).

It is important that this question, necessary to man, the metaphysical question, be really the question about the whole of being. "Man can never rest his thinking or his acting with

191

this or that alone. He seeks to know what everything is in the very unity in which things always confront him. He poses questions about ultimate horizons, about the unified ground of all things and, to the extent that he knows all particular things as being, about the very being of all being, viz., he does metaphysics. Even should he ignore, or explicitly deny, such a mode of questioning, he nevertheless gives an answer to this question. He declares the question to be arbitrary, or meaningless, and has thus given an answer, viz., that being is something that is arbitrary, dark or meaningless in each and every being. Or, a determinate being is explicitly designated as being as such, e.g., material substance or economics, the life-impulse or death and nothingness. For whenever a man lets his entire existence, his very life's blood, flow completely into such a being, he declares, through this absolute positing of a determinate being, that this being is the focal point of all that he is and of all that is around him, everything else being either a means toward or an extension of this one thing. Consequently, he asserts what he understands (and intends to understand) by being, viz., he does metaphysics" (HW, pp. 44f.). Whence, then, can the metaphysical question derive its valid answer if it is to refer to everything? Because this question is all-encompassing, "the starting point for the answer to the universal question about being can be nothing but the question itself. . . . The starting point of metaphysics, therefore, is the question about what the very being of being itself is, in the very necessity with which the question is posed by man. For if the question were not presupposed as actually and necessarily posed, then a man who could not decide whether or not to pose it, or to recognize it as posed, would have closed off the very possibility of moving toward an answer" (HW, p. 46). This, however, would imply the impossibility of the function which expresses this question and its answer as the condition of possibility for the actual life of man (as we saw above), and the answer itself would negate itself if the attempt were made to deny it every possibility of validation. "An '*epoché*' with respect to the answer concerning being, therefore, is not possible, because the question about being necessarily belongs to the existence

192

of man. Consequently, man necessarily poses the direction toward an answer (and thus, implicitly, the answer to the question about being itself) in his very existence" (HW, p. 46). But how is the question about being itself possible? "In order to be the one who questions the whole of being, man begins with his goal, because he must know about the whole of being if he is to pose a question about it, and to recognize precisely in his questioning that he is not himself the goal, but only a finite human being" (GW, p. 74). The question about being must already know about being in order to be a question. "Every question has a direction [ein Woher], a principium for a possible answer, because a question that seeks no answer is self-defeating. . . . Therefore, it necessarily includes a determinate base, an unequivocal ground, on which it can, and must, be posed, from which an answer must begin, because otherwise every answer would be correct, even the most arbitrary ones" (HW, p. 45). The base from which the question stems, however, is itself a knowledge, a foreknowledge of the question, i.e., it has the character of an answer, not a question. For "the direction of the answer cannot itself be in question if it is to be the ground upon which the answer can be secured" (HW, p. 45). Consequently, "with the question about the very being of all being there is expressed a preliminary knowledge about being as such" (HW, p. 50).

The result of all this is significant. "Since the question about being as such puts everything in question, the knowledge contained in the question cannot think about what is known, as such, as something different from what is questioned. Being as questioned is, in its very need to be questioned [in all seiner Fraglichkeit], already being as known. . . . If, however, being, in the same context and in every respect of which a question can be posed about it in metaphysics, is already something known, then the fundamental knowability of all being is implicitly affirmed with it" (HW, p. 51). This implies further that every being, as the possible object of some knowledge, has essentially, with respect to itself and because of its very being, an inner reference to some possible knowledge, and thus to some possible knower. . . . If, however, this inner relatedness

193

of all beings to some possible knowledge is an *a priori* and a necessary proposition, it can only be such because being and knowing constitute a basic *unity*. Otherwise this relationship of every being, with respect to itself, to some knowledge could at best be a factual relationship, but not a determination of all beings already given with the essence of being. . . . Being and knowing, therefore, are correlative because fundamentally, in their ground, they are the same. This is simply to say that being as such, to the extent that it is being, is knowing, i.e., knowing in fundamental unity with being, and therefore the knowledge of the being which is the knower himself" (HW, pp. 51f.).

This transparency (*Gelichtetheit*) of being, the fundamental knowability of what is questioned, does not yield the answer for why man must question. "The possibility of questioning being [*die Fragbarkeit des Seins*] represents being as self-presence, as the fundamental unity of being and knowing. The need of this very same being to be questioned [*die Fraglichkeit des Seins*], however, would appear to negate this determination" (HW, p. 60). The discussion of this aporia leads to the restriction that only "to the extent that a being is, or has, being" is the identity of being and knowing realized. "Because being is an analogous concept, viz., analogous with respect to the same ground from which the first proposition stems, not every being is 'knowing' in the same sense and to the same extent, nor is every being in the same sense 'true.' Thus a being is thinkable, and even actually affirmed as present, which is not as such an inner moment of a knowledge of 'absolute consciousness'" (HW, p. 65).

Beginning with the posing of a question serves not only as an indication of the fundamental relation between being and knowing, but as a warning against misunderstanding the relatedness between them as a pantheistic idealism. That is to say, "not only the possibility, but also the need of being to be questioned, belongs to the fundamental human situation, because man must *question*. Consequently, man is not absolute consciousness: rather, to the contrary, in his metaphysics, viz., as 'transcendental consciousness,' he is *finite* spirit" (HW, p. 65).

194

THE STRUCTURE OF RAHNER'S PROCEDURE

We shall now attempt to characterize Rahner's procedure with respect to this first step in his method of demonstration. We find here again the *phenomenological* description of the sense-orientation of the conscious act of human knowledge as the starting point, although it is the *question,* and not (as in the case with Lotz) judgment, which is in the foreground. Of course, there is an inner connectedness between judgment and questioning with respect to their possibility, because a judgment can be conceived as an answer to a possible question and because a question as such presupposes a knowledge that can be expressed in a judgment and requires the fundamental possibility of an answer (which, again, takes the form of a judgment) as a condition of possibility. It remains, therefore, for the conclusion of questioning to vindicate the justification of the validity of judgment, whose conditions of possibility come under analysis. This does not completely involve the necessity of a *retorsive* proof of the starting point, since questioning must only be made reflectively conscious in its irrepressibility, which Rahner does.

As with Lotz, the development of the *analysis,* in distinction from Maréchal, does not consist in an investigation of the characteristic which the knowing self must possess in order to be able to perform the immanent activity of knowledge, but rather in a demonstration of that which must be affirmed in order that the conscious activity not negate itself. Due to the phenomenological quality of the procedure, the conditions of possibility are conceived as contents of knowledge which are questioned (earlier than in Lotz) in terms of their possibility with respect to the knowing subject. However, this difference with regard to Maréchal should not be overemphasized, because in Maréchal's transcendental critique as well, the conditions of possibility in the subject, which determine its act of knowledge, are not conceived ontically, but as functions which internally determine objective consciousness as such and are represented in its conscious structure. As we have already seen

195

with regard to Lotz, this difference consists largely in the fact that, first of all, with Maréchal, these conditions of possibility are not accentuated according to the content which they possess in knowledge, and secondly (as is the case also with Rahner), the relation of knowledge to being does not come to light only at the end of the analysis, but in the very first step, although it is developed more thoroughly in the course of the analysis.

The primary element is, again, the inner tension of the elements demonstrable in the act of knowledge which, because of the true legislative power of this act, desires its solution, without which the actually present act would not be internally possible. For example, the restriction pertaining to questioning, viz., with respect to the possibility (*Fragbarkeit*) and need (*Fraglichkeit*) of being to be questioned, not only lead to the identity of being and knowing, but to the finitude of human knowledge. In subsequent steps, this leads "to the completion of the transcendental deduction of the transparency [*Gelichtetheit*] of being in such a way that it becomes the transcendental deduction of the intimate self-presence of being [*des Beisichalleinseins*], viz., of the inaccessibility of the eternal light, which it has in, and in terms of, itself" (HW, p. 93), i.e., the transcendence of the absolute, of the unlimited.

THE REFERENCE TO THE STARTING POINT

The reference to the starting point, viz., the more complete evaluation of the aspects contained in it and, as a result, the elaboration of the fundamental understanding of being, is not only used by Rahner but is recapitulated exactly as the methodology indicates it should continue. At each partial step only one aspect can be treated and evaluated. However, each partial result, once attained, takes its place in the whole through the relations which the aspect which it treats has to the other aspects of the starting point.

Two methodological principles emerge here which regulate the transcendental development of the starting point. We shall refer to them as the principle of abstraction and the principle

196

of integration. The *principle of abstraction* is to give expression to the justification as derived from *one* moment demonstrated in the act, from which one begins, although it is derived in particular steps of the transcendental development of the conditions of possibility of this act, since it is impossible to comprehend all of them fully at once. Naturally, the development, whose course is fixed by this one moment, receives its power of demonstration not from this one moment alone, but from the relationship in which it stands with respect to the other moments demonstrated in the act. These, however, enter into the development of the steps of the demonstration only to the extent that they promote the analysis, while the course of the analysis is determined through the one special moment. Thus the development of questioning, from the special viewpoint of the moment of the possibility (*Fragbarkeit*) of what is questioned, leads to the transparency (*Gelichtetheit*) of being. Our success in this endeavor depends on the demonstrated necessity of a meaningful question about being for the possibility of conscious life. That this question about being, as a question, is necessary, and that our noetic relationship to being is also determined by the need of being to be questioned (*Fraglichkeit*), are ignored for the moment.

The principle of abstraction, in order not to go astray, must be completed by the *principle of integration,* viz., that the meaning and validity of the conditions of possibility are fixed by the relationship of this moment to the other moments of the act from which the transcendental analysis begins. Thus the result of a partial investigation worked out under the principle of abstraction must be reconsidered in terms of the starting point so that it may be ordered, from that point of view, with other results and gain its full and proper meaning. By reconsidering the demonstrated transparency of being in terms of the starting point, it will, with respect to the need of being to be questioned (*Fraglichkeit*), be more exactly fixed with regard to its applicability to the explanation of human knowledge. This also excludes any sort of idealist misunderstanding. The principle of integration, therefore, avoids the dangers which infect abstract speculation, which does not maintain a sufficient enough relation to its starting point and thus easily neglects the limits of the senses and the applicability of its results. *Concrete speculation,* on the other hand, which, as based on the principle of integration, not only begins with the given act of questioning and develops the conditions of the act, which the act itself indicates as its conditions of possibility, but also gives attention to the reference of these conditions to the concrete act (which establishes their own possibility) and their relations to other conditions of possibility, avoids, first of all, the danger of absolutizing one particular point of view, and secondly, brings speculation closer to its goal. For the effort to understand the concrete act of questioning, which occasioned speculation in the first place, did not begin in order to find its ultimate rest in speculation, but in order to understand better, with its help, the concrete act itself. While abstract speculation easily loses itself in the realm of abstractions, concrete speculation enlists the aid of abstraction with the aim of thereby understanding concrete reality. This coincides with the purposes of phenomenology and existential philosophy, without absolutizing any one aspect and thereby transcending the necessity of metaphysical discourse. The strength of Rahner's thought, it would seem to us, lies in this mode of thought which we have called concrete speculation, which, especially in the area of theological speculation, has yielded rich and abundant results.

THE *A PRIORI*

We shall now briefly examine Rahner's view of the relationship between *pre-knowing* and the conscious act of questioning and his conception of the *a priori* determinability of knowledge, because the possibility of metaphysics, as he sees it, consists chiefly in the fact that although knowledge about the metaphysical is posited in all modes of knowledge about the experiencable, as the *a priori* condition of experiential knowledge, it does not itself possess experienceable objectivity. Metaphysics "is neither 'realistic' nor 'inductive,' in the common meanings of the terms, because the *lumen intellectus agentis* is essential for its possibility. Because this light is the *a priori* and purely formal condition of the objectifiability of the world, metaphysics does not consist in the perception of a metaphysical object, e.g., being as such, but in transcendental reflection on that which is co-affirmed in knowledge of the world, i.e., in affirmation of the physical. . . . If man in doing metaphysics transforms that which he co-affirms in the prehension (*Vorgriff*), which makes his knowledge of the world possible, into the 'object' of his knowledge, he thereby converts it necessarily into the only kind of represented object that he can have, viz., he represents it as a thing, as things are in the world, because no object at all can be represented without *conversio ad phantasma*. However, to the extent that this representation of the metaphysical 'object' is itself made possible through prehension (*Vorgriff*), prehension denies that it is represented, and thus man, through his prehension in judgment, to this extent denies the contraction of *esse* to *ens mobile*. In judgment, then, he can deny such contraction through negation (*remotio*), and, in judgment, think the metaphysical object *per excessum et remotionem,* without directly representing it as such" (GW, pp. 397f.).

The relationship between the mode of knowledge (*Wissen*) which grounds the possibility of experiential knowledge and this knowledge itself is described by the words "inclusive" (HW, pp. 46f.), "co-known" as the "constitutive element" contained in the object known, which "belongs to it as known" (GW, p. 223), "direct, non-explicit and non-reflective knowledge (*Wissen*)" (HW, p. 47), "co-awareness" (HW, p. 47), through which something is "confronted, but not exhaustively known" (HW, p. 49), not in "objectively thematic awareness, but non-objective, unthematic awareness, which cannot be drawn outside of itself in its pure apriority to reflective knowledge, so that true thematization, reflective elaboration and categoreal development of this *a priori* knowledge of the absolute, viz., a 'proof of God's existence,' is not superfluous, but is rather made possible by . . . and is demanded by the very characteristics of this *a priori* knowledge" (GW, p. 191). This "previous condition," of course, must not be conceived "in terms of temporal priority" (HW, p. 47).

As with the other representatives of the transcendental method, these expressions should be construed as indicating the peculiar relationship between the "pre-knowledge" (*Vorwissen*), which makes explicit knowledge possible, and this explicit knowledge. On the one hand, these expressions deny that this pre-knowledge and its content are the subject and "hence the intended object" (HW, p. 47) of the explicit knowledge which they make possible. If this were the case, then there would be no need of a transcendental development and thematization of this pre-knowledge, because human knowledge would then no longer be discursive, but intuitive, viz., man would no longer be "spirit in the world" (*Geist in Welt*), but pure spirit. On the other hand, these expressions mean that nevertheless there exists an influence upon explicit knowledge which is not simply a purely causal, or ontically conditioned, influence which in no way enters consciousness, but an onto-logical, transcendental influence which can be characterized by the following properties. First, that which is explicitly affirmed is not affirmable if the transcendental condition of possibility is not also affirmable. Second, this connection is not mediated by a principle drawn in from without, as it were, but rather the immanent legitimacy of the affirmation of that which is explicitly affirmed itself refers to these conditions, because its very meaningfulness is negated if it is not understood in terms of these conditions. If it is to be understood, however, it and that which is known thematically through it, cannot, with respect to its very affirmability, be separated from the affirmability of something else, viz., the transcendental conditions of possibility. Third, however, this means that these conditions of possibility directly condition the conscious affirmation of that which is thematically known, insofar as this affirmation is conscious and is known as an affirmation, i.e., is known as capable of a self-exposition of this knowledge, in which not only the dependence of the possibility of affirmation on the affirmability of the transcendental conditions becomes clear, but the affirmability of such conditions is vindicated. This means, then, that something is contained in the act of thematic knowledge which, precisely to the extent that it is known, exerts an influence on the conscious act, although it is not thereby thematically and explicitly known, but must first be elaborated in order to become thematic. If it were not contained in the act of consciously thematic knowledge in some mode of knowing, then the act could not be understood as vindicated and at the same time constituted in its vindication by the vindicated affirmation of the conditions. It does not really matter which words are used to describe this relationship between the previous understanding of being and self-understanding as explicit knowledge. But awareness of the characteristics of this relationship is important because it is the only way in which the possibility of a transcendental procedure can be understood (although the concrete act of this procedure does not logically depend on the previous recognition of this state of affairs, but rather demonstrates it).

As we have already shown, the necessity of such a previous knowledge does not exclude the possibility of appealing to the evidence of an object to vindicate the determinate knowledge of an object of external or internal experience. Rather, the fact and the possibility of being *evident* finds its complete explanation in transcendental analysis. The attempt to stress one at the expense of the other violates the principle of integration by absolutizing invalidly one aspect which reflection on the act of knowledge can secure.

The previous understanding of being indicates how it is that affirmation is vindicated only if the very being of what is judged is made manifest or dis-closed. It is only because knowledge is oriented *a priori* to the realm, or horizon, of being that it can be related validly to something only to the extent that it participates in being. Since the foundational, necessary structure of what is possible within the horizon of being is included in the understanding of being, the necessary relationships between objects, as grounded in being, can be comprehended through a comparison of the concepts which determine the objectivity of this realm. Consequently, since the previous understanding of

201

being, and that which is included in it, can be demonstrated transcendentally as the conditions of possibility for the act of knowledge, intuited synthetical judgments are also deducible *a priori* through this transcendental analysis without prejudice to the recognition of their intuitiveness. Of course, a transcendental deduction of the particular contingent things given in experience is not possible. The reference to insight here is irreplaceable. Transcendental analysis can demonstrate that human knowledge is referred to such evidence and what rules this reference to what is evident must follow. Rahner works this demonstration (in *Hörer des Wortes*) into a deduction of the historicity of man, who, in his very relation to the absolute, is oriented attentively to the word of God.

This deduction of the *necessity of the contingent element* in human knowledge and the relationship of contingency to necessity carries important implications for the foundations of empirical science (both natural and cultural science). We shall point out a few instances.

The diversity of the *special sciences* can be explained in reference to the many points of view from which what is given in the world can be understood. The understanding of particular aspects of experienceable being makes it possible, with respect to the approach suggested by the point of view adopted, to gather further experiences and thus to come to know reality better from this point of view. The relation to other aspects of reality, and to the other sciences, the foundations of the interpretation of the results of science with respect to being, corresponding to the ultimate goal of human knowledge, and the applicability and regularity of the particular approach adopted, are determined according to the original understanding of reality in its diversity and according to the previous understanding of that aspect of reality to which each science is particularly related. "Every special empirical science includes, *a priori* to the undertaking of research, a previous law according to which it tries to discover the determinations of its object" (HW, p. 10). "A special science rests basically on a ground which it has not itself established, because such a ground constitutes its very possibility to be" (HW, p. 11). "Thus from the mere conclu-

202

sions of a science one can understand how its object is determined in the particular, but not why and with what right it conceives its object in a determinate way *a priori* to research so as to be able to determine it at all. The organization of a science instructs us on how it operates, viz., its method, but ultimately not why and to what end man becomes so involved in it" (HW,, pp. 10f.). Rahner then shows that, from this ground, the seemingly unimportant question concerning the relation of two sciences to each other ultimately leads to a question which can be answered only with respect to the previous understanding of being and man's own self-understanding, viz., "the metaphysical question concerning the one fundamental ground which supplies a basic foundation to both sciences in their respective objects and in the necessity of each special science and thus places both sciences in a determinate relationship to each other" (HW, p. 13). Thus a transcendental metaphysics shows itself to be necessary with respect to the question concerning the relationship between the sciences arising from the diversity of the special sciences in the unifying knowledge of man. The result of such an investigation is the transcendental deduction of the principles of the special sciences, i.e., the development of the previous understanding of being with respect to the starting point of a particular science.

We see other examples in the application of the development of the previous understanding of being to the understanding of *historicity* and the linguistic formulation of human knowledge. Rahner emphasizes the historicity of man in *Hörer des Wortes,* and Lotz expands this point in several articles[21] concerning the conditions of the historicity of man, in which the narrowness of historicity is contrasted with the absolute value of human knowledge. Lotz also attempts to give a transcendental demonstration of the properties of human *language* and the laws governing its relation to human knowledge.[22] Rahner makes use of

[21] J. B. Lotz, "Zur Geschichtlichkeit des Menschen," *Scholastik,* vol. 26 (1951), pp. 321–341. Also, "Geschichtlichkeit und Ewigkeit," *Scholastik,* vol. 29 (1954), pp. 481–505, and Von der Geschichtlichkeit der Wahrheit," *Scholastik,* vol. 27 (1952), pp. 481–503.
[22] J. B. Lotz, "Zur Phänomenologie und Metaphysik der Sprache," *Scholastik,* vol. 31 (1956), pp. 496–514.

THE TRANSCENDENTAL METHOD

the nature of language,[23] not merely as the expression of an entirely determinate and explicitly specifiable area of knowledge, but one which has concrete meaning only in connection with what is inexpressible, for the deepening of an understanding of the development of dogma.

[23] Karl Rahner, "Zur Frage der Dogmenentwicklung," *Wissenschaft und Weltbild,* vol. 7 (1954), pp. 1–14, 94–106.

10. CRITICAL OPPOSITION TO THE TRANSCENDENTAL METHOD

As we have seen, the transcendental method according to Maréchal consists in an operative analysis of the necessary characteristics of the object of knowledge. This requires the use of terms from the metaphysics of knowledge (in the narrow sense). This method, with explicit reference to Kant and the German Idealists, the classical representatives of the transcendental method, begins with the reflection on the consciousness of objects, demonstrates the *a priori* conditions of possibility which manifest themselves here and derives from them the necessary *a priori* determinations of the object of knowledge as such. Because an object is possible only with respect to these conditions, and because, as Maréchal shows in opposition to Kant, they are such that they include an affirmation of the absolute order of being and because this affirmation is necessary and constitutive for every object, then all objects must in some way be related to the absolute, viz., the real, order of being. Once this result is attained, the terminology of the metaphysics of knowledge can be used in a much richer sense. Conscious knowledge is taken to be the reception of what is given in the dynamic orientation of the subject of knowledge to the absolute. This means that what we experience as evident and can describe as such becomes metaphysically understandable. But it does not make an investigation of the relation of particular objects to the absolute of being superfluous, and much less so a criteriology which regulates the elaboration of what is given as governed by conscious effort.

When Maréchal published his ideas, his original way of comparing Kant and Thomas found great admiration, but it also met with great hesitation with respect to some of its essential points. His grounding of the validity of the knowledge of being was presented with the trappings of a metaphysics of knowledge, but how can metaphysics critically vindicate the very foundations of metaphysics without slipping into a logical circle? He also demonstrated the fundamental relation of every mode of objective consciousness to reality, but how can this procedure be reconciled with the undeniable fact of error, or the lack of conformity with an object? The transcendental argument begins essentially with Kant's premises, viz., from an investigation of the necessary structure of knowledge as conditioned by the subject, but how can this procedure lead to a vindication of the reality of what is known? Would not such a venture, precisely for this very reason, remain trapped within idealism and subjectivism, as was the case with the classical representatives of the transcendental method? How can this procedure possibly avoid the errors included in the illegitimate transfer from necessities of thought to reality, either as the confusion of the logical and real orders or of the orders of subjective, psychological necessity and objective, essential necessity? Does not this whole attempt to relate conscious knowledge to a pre-conscious dynamism of the understanding lead to a falsification of the essentially receptive character of knowledge? A thorough investigation of the scope of these objections as found in the various reviewers and critics of Maréchal's writings would carry us beyond the framework of this work. We must content ourselves with an investigation of the structure of the transcendental method, and thus for our purposes it will suffice to cite the typical kinds of objections, as presented by the most significant of these critics, and to examine their legitimacy.

The most persistent objection is that it is false to attempt to ground realism in a way that would begin with the immanent object. History shows, so argues Etienne Gilson,[24] that this procedure cannot lead to a vindication of realism, as is abundantly evident with regard to Descartes and Kant. M. Casula

[24] Etienne Gilson, *Réalisme thomiste et critique de la connaissance,* Paris, 1939, pp. 131–155.

206

opposes Maréchal's starting point even more strongly.[25] He tries to show that beginning with the phenomenal object cannot, by its very nature, lead to realism, but can only lead to transcendental idealism. The transcendental method and the *a priori* not only neglect the real validity of knowledge, but exclude it necessarily. After all, how did Kant arrive at the transcendental method? He was face to face with the antinomies of metaphysics (MK, p. 94) and attempted to resolve them through the "Copernican revolution," viz., he tried to show that the antinomies could be resolved by replacing the conception that knowledge is ordered to objects with the assumption that the object known is ordered according to the subject. The implications of this position, however, show that synthetic *a priori* knowledge in mathematics and natural science can be vindicated and the antinomies of metaphysics resolved because this vindication limits synthetic *a priori* knowledge directly to the realm of phenomena to the exclusion of things-in-themselves so that metaphysics falls into antinomies by confusing phenomena and things-in-themselves (MK, pp. 69, 82, 95 and 111). According to Casula, however, this shows that the entire position of the transcendental method treats the phenomenal object from the beginning as the product of the subject to the exclusion of the ontological thing-in-itself. Thus the *a priori,* the totality of the conditions of the subject which determine the object of knowledge, is necessarily subjective (MK, pp. 75–96). Consequently, all contact with reality is broken and the conclusions of the transcendental procedure remain enclosed in what is immanent (MK, pp. 84, 110) in such a way that the transcendental method essentially excludes the ontological (MK, pp. 97f.).

Casula distinguishes two ways in which the phenomenal object can be taken with respect to the ontological object, viz., in the proper or the improper sense. If the phenomenal object abstracts from the ontological object in the improper sense, this means that the understanding knows real being, the ontological object, but by affirming the phenomenal object it neglects this relation to real being. If the phenomenal object abstracts from the ontological object in the proper sense, this means that the

[25] Casula, *Maréchal e Kant,* Rome, 1955.

understanding knows the phenomenal object, but not real being, which could at best be arrived at later from the phenomenal object.

With this distinction in mind, Casula formulates his objection against Maréchal in terms of the following dilemma (MK,
pp. 115f.). Either the phenomenal object, which is the starting
point of the transcendental method, aims at the ontological object only figuratively, or it does so in the proper sense of the
word. In the first case, the phenomenal object presupposes the
real object, which Kant would consider pure dogmatism. In the
second case, we find a sharp opposition to the Thomistic conception of knowledge, viz., that we do not merely apprehend the
phenomenal, but the real, with our reason. Consequently, the
transcendental method cannot accept the critical position without contradicting the Thomistic conception of knowledge and
the actual nature of knowing.

Thus if Maréchal chooses to consider both factors as unified,
it is because he interprets Thomas and Kant in a wilfull manner. Thomas is distorted in the process because according to
him the active intellect not only makes the intellectually conceivable content in the really experienced thing *visible,* but
adds the intellectual content of knowledge to what is given in
pure phenomenal experience. Besides insight, there is a positing
or constructing (MK, pp. 61, 117), because the formal object
of the power of knowing is not the viewpoint under which the
given object is apprehended, but the law of an *a priori* rule
which is related to the phenomenon when it becomes the object
of this faculty.

On the other hand, Casula contends that Kant's anti-ontologi-
cal position (MK, p. 82) and the rejection of the transcendent in
favor of the transcendental as accomplished through the Copernican revolution are ignored (MK, p. 110). Only in this way
is it possible for Maréchal to regard the *a priori* not merely
as a purely logical function but as grounded in the real power
of knowing, which is directed to the unlimited unity of being and
confers determinacy on the object which coincides with reality.
This, however, forces him to abandon one of the essentials of
Kant's transcendental method, viz., the foundation of the validity

of knowledge. Kant vindicates the validity of knowledge by identifying the *a priori* element of knowledge in the subject with regard to the object as phenomenon (MK, p. 111). The exclusion of the real object thus enters constitutively into the very foundation of the validity of the transcendental method, for if the phenomenal object is viewed as an object of knowledge constituted by the subject, then conclusions about the object of knowledge are derivable from the *a priori* forms. Casula's point, then, is that a comparison of Thomas and Kant, such as the one Maréchal attempts, is possible only if both are taken from their respective point of view.

THE POSSIBILITY OF A
TRANSCENDENTAL THOMISM

A comparison of this objection with the analysis of the transcendental method which we have already given forces us to conclude that Kant's transcendental method is really anti-metaphysical. This is true of his conclusions as well as of the epistemological viewpoint which prompted him to employ this method. A reflection on the nature and the scope of this method, however, should distinguish between the actual, concrete, more or less complete *expression* of the method and its basic *structural law*. Maréchal tries to ground the basis for this distinction in his historico-comparative propaedeutic. Within the historical perspective, it is understandable why Kant sees the transcendental method as anti-metaphysical and why Kant's successors were able to develop the method further without arriving at a realistic metaphysics. Historically, it is entirely possible to separate the basic structure of the transcendental method from particular instances of its special adaption. It is then possible to ask whether or not this method is capable of correcting erroneous views which crop up in some of the concrete expressions of the transcendental method. This is exactly what Maréchal attempts to do with respect to the anti-metaphysical and idealist views which have been connected with the method in relation to Kant and German Idealism.

Second, it is then clear that the word "transcendental" must not be encumbered with Kant's whole theory of knowledge. "Transcendental" means that type of experience which, through an analysis of the *a priori* conditions of possibility for the consciousness of objects, allows us to derive the nature of this object. Thus it is not Kant's theory that is adopted, only his method, and this only in its essential characteristics, not in its concrete details. Maréchal's comparative investigation into the history of philosophy shows that the notion of a Copernican revolution resulting from the *Critique of Pure Reason* must be distinguished from the program of a method for analyzing the immanent object. The essential characteristic of this method, without which it would fall into self-contradiction, do not coincide with Kant's concrete elaboration of this program.

Third, we must determine the aspect from which Thomas and Kant can be compared with each other. This aspect cannot be Kant's concrete conclusion, viz., his theory of knowledge, which interprets the hypothesis of a "Copernican revolution" in a way which radically excludes the real object in favor of the immanent, phenomenal object. The *point of comparison* rather lies in the relation of the immanent object, in the sense of the actually known object, to the subject. This relation, which is discussed in detail by both Kant and Thomas, is thus the topic of the investigation attempting to give a methodical evaluation of this relation. This does not depend on Kant's own conclusions; rather, it shows independently of his conclusions, the true legitimacy of the transcendental procedure, without which Kant's procedure would not be possible, even though Kant himself was not aware of this true legitimacy. Maréchal takes up this point in the second book of the fifth volume of his main work, which is centered around a metaphysics of knowledge and basically tries to show, through the metaphysics of knowledge scattered throughout the works of St. Thomas, the fundamental unity between the transcendental method and Thomistic thought. Logically independent of this attempt, the third book shows that the resultant transcendental analysis does not lead to the anti-metaphysical conclusions of

Kant, but to a vindication of the fundamental relatedness of human knowledge to the order of real being.

Fourth, Casula's dilemma is resolved as soon as we recognize that we must distinguish the conception of knowledge in its totality from the determinate, methodical way in which we arrive at this conception (corresponding to the distinction between the second and third books of Maréchal's fifth volume). It should be noted that Casula does not give sufficient stress to this distinction, although otherwise he seems to present Maréchal's metaphysics of knowledge in a thorough and precise manner. He thereby plays down the methodological uniqueness of the transcendental procedure, which allows him to pose his dilemma, viz., that the object of knowledge is either the real object or only the phenomenal object such that, in the first case, the phenomenal object is merely an abstraction from the real object and therefore does not ground it because it presupposes it, and in the second case, knowledge would be falsified. This dilemma arises if the concern is with a *total conception* of knowledge, viz., with a complete metaphysics of knowledge, but not if the concern is rather with the *methodological vindication* of the real value of knowledge, for it can certainly be the case that we have a conception which we do not logically presuppose, but rather want to prove, viz., that knowledge is necessarily directed to real being even though we only take notice of knowledge insofar as it is the awareness of an object by a subject. At the start of epistemo-theoretical reflection, it cannot yet be asserted that this awareness of objects is related validly to real being. It is precisely from this point of view that Maréchal, with the aid of the transcendental method, tries to show that the assumption that knowledge is not validly related to real being, but merely to the phenomenal object to the exclusion of what is real, stands in contradiction to the conditions of possibility to which the act of knowledge is related. Maréchal elaborates this point not only in the fifth volume (V, p. 517), but also in a detailed response to an objection by Maritain.[26]

26 Jacques Maritain, "Note à propos des 'Cahiers' du R. P. Maréchal," *Revue Thomiste,* vol. 7 (1924), pp. 416–425. Since Maritain had raised

Consequently, we can take the first part of Casula's disjunction and say: The phenomenal object is related to the real object only in an improper sense. However, in critical reflection this relation to the real object is not logically presupposed, but rather demonstrated as the condition of possibility for the consciousness of objects. This allows Maréchal to avoid both dogmatism on one side and a contradiction with respect to the relation of knowledge to reality on the other. In his letter to Maritain,[27] Maréchal asks why we should not "begin with the phenomenal object, from a methodological point of view (*ad modum quaestionis solvendae*) and polemically (*elenchice*), as something given, since this is admitted by those who reject every mode of determinate metaphysics, and then attempt to show that a purely phenomenal object cannot be an object [in consciousness]. . . . This is the leitmotiv of my fifth volume."

Fifth, Maréchal does not at all claim that the phenomenal object is the only possible, or even the natural, starting point. It is no doubt more natural, as well as possible, to begin with the spontaneous affirmation of being in natural knowledge, which can be described as the "perception" and "reception" of real, perceptible being as sensibly (but nonetheless intellectually) perceived. To this extent the "classical critique" is correct. The current status of the problem, however, as it has emerged from the historical development of modern thought, makes it more advisable to validate the claims of natural knowledge through a transcendental analysis of the *a priori* conditions of possibility of the consciousness of objects. This has a polemical function, specifically with regard to those who only recognize the phenomenal object, as well as a systematic function, to the extent that both the philosophical questions posed by the modern problematic and the relation of knowledge to being are clari-

against Maréchal's starting point the objection that the phenomenal object as separated from being must be something not understandable since the phenomenon can only be thought as a consequence of being, Maréchal answered (in a letter quoted on page 418): "Actually, my rejection of Kantianism is grounded in the inner contradiction of the (purely) phenomenal object."

[27] *Op cit.*, p. 418.

fied.[28] When Maréchal speaks of "the starting point of metaphysics" in the title of his five volume work, we must not then think that he is referring to the phenomenal object. He means the affirmation of being. The starting point of metaphysics, therefore, is not the starting point of transcendental analysis, but rather its goal!

Sixth, when Maréchal examines the consciousness of objects according to conditions of possibility and when these are shown to be determining conditions of actual knowledge, i.e., that the object, insofar as it is known, is posited by the subject, this does not contradict the receptive character of knowledge, for this position does not deny that of which we are conscious in knowledge and which we describe as the grasp of a given object, but grounds it more securely. The *positing* character of knowledge, as presented by Maréchal, does not exclude its *receptive* and perceptive character, but rather presupposes it and clarifies it. Maréchal's approach to the theory of knowledge is distinguished from others in that he does not simply accept the legitimacy of the claim of knowledge to grasp real being through a mere appeal to what is evident, but derives the validity of this evidence from the conditions of possibility of the act of knowledge. If the constructing or positing of the object of knowledge through the participation of *a priori* forms is radically opposed to the reception and perception of the real object of knowledge, then we forget that both are two complementary aspects under which knowledge can and must be viewed if we wish to gain a sufficient understanding of it. These two aspects do not exclude each other, but reciprocally expand each other, viz., the aspect which transcendentally makes knowledge possible (or, from the metaphysical point of view, the epistemologico-metaphysical explanation of knowledge) and the aspect of the phenomenological description of knowledge.

A confusion of these aspects occurs when the idealist rejects the receptive aspect in favor of the positing character of knowledge, or when the realist considers the positing character im-

[28] Cahier V, p. 517, and in the letter to Maritain referred to above, pp. 416, 418.

possible because of the receptive aspect of knowledge. The exponents of transcendental analysis in contemporary scholastic philosophy manage to avoid this confusion because they begin with a phenomenology of the act of knowledge in which, among other things, they guarantee its claim to grasp reality. However, the structural elements which manifest themselves in the act of knowledge refer to *a priori* conditions of possibility from which ultimately they are able to derive the fundamental validation of the claim of knowledge to grasp reality. Consequently, with the aid of transcendental reflection what is included in the direct act of knowledge is made explicit and evaluated with respect to the assessment of direct knowledge. This outlines a fundamental law of reflective and abstractive thought, viz., the function of the abstractions of reflection for the direct knowledge of the concrete.

This analysis allows us to conclude with justification that Casula's objections do not succeed in showing that the transcendental method is actually impossible, or basically alien, with respect to Thomistic thought.

VINDICATION OF THE TRANSCENDENTAL PROCEDURE

Other critics, such as M. D. Roland-Gosselin, J. de Vries, A. Pechhacker and A. Brunner, grant that a critical vindication of knowledge is justified, and even necessary, but for various reasons they find Maréchal's procedure lacking. Their objections may be summarized in the following points.

(1) The analysis of knowledge, especially of judgment, the central act of knowledge, is presented incorrectly by Maréchal.

(2) Maréchal does not consider the role of what is evident, viz., the intuitive element in knowledge.

(3) Consequently, he disregards the only possible way of giving a final logical grounding to the objectivity and reality of knowledge, i.e., the correspondence between thought and being,

viz., through the direct reception of immediate reality, in cases where this is possible.

(4) It is thus unnecessary to require an *a priori* for the knowledge of being.

(5) To claim that such an *a priori* discloses reality presupposes the validity of the principle of finality which, in turn, presupposes the validity of the knowledge of reality and the demonstration of certain fundamental metaphysical insights. The *a priori* is thus not applicable to the critical demonstration of the fundamental relation of human knowledge to reality since it would lead to a logical circle.

(6) This means, further, that the transcendental method must presuppose the validity of basic concepts and principles in order to arrive at its conclusions, and these conclusions should constitute the justification of this validity.

(7) The transcendental method thus falls into the unusual fallacy of trying to demonstrate simple knowledge by presupposing a much more complicated mode of knowledge.

(8) The inclusion of the existence of God as the final goal of the dynamism of the understanding unnecessarily complicates the critical proof.

(9) This results in casting doubt on the usual proof for the existence of God.

(10) Finally, Maréchal's conception of the supernatural character of the ultimate end of the natural orientation of man gives rise to hesitations with respect to the very method which he employs.

If we contrast these objections with the analysis of the transcendental method as we have studied it so far in connection with Maréchal and his followers, we find that they confuse the nature of transcendental analysis with a pure intentional analysis of knowledge. We must not forget that there is more than one kind of noetic analysis.

There is a mode of noetic analysis which tries to determine what the intention of knowledge is concerned with and what is expressed in judgment. This *intentional* (that is to say, descriptive or phenomenological) analysis is only concerned with those elements of knowledge in consciousness which can be made expressly conscious through direct reflection on that which is intended in knowledge and which can be determined by grounding knowledge in an intuition into the state of affairs which it actuates. There is, however, another mode of noetic analysis which views the functions operative in knowledge as activities which are distinguished from each other and from other object-related activities through the various ways in which they relate to objects. Such an *operative* analysis investigates how the objects to which these various activities are related stand with respect to each other and which properties they must have in order that the activities constituted in relation to these objects can be constituted with respect to their actual relations to each other.

This latter method makes it demonstratively clear that the activity of knowledge is so constituted that the affirmability of the content of judgment excludes the possibility of affirming its contradictory. The affirmability of a state of affairs, as opposed to mere sensible perception, excludes the possibility of the relativization of this affirmability since a comprehensive knowledge of this affirmability cannot possibly render itself relative. This means that the affirmability of a determinate object can be non-relative only if the necessary conditions of this object are affirmable. In this way (which we can only sketch here briefly since a more exact treatment would have to show the different presentations and points of view among the various exponents of the transcendental method), we arrive at the affirmability of the principle of contradiction, of the transcendentality of being and of the existence of the absolute as necessarily connected with the possibility of judgmental affirmation.

Operative analysis, therefore, as distinct from intentional analysis, does not simply move from consciousness to what is intended in knowledge, but from reflection to the true validity and various implications of the functions of knowledge. That which must belong to objects in order to make the structure of the object-relatedness of the activity of knowledge possible, is not merely demonstrated, but, since it is often not open to direct reflection, *dis-closed*.

216

THE FUNCTION OF EVIDENCE

Two entirely different roles with respect to what is evident appear in these two modes of noetic analysis. In intentional analysis evidence serves as proof of the validity of knowledge, viz., of the realization of its intention. In operative analysis, however, no explicit notice is taken of the traits of objects which appear as evident. What is evident is presupposed only to the extent that it is a constitutive element of a mode of legitimate knowledge, viz., only to the extent that it is an activity of knowledge in the full sense of the word. The properties that necessarily belong to the object of such a mode of knowledge, however, can only be derived by means of an operative analysis. To this extent, then, operative analysis is contained in what is evident.

The validity of the affirmability of what is derived by operative analysis as the necessary presupposition of every possibility of noetic activity is grounded in the fact that otherwise the very activity of knowledge which would cast doubt on the validity of these presuppositions would not be possible. This retorsive move leads to the demonstration of the reductive attainment of the presuppositions of knowledge to the extent that they are presuppositions of every mode of knowledge, including the validity of any mode of knowledge which would cast doubt on some other mode of knowledge. Consequently, whatsoever must be *necessarily* presupposed for all modes of knowledge must be *legitimately* presupposed.

This demonstration of validity does not require insight into the actual constitution of these presuppositions, but only insight into the structure of the noetic activity which necessarily includes these presuppositions. Insight is thus not taken as the criterion of the metaphysical validity of knowledge, but only as one of the regulative factors of knowledge. The mode of validity proper to knowledge which is regulated in this way appears only in the result of the entire operative analysis.

We are already somewhat familiar with these two structural elements of transcendental analysis, viz., operative analysis and

217

retorsion. We shall now see if they allow us to answer the objections which are presented earlier.

From the point of view of intentional analysis, we would have to divide a grounded judgment into (a) a representation of a state of affairs, (b) a direct or indirect perception of a state of affairs and (c) the personal reception of the representation of a state of affairs as grounded in the perception of this state of affairs. With regard to the meaning of the copula, viz., the form of judgment which unites the concepts which represent the state of affairs, it can only be said that through it the factual identity of the content signified through the concepts gains expression without signifying a grasp of the absolute ground of the total order of being.

This does not exclude the possibility that a broader investigation, such as the one attempted by de Vries (Cr., pp. 285–288; U., p. 395), may come to the conclusion that the meaning of the activity of judgment aims at true knowledge, viz., a correspondence between thought and states of affairs such that all states of affairs are ultimately grounded in real being, although Pechhacker cautions that this should be referred to as "co-affirmation" in judgment, since not everything is co-affirmed in judgment which belongs of necessity to its object (Ver., pp. 106f.). This indication serves to show that it is meaningful to extend the *analysis of judgment* further than is possible through a simple intentional analysis of what is directly signified in judgment. However, this requires a different analytic mediation.

Operative analysis is such a mode of mediation which allows for the manifestation of the traits which necessarily belong to the object of each valid judgment. It does not investigate how the intentional analysis which is thought when the validation of a judgment is considered from the point of view an insight into a state of affairs is justified. Rather, it seeks to know which characteristics must belong to the object of knowledge in order that this knowledge can have the structure and the fundamental interconnections of other activities which we actually discern in it.

This procedure allows us to understand (if we leave open for a moment the question of finality because of the misunderstand-

218

ings it can lead to) why the properties of the object of knowledge necessarily dis-closed by this analysis are referred to as "co-known" or "unthematically co-affirmed," because these "co-known" traits of the object are such that they work determinately on our object-related constitution. If they were not affirmable we could not demonstrate in knowledge the actual structure of knowledge, i.e., affirmation itself would not be possible if the affirmability of these traits could not also be established. It is in this sense that they are "co-affirmed." Of course, I am not aware of all these "co-affirmed" interconnections in the sense that a simple intentional analysis could expose them to me, but at the same time attention to the implications of the affirmability of an object can show that these interconnections are validly affirmable if the affirmability of the object proves to be valid.

OPERATIVE ANALYSIS OF WHAT IS EVIDENT

Several avenues of approach are open here. An appeal could be made to *what is evident* as a sufficient grounding of the affirmability of the object with the consequence that everything which can be demonstrated to be necessarily connected with the affirmability of this object is, for this very reason, also counted as affirmable. However, turning this statement around it could be said that since the proof of the validity of judgment can guarantee only the components directly accessible to intentional analysis through recourse to insight into the asserted state of affairs, the question arises whether the elements necessarily connected with the affirmability of this state of affairs through later developments, although not explicitly considered in the grounding evidence, are also validly affirmable. Does evidence extend that far? Or rather is it not the case that linguistic formulations, preconceived notions and other similar distortive factors would have to be included in evidence?

It is a matter of fact that many modern epistemologists have had such a mistrust, causing them to discount the value of evidence altogether, because it seems that the affirmability of what is open to insight carries with it undesirable consequences. For instance, empiricists hold that in such a case more must be comprehensible than can be comprehended of real being through the senses and therefore they deny the validity of universal and necessary contents of knowledge grounded in insight. Likewise, Kant holds that insight does not guarantee the real validity of synthetic *a priori* judgments without which we are left with insoluble contradictions and are incapable of explaining the possibility of scientific knowledge.

Keeping this in mind, we can clearly see that an investigation into the ramifications of the affirmability of an object is by no means useless since it would serve as a reflective validation of that which is included in what is evident and would also make possible a fruitful dialogue with epistemological positions which have reservations with regard to the simple appeal to what is evident. Since intentional analysis gives scant attention to these problems, which confront us and which philosophy cannot deign to ignore, the need arises for another mode for noetic analysis.

Because transcendental analysis as operative analysis deals with the implications of the evident affirmability of an object in order to reveal the structure of objectivity which it necessarily involves, in which the validity of the affirmability of this structure of objectivity is demonstrated by means of its retorsive element, it is also an elaboration of that which can be grounded through what is evident. This entails the validation of what is evident as a criterion of truth over and against those objections which can be drawn up against evidence from the ramifications of knowledge as actually grounded in what is evident.

THE DEVELOPMENT
OF ACTUATED KNOWLEDGE

In order to clarify in what sense the conditions of possibility of knowledge are *"implicitly"* contained in knowledge, we must distinguish the way in which these conditions are present in knowledge from the way in which they can be brought to explicit awareness. They are made explicit to the extent that implications are drawn from the assertability of an object. These implications, however, are not simply such that they are drawn from the content of what is asserted, but rather from the very act of asserting this content. Furthermore, they are not simple, direct implications but, for the most part, actual conclusions. Yet whatever can be concluded to depends on premisses under which knowledge can be subsumed.

These premisses can stem from a simple reflection on the act of knowledge, in which case we have a mere self-exposition of knowledge; however, the conclusions could also be derived from a general metaphysics, in which case we come to a metaphysics of knowledge or a psychology of knowledge. The conditions of possibility of knowledge disclosed in this way do not concern us here so long as the metaphysical premisses themselves are not derived from the self-exposition of knowledge. That which concerns the transcendental method is the *self-exposition of knowledge*. This, of course, leads to a metaphysical self-understanding of knowledge, as we have seen in Maréchal, viz., the transcendental critique employs only those concepts which can be disclosed in a direct reflection on the act of knowledge and which determine the structure of the act of knowledge, i.e., concepts which result directly from such a critique.

The expression of reflection is dependent on conceptual forms which are derived from direct knowledge. Of course, we can determine the meanings of the words by means of which these concepts gain expression through reference to what appears in reflection. Such determination is in fact essential for a clear reflective method. However, it involves the danger of false objectification, which every reflective method must beware of succumbing to. The error of false *objectification* consists in not using words in the senses indicated by reflection, viz., letting other meanings slip into the conclusions which are normally connected with these words. This error is committed, for example, by empiricism when it identifies what is sensibly given in direct consciousness with that which can be explained by a psychology of perception.

221

Another procedure for explicating knowledge is possible which does coincide with such a false objectification and which is not simply a mere self-exposition of knowledge, but which grasps this self-exposition in a determinate conceptual form which is taken to be introduced from without. This procedure puts forth analytic disjunctions whose members include conclusions concerning knowledge and which can be distinguished through comparison with actual knowledge. This suggests a way of interpreting the logical structure of Kant's Copernican revolution (B, 17f.). As an analytical disjunction, we have: The ground for the correspondence between thought and object lies either outside of or within the knowing subject. The conclusions of the members of the disjunction with respect to knowledge are the following. In the first case, perceptions and concepts are oriented toward objects. Then we must explain how we can know anything about objects apriorily, for if the ground of the correspondence lies in objects, viz., in things which can be approached through experience, then I can discern nothing in them that would be valid independent of an experience of them or which could not be grounded in experience. In the second case, however, the ground lies in the subject such that objects in experience are oriented toward our concepts, in which case we can understand how modes of knowledge expressed in synthetic *a priori* judgments can be valid of object-oriented thought. These conclusions exclude the first member of the disjunction in favor of the second. The second member of the disjunction offers an exposition of knowledge. We shall call this procedure, whereby knowledge is presented as a conceptual determination involving the introduction of a conceptual disjunction and the exclusion of one of its members, a *categoreal development,* for this can be taken to be the development of something not yet sufficiently conceived categoreally with reference to the categoreal schema outlined by the concepts of the disjunction. Since this development is quite important for an understanding of the logical structure of the transcendental method, we shall examine a few of the properties of categoreal development.

To begin we must determine some of the logical conditions

of the conclusiveness of this procedure. First, the disjunction must be complete and the concepts of the disjunction must be meaningful. If the procedure is to aid the self-exposition of knowledge, then the concepts must be shown to be structural elements of the act of knowledge and the completeness of the disjunction must either be analytic or grounded with reference to the results of a previous self-exposition of knowledge. If the meaningfulness of the concepts or the completeness of the disjunction are grounded in some other way, the categoreal development may be valid, but it would not suffice as a transcendental self-exposition.

Second, the conclusions drawn from the members of the disjunction must actually be conclusive. If these conclusions are drawn from subordinate premises, the character of the procedure depends on the grounding of the premises. If they are grounded in the self-exposition of knowledge, then the procedure remains a self-exposition. Of course, the procedure loses its conclusiveness if the conclusion involves a fluctuation in the meaning of the concepts.

If these conditions are met there can be no objection to the validity of this procedure, but care must be taken so that in the assessment of the results that which is found in knowledge through this exposition is actually an element of knowledge, although not in a conceptually developed manner. This consideration signifies, more than self-understanding can, that the properties of a thing which are conceptually conceived are actually in the thing according to the concrete content of its meaning and not in the abstract conceptual mode in which it is thought. It clarifies matters to the extent that analysis is shown to be concerned not only with the fact that something is realized in knowledge, but that it is somehow also "co-known," viz., that along with knowledge the affirmability of what is "co-known" is recognized through the act of knowledge. This recognition arises through the act and is also operative in the conscious act whereby it is meaningful to speak of something that is contained in knowledge as such. This recognition, however, cannot appear in conceptually explicit form in determinate judgments, even though we can become clearly conscious of what is recognized in this way only in a conceptually and judgmentally explicit form, viz., through the self-exposition of knowledge or through categoreal development. This exposition, however, can take on many fundamental conceptual forms, and although what is "co-known" can be expressed in reflective clarification only in a determinate conceptual form, what is expressed is not necessarily contained in what is co-known in precisely this conceptual form, since it depends on the way in which what is thus included is drawn out and developed.

Since there can be no explicit human knowledge without concepts, we find here further grounds for caution in using the designation "co-known." At the very least we can see here a connection with perception and with evidence as pre-predicative knowledge. If we then consider that transcendental analysis is determined in its relation to evidence insofar as it develops and clarifies what is included in the insight which grounds knowledge, we might validly refer to what is "co-known" as "co-perceived." This would allow for the fact that what is included in knowledge concerns something that must first be categoreally developed.

However, this expression is also not completely satisfactory because then the relation of dependence with respect to the absolute would have to be characterized as "co-perceived," which would not reflect the typical employment of the word "perceive." It would perhaps be best to begin with a metaphysical description of knowledge as an apprehension of an object. It is possible to know something without knowing explicitly everything that is contained in what is apprehended. Thus the real validity of this concept can be vindicated in terms of the intentional grounding of knowledge through insight, viz., that a concept is realized in a confronted real object even though it is only through subsequent reflection that it is discovered what grounds everything in this concept is essential relationships. If I have a concept, then I have apprehended the constitution of meaning which it determines, but I do not completely and explicitly know it. Knowledge of what is apprehended, taken in this sense, is increased through subsequent reflection in which the essential properties of what is determined through this concept are determined. This increase does not alter a thing with respect to the real validity of the concept, although these traits are not included in what is immediately evident but are known later as necessarily connected with it. This procedure resembles an intentional analysis of knowledge to the extent that more is apprehended in knowledge than I am explicit aware of, while at the same time this "more" is apprehended in such a way that it can operate on further knowledge. Consequently, we shall refer to those components of which we are not explicitly aware in knowledge, but which are actual to the extent that they operate in knowledge and can thus be developed through subsequent reflection and exposition, as *"co-apprehended."* Since conscious attention is not immediately directed to what is "co-apprehended," it is not thematic in knowledge, and therefore we may characterize what is "co-apprehended" as *unthematically* known.

Insofar as it is also described as a positing, the co-apprehended can also be referred to as *co-posited.* This expression will help us guard against a common misunderstanding, viz., that we are dealing with something that is directly demonstrable through reflection. However, this expression will inevitably face the objection that it misrepresents the receptive character of human knowledge and is thus at the very least misleading.

The description of judgment as positing, of course, relates more to the operative analysis of knowledge, i.e., it expresses the nature of the activity of judgment such that a mode of ultimate validity and absoluteness is attributed to what is affirmed. That is to say, if the activity of thought wherein what is thought is only pondered is compared with an activity of thought wherein what is thought is affirmed, then a certain ultimate validity is attributed to what is thought through this affirmation; that is, it gains a specific rank in the order of that which must be taken into account with respect to the activity of thought.

If, however, something whose affirmability has been granted is described as "posited," this means that everything whose affirmability must be guaranteed in order that affirmation itself be possible, namely, everthing which is "implicitly co-affirmed," can be referred to as "co-posited." Thus we can describe the traits of each object as such as "co-posited" or "co-apprehended" in knowledge through the self-exposition of knowledge. These expressions should therefore be taken to mean the same thing even though the modes of description are derived from two reciprocal aspects of knowledge.

In summary, we can see that it is not necessary to restrict the *analysis of judgment* within the narrow limits of intentional analysis. Through transcendental analysis it is possible to regard the function of the copula in judgment not merely as the expression of the categoreal synthesis of judgment but as an objective synthesis in relation to the absolute. However, in operative analysis it does not suffice merely to declare the reality of the objective domain in which everything that is assertible is ultimately grounded because from the operative point of view reality, as opposed to phenomenality and ideality, can only be conceived through its non-relativity, viz., through the absolutivity of the positing of reality as known. However, this means that the possibility of the absolutivity of the non-relative positing of what is finite and conditioned as such can be included in the relation to the absolutely unconditioned. Consequently, an activity which does not tend toward the absolute cannot relate to what is real as such since knowledge of the real extends to knowledge an absolutivity which would not be possible without a foundation in the absolute.

Thus *Maréchal's critique of the analysis of judgment,* as well as that of those who have been influenced by him, is grounded in the realization that the results of transcendental analysis (which is an entirely different means of analysis than intentional analysis) nevertheless corresponds completely with the norms of intentional analysis.

THE VINDICATION OF WHAT IS EVIDENT

It should have become clear by now that the charge that Maréchal disregards the role of what is *evident* and thus rejects the only possible way in which knowledge can be vindicated no longer carries any force. We have seen above that Maréchal employs the evidence of the performance of the act of judgment as the starting point of his transcendental analysis. He does not derive the function of what is evident, viz., the validity of knowledge as truth defined as a correspondence with a state of affairs grounded in real being, directly from the awareness that real being is manifest in what is evident, but rather from an operative analysis of knowledge derived from what is evident. This procedure allows him to derive the constitution of the essence co-apprehended in what is evident without explicit reference to the evidence of this constitution. However, this procedure does appear to be capable of indicating in individual cases the degrees of evidence at hand and whether the concern is with a mode of knowledge whose conditions of possibility can be given through transcendental analysis. This makes it abundantly clear why Maréchal insists that he is not concerned with a detailed theory of knowledge but only with a determination of the universal structures within which an object of knowledge is possible and, further, that we actually possess such a mode of knowledge and therefore that we know the existence of reality structured in this way. He does not at all take up the question of the criteria according to which the actual knowledge of facts can be taken to be sufficiently grounded.

THE MEANING OF THE *A PRIORI*

Just as it is not correct to reject the conception of knowledge through operative analysis as "positing" in favor of a conception of knowledge as perceptive, so the appeal to the immediate givenness of a situation does not render the acceptance of the *a priori* unnecessary. It is meaningful to ask which traits of the object are co-posited in every mode of knowledge with regard to those traits which are co-apprehended in every mode of evidence. We have already seen that insights into essence would not be possible as synthetic judgments *a priori* if nothing were co-apprehended. However, what is co-apprehended can be transcendentally derived by means of operative analysis and retorsion. This means, first of all, that it is a necessity given with the essence of the activity of knowledge that these traits correspond to the object of knowledge. Thus the concern is not with a mere logical *a priori* but with the foundations of this logical *a priori* in a necessary structural mode of the activity of knowledge; in other words, the concern is with an epistemological, or more precisely, an epistemologico-metaphysical *a priori*. However, secondly, the transcendental derivation indicates that the traits which correspond to the object in the activity of knowledge are validly identified with this object since they are traits which belong to objects as such, viz., determinations of being. This lends a "dis-covering" character to the epistemological *a priori,* i.e., it gives us access to the real structure of the object of knowledge. It is because knowledge possesses such an *a priori* that it can possess an insight into the constitution of essences. If it did not have this *a priori* knowledge would no longer be intellectual but the mere reception of unconnected individual impressions, for if the question about the real validity of knowledge were not possible, then it would be impossible to appprehend the meaning of this question.

However, it is not necessary to pose the question about the *a priori* if we are not restricted to intentional analysis and cannot question the deeper epistemologico-metaphysical understanding of the activity of knowledge. This is possible only if the problematic sphere of philosophy is arbitrarily restricted, thereby avoiding problems which the evolution of modern thought has placed before us and which require an operative analysis of knowledge. If we do choose to deal with these problems and to pose the question: Is it not the case that the nature of knowledge is such that it must necessarily affirm certain traits in the object?, then we pose the question about the *a priori*. If it is then determined that these traits necessarily belong to the object through real being, in which all objects are grounded, then we are dealing with a "dis-covering" *a priori*. We do not come to know this *a priori* merely through a reflection on the content of knowledge, in order to show that the concept of being is transcendental, but through a reflection on the object-related activity in terms of which we derive the traits that must necessarily be attributed to the object, if not our knowledge but rather the doubt concerning the real validity of knowledge is to be negated, since transcendental deduction has already demonstrated the essentials of the real validity of the formation of the object of knowledge as stipulated by the *a priori* structure of knowledge.

TRANSCENDENTAL ANALYSIS AND CRITICAL REFLECTION

Since the transcendental method does not try to replace (and is not capable of replacing) a criteriological verification of particular modes of knowledge as related to reality, it is incapable of deciding whether there is valid knowledge in particular cases. In other words, it is concerned with a mode of knowledge whose validity, as co-apprehended, is arrived at by means of transcendental deduction. Furthermore, the transcendental deduction of the necessary relatedness of each object of knowledge to the absolute real ground of all being does not explain how this relation is determined in particular cases. It can, of course, be the case that an object is a mental fact, since this kind of object is ultimately grounded in the real order of being, but it cannot be the case that there are only mere mental facts and no reality. If this fact is accepted, then the usual objections raised against the transcendental method, viz., with regard to the possibility of error and the non-reality of objects of knowledge, are left wanting. However, all this clearly shows the limits of the transcendental method, namely, that it is not a universal solvent, and the need for supplementing it with an intentional analysis.

THE ROLE OF THE DYNAMISM OF KNOWLEDGE

What is the status of the logical dependence of transcendental deduction and of the demonstration of the real validity of *a*

229

priori structures on the value of the principle of the certainty of the attainment of an end and on the existence of God? How does the principle of finality function in the transcendental method?

The application of transcendental deduction as retorsion leads to the direct derivation of the real validity of statements. Here there is no need for recourse to the principle of finality, nor is there concern for the orientation of the capacity for knowledge. Rather, the fulfillment of the validity of knowledge is shown directly through retorsion. This is the advantage of retorsion, but it has a disadvantage insofar as the inner structure of the activity of knowledge is not sufficiently clarified. The demonstration extends only to the mere fact of the necessary validity of knowledge, not to the ground in terms of which this validity can be understood.

If transcendental analysis is structured so that there is a direction to the natural orientation of knowledge at the base of noetic activity—to the extent that it is manifest in noetic activity, then we come up against the question whether a fulfillment of this orientation is possible—that is, necessary. This question, at least in Maréchal's transcendental critique, is not posed and answered in universal concepts, but with reference to the noetic activity directly manifest in reflection. By comparing the universal form which characterizes judgmental knowledge as such with the form which determines a particular judgment, presented as a partial fulfillment of the orientation of noetic activity, we reach the conclusion that the universal form of knowledge, which in itself corresponds to a complete knowledge of absolute being, is a constitutive element in each particular mode of knowledge such that if the orientation of knowledge toward absolute being were incapable of fulfillment, then a partial fulfillment of this orientation would also be impossible. However, not only is such partial fulfillment an actual fact, but it is the case that possible partial fulfillment, viz., the possibility of valid knowledge, cannot be questioned from the point of view of the impossibility of such partial fulfillment. The possibility of fulfillment with respect to the orientation toward knowledge in this connection is nothing but the affirmability of that toward which the possibility of fulfilling the orientation tends. Thus the affirmability of the absolute is the condition of possibility of every mode of affirmability. This means that the particular judgment is possible only through a co-apprehension or co-positing of the relation of dependence upon the absolute.

THE POSSIBILITY OF THE GOAL

By the possibility of fulfillment we mean simply the real *possibility of the goal* of the orientation of an active faculty, not whether the conditions necessary for the *actual performance* of the corresponding activity can be realized. Thus reason as such is directed to the knowledge of all being, but with respect to a finite, viz., human reason, the realization of this orientation is bound to other conditions which constitute its fundamental limits. Consequently, the objection raised against the possibility of the goal of this orientation of reason is a poor one if it claims that a knowledge of all being is impossible for man, for in the development of the proof the concern is only with the possibility of the goal of the orientation of reason as such. If this goal were not possible there could be no uniquely human reason, but at best only a more developed sense knowledge whose formal object would not be being as such. In this case, however, no reflection, and no question, concerning the validity of knowledge would be possible.

That the goal of the natural orientation of an active faculty must be really possible and that this goal determines the form of the activity (which, with respect to an object-oriented activity, corresponds to the formal object of the activity) is actually only a clarification of the meaning of the propositional concepts, for an active faculty is defined with respect to its real orientation toward the realization of its activities. Under the goal of such an orientation we understand that toward which this orientation tends. If the goal were impossible, then there would be neither an orientation toward an activity (and hence no activity) nor an orientation toward another possible goal (and hence a different activity). If an activity is determinable, then the question cannot be whether its goal is really possible but what its goal is (or, in other words, whether the goal which we project as the goal of this activity is capable of fulfillment, i.e., whether the goal which we accept is really the goal of the activity). We can, to this extent, agree with Maréchal when he refers to the principle of the possibility of the goal as "analytic." But how can we determine what the goal is? Because of their conceptual determination, there is an exact correspondence between the goal of an orientation, the orientation itself and the form of the activity of a faculty with this orientation. Consequently, the universal form of the activities of a faculty corresponds with the final goal of its orientation. Thus the comparison between the concrete form of the activities of a faculty and the form which is common and essential to them all yields the means by which to characterize the activity which is viewed as the ultimate (subjective) goal of this faculty.

This goal, with respect to reason, is not simply true knowledge in the sense of a correspondence with real being, for in order to be able to say, from the analysis of the activity, what real being is, operative analysis must reveal how the distinction between object-related activities which relate to real being and those which relate only to appearance manifest themselves in the structure and coordination of these activities. With regard to the specific modes of operative analysis employed by the individual exponents of the transcendental method, it is clear that the mode of knowledge toward which reason as such is oriented, to the extent that the possibility of individual knowledge is internally dependent on this orientation, is the complete knowledge of being, the object of which is an absolute being as the final goal or ultimate ground of all being. The degree to which this goal is attainable, in relation to the concrete conditions of human reason, is left open. However, insofar as this goal operates constitutively within the intellectual activity of knowledge, the complete knowledge of this goal is not included in noetic activity, but this activity does include the orientation toward this goal and thus the affirmability of the object of this knowledge, viz., the absolute being.

THE DYNAMISM OF KNOWLEDGE AS CATEGOREAL DEVELOPMENT

The inclusion of the absolute being in the transcendental grounding of knowledge can be conceived as a categoreal development of the noetic character of absolutivity. To the extent that the question is how noetic activity can be understood in terms of the orientation of the faculty of knowledge which performs it and the goal of this orientation, we see that noetic activity could not have the structure which necessarily belongs to it if it were not oriented toward absolute being in such a way that this absolute is co-posited or co-apprehended in every mode of knowledge even though it is not explicitly in awareness. To the extent that the concepts and presuppositions necessary for this categoreal exposition of knowledge can be demonstrated on the basis of a reflection on noetic activity, we have a self-exposition of knowledge.

Consequently, the absolute is not introduced in order to guarantee the possibility of the fulfillment of the determinate orientation of knowledge. Since the principle of the certainty of the goal is not introduced into the proof, but rather the principle of the possibility of the goal, which is logically demonstrable independently of the existence of a personal, all-knowing and good God, the existence of God is not logically presupposed. The absolute appears as the possible and co-posited omega point of the orientation of reason, viz., as the result of the attempt to make explicit in concepts what is actuated in knowledge, the legitimation of which is grounded in a reflection on knowledge. Consequently, it is possible to answer questions about the possibility of the knowledge of being which are formulated in the very same categoreal manner. This is precisely Maréchal's position.

The *intentional critique* (A) begins with the determination of the claim of judgment (1) and vindicates the validity of this claim (2) by showing that the existence of what is asserted is manifest in what is evident (3). The focal point here rests on the fact that in judgments of states of affairs, which are directly

233

WAYS OF GROUNDING VALIDITY

We can outline the different attempts to demonstrate the validity of the claim of judgmental knowledge to non-relative validity, i.e., to truth, in the following schema:

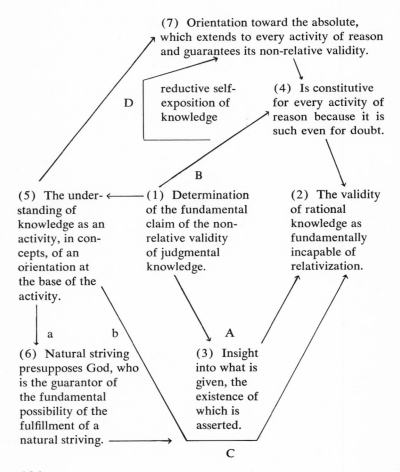

(7) Orientation toward the absolute, which extends to every activity of reason and guarantees its non-relative validity.

D   reductive self-exposition of knowledge

(4) Is constitutive for every activity of reason because it is such even for doubt.

B

(5) The understanding of knowledge as an activity, in concepts, of an orientation at the base of the activity.

(1) Determination of the fundamental claim of the non-relative validity of judgmental knowledge.

(2) The validity of rational knowledge as fundamentally incapable of relativization.

a   b

A

(6) Natural striving presupposes God, who is the guarantor of the fundamental possibility of the fulfillment of a natural striving.

(3) Insight into what is given, the existence of which is asserted.

C

accessible to consciousness, such as acts of consciousness, the existence of what is asserted is immediate. Everything that is co-apprehended in this insight, since it can be studied through subsequent reflection on the meaning of concepts and through comparison of concepts, is given little attention here. Likewise, the character of the activity of the noetic act is not included.

Retorsion (B) begins with the determination of the claims of noetic activity (1). The non-relative validity of knowledge is demonstrated (2) by showing the fact of the fundamental necessity of such non-relative validity. If the attempt is made to call it into doubt it immediately comes into contact with the claim to non-relative validity (4). Thus to the extent that reason is at all active it proves itself to be capable of a mode of knowledge of fundamental non-relative validity. The pursuit of retorsion leads to the more careful determination of this capability. Retorsion can be distinguished from the appeal to what is evident in that retorsion does not demonstrate the fact of the realization of the claim of knowledge *a posteriori,* but demonstrates the necessity of the possibility of the fulfillment of this claim apriorily. In the act of retorsion it becomes clear that the affirmability of whatever belongs to noetic activity with such necessity that the very attempt to deny it, or place it in doubt, presupposes its affirmability, is validly affirmable. However, since knowledge claims to recognize as validly affirmable only what actually is, it follows that whatever knowledge necessarily posits is also actual. Legitimate affirmability as well as the actual existence of what is thus affirmable follows from the affirmability necessarily grounded in noetic activity. This is the fundamental principle of the transcendental justification and foundation of knowledge.

One might object to this principle by claiming that the transcendental method, on the basis of its own mode of questioning, could only arrive at *a priori* forms of thought, that is, to the necessity of thought, but could never attain the validation of the content of knowledge. This objection holds only if we ignore the connection between the thought which we reflect upon and the thought with which we make this reflection. The real validity of what is necessarily affirmed can be derived only if we can demonstrate the connection between thought and being either by referring to the intuited givenness of the state of affairs or (something which is easily overlooked) by demonstrating that it belongs to the necessary conditions of judgmental thought, i.e., due to the legislative power of thought only that can be asserted with necessity which is grounded, directly or indirectly, in an insight into the state of affairs. If it can be shown that something is necessarily affirmable, then it follows that it can be grounded in an insight into the state of affairs and thus can be validly asserted even though at present it cannot actually be taken to be an insight into the state of affairs. This demonstration clarifies how transcendental analysis does not stand in concurrence with what is evident, but can be a means of showing what can be grounded in what is evident without having to appeal to what is evident as a criterion of the ontological validity of what is to be grounded in particular cases.

In light of the fact that because of consciousness (which accompanies the act of knowledge) there is an inner connection between object-oriented thought and the reflection related to this thought, it is not necessary to derive the connection between insight and the necessity of thought. As retorsion shows, knowledge is constituted in this consciousness in such a way that there is an awareness of the fundamental justification of its claim to validity. If it is claimed that this awareness is not possible because the real validity of thought can never be demonstrated by means of a reflection on thought, but only through a comparison of the facts, several points must be made clear. First, this assertion would contradict the fact that retorsion can demonstrate this validity. Second, retorsion does not exclude the possibility that acceptance of the fundamental justification of the claim of the act of knowledge to validity, as explicated through retorsion, is itself grounded in a mode of evidence even though an explicit appeal to this evidence is not necessary for the retorsive demonstration of this validity. Third, we would not be excluding merely a purely subjective necessity of thought, but a necessity which is essential to the thought about factual situations, although the relation to factual situations is made explicit only through reflection.

If the real validity of that which corresponds to the object with *a priori* necessity is to be demonstrated, it is not necessary first to refer to the fact that knowledge is meaningful and to the possibility of the fulfillment of its orientation; rather, these conditions can be derived as the condition of possibility of the nature of knowledge as determined through retorsion, that is, as the conditions of possibility explaining the why of what is determined through retorsion. The development of these conditions of possibility is therefore a further self-exposition of that knowledge which accompanies all knowledge. If the existence of God is seen to be necessary for the constitution of the possibility of fulfillment, then this is derived as implicit in the conditions of possibility. This would mean that no mode of knowledge is possible; in other words, nothing would be affirmable, if the existence of God were not also affirmable. Nevertheless, the acceptance of the validity of knowledge does not consist in a direct appeal to the acceptance of the existence of God.

This way of grounding validity can be compared with the *epistemologico-metaphysical* way (C) which de Vries proposes at the conclusion of his *Critica*. The starting point here is the determination of the essential claim of judgment (1). This leads to the supposition of a corresponding natural orientation of the faculty of knowledge (5). Two lines of development are then pursued. First (a), with the help of a principle of causality already vindicated elsewhere, God is proven to be the intelligent prime cause of a natural orientation, that is, as the guarantor of the fundamental possibility of the fulfillment of natural striving (6). Second (b), from the striving of knowledge (5) and its possibility of fulfillment (6), the fundamental possibility of the fulfillment of the claim of knowledge to truth, that is, its non-relative validity, can be demonstrated.

Such a procedure is certainly possible, but how can the recourse here to the principle of causality and to the existence of God be necessary? Such recourse would fail to recognize that a

237

statement which is referred to the existence of God as its ground must also be capable of being grounded without explicit appeal to the existence of God because every statement about God which is employed as a premiss for a further proof must itself be grounded in premisses which do not deal explicitly with God. The reason is that God is not directly accessible to our mode of knowledge, rather only as mediated through finite knowledge. If we cannot derive that which can be derived from the statement about God from premisses which produce the statement about God, then the proof is not conclusive. Therefore, the explicit appeal to God is replaceable by statements through which we can ground the statement about God. In this case, it is the principle of causality and the fact of natural orientation. Thus it is the appeal to these statements which is decisive in the proof of the validity of knowledge under discussion at present and not the appeal to the existence of God. We must admit, however, that the replacement of the statement about God through the premisses which ground this statement bears two disadvantages. First, the proof tends to become more complicated and less obvious. Second, if the actual state of affairs is less clearly presented, it diminishes the metaphysical understanding which one receives when the relation to the primal cause is made explicit.

Why does this mode of proof presuppose the principle of the certainty of the end (which in turn presupposes the principle of causality)? To see why, we can refer to Maréchal's proof (D). This mode of proof also begins with reflection on the act of knowledge and its claim to truth (1). This reflection leads to the demonstration that a self-knowing act which negates itself if it does not come to an understanding of itself can be nothing but an act of a faculty which is oriented to the knowledge of truth. Therefore, the orientation determines the universal form of the act (5). It is then shown that this orientation cannot be the form of a mode of knowledge which necessarily makes the claim to non-relative validity unless this orientation tends to the absolute as the ultimate objective goal such that every mode of particular knowledge is supported by this orientation and thereby receives its fundamental non-relative validity

(7). Therefore, if true knowledge is not fundamentally impossible, knowledge can be meaningful only if the absolute is affirmable and only if particular affirmations occur because of this affirmability. This fundamental possibility of knowledge is constitutive for every mode of objective consciousness, even for that which casts doubt on the validity of knowledge or on the affirmability of the absolute (4). Consequently, the fundamental non-relative validity of knowledge, viz., the affirmability of the absolute, is the condition of possibility for every mode of objective consciousness (2).

How is this proof (D) of the validity of knowledge, as the self-exposition of knowledge, possible without the explicit presupposition of the principle of causality, as was the case in the previous mode of proof (C)? This difference between the two modes of proof can be explained by means of another difference, viz., the retorsive element (4) plays a decisive role in the last mode of proof, but not in the previous one. Through the retorsive element there occurs a development of the undeveloped awareness of the validity of knowledge already contained in the act of knowledge which gains a yet deeper development in the conceptual sphere through the terminology of the orientation of the understanding and its goal, which makes possible an epistemologico-metaphysical understanding of the knowledge supported by this validity. If the concern is with the absolute, this concern does not serve primarily as a demonstration of the validity of knowledge but as a means toward the more complete development of the co-apprehended validity.

Since the previous mode of proof (C) does not make sufficient use of the demonstrative force of retorsion, it is forced to employ other means of proof. First, the possibility of the fulfillment of noetic striving must be proven, which is again a reference to the principle of causality (for the proof of the existence of God). This shows how transcendental analysis can function without dependence on principles demonstrated elsewhere. The force of its proof does not lie in the concepts with which the development proceeds, but in the self-understanding of the act of knowledge which is elaborated in this conceptual material. The concepts offer only the material for an analytic disjunction, which is to be distinguished from the knowledge of the act in terms of itself (cf. V, pp. 503f.). The instrument for this distinction appears in its purest form in retorsion. Because of this conjunction of conceptual clarification and retorsive distinction, and because of the different possible accentuations of both, it is obvious how the transcendental method can receive such different expressions as we find in Maréchal on one side and Isaye on the other. Another possibility for the differentiation of the transcendental method is given in the categoreal material through which the exposition of self-cognitive knowledge can be completed. This point of view will be important shortly as we continue our study of the transcendental philosophers.

CONCLUSIONS

As a result of these considerations we can adopt the following position with respect to the objections, viz., the *dis-covering* character of the *a priori,* because of the retorsive element of the transcendental method, can be demonstrated without presupposing the justification of other principles. In this way we avoid a circle since the reflective justification of the metaphysical validity of knowledge is a result of the transcendental method in such a way that its metaphysical validity does not have to be presupposed, either universally or with regard to individual principles. Rather, the metaphysical validity of the statements which are grounded through the self-reflection of knowledge is only asserted as a conclusion. The only presupposition to the development of the proof is the indication that only a mode of thought corresponding to the self-legislative power of knowledge is guaranteed, the full validity of which need be referred to only at the end of the procedure.

Because operative analysis requires a certain overview of the modes of human activity and because categoreal development presupposes a more detailed analytic structure of concepts, it actually begins with rather complicated notions. This fact, together with its unique logical structure, accounts for its *difficulty,* but this disadvantage ·is counterbalanced by the advantages of its philosophical utility. However, these presuppositions of the transcendental method are not logical presuppositions which resolve a critical problem, since this concerns merely the understanding of phenomenologically demonstrable structures and the terminology by means of which they can be conceived. However, should critical questions be raised in this regard they can (at the very least with the help of retorsion) be reduced to simpler modes. If these "presuppositions," because of their complexity, appear to be too difficult from the didactic point of view, it is possible, through retorsion, to work out a more elaborate reconstruction of the intermediate results. Such a reconstruction, at any rate, counters the objection that the transcendental begins with complicated results in order to demonstrate simpler modes of knowledge which themselves were the focus of skepticism; in other words, the assumption is that these complicated results actually presuppose these simpler modes of knowledge logically. It may seem to those unfamiliar to the ways of philosophy that we should first seek to clarify the simpler modes of knowledge and then to demonstrate the more complicated results. However, one phase of the philosophical situation is such that beginning with complex modes of knowledge which are also totally acceptable to non-philosophers, the fundamental vindication and significance of what is evident is placed in doubt as a criterion of truth to such a degree that the act of awareness of what is evident is shaken as a foundation of knowledge. Consequently, it is no longer possible to complain that a method which demonstrates the fundamental epistemological and metaphysical statements as conditions of the very possible of casting the vindication of knowledge into doubt, thereby undermining the starting point of its critics, is unnecessarily complicating the procedure.

The primary transcendental (retorsive) grounding of the validity of knowledge does not require explicit reference to God as the goal of the orientation of the dynamic of knowledge, but only a proof that gives, along with the demonstration of the validity of knowledge, an understanding of this property of the nature of knowledge. We have already seen, most explicitly in Maréchal, that the supernatural perception of God, as subjective goal, does not have to be required.

Finally, we shall take a look at the objection that Maréchal was too taken up with the knowledge of things as mediated by sense knowledge and therefore did not consider the way followed by the critique which operates through intentional analysis, viz., first of all to justify the knowledge of what is directly evident as essential and as given to consciousness, and then, with the help of this justification, to ground the mediate knowledge of the world. The only thing that needs be said in this regard is that there is no necessity that Maréchal follow this way. He does, of course, begin with reflection on the direct awareness of noetic activtiy, but he uses this awareness (in distinction from intentional analysis) not in order to demonstrate the knowledge of this awareness as true in the sense of correspondence, but rather in order to construct a transcendental analysis and hence to introduce a grounding of the validity of noetic activity, which is then shown to be oriented to objects of the world. Success in this venture has the advantage of drawing the objects of direct and spontaneous human knowledge under transcendental analysis. The objections raised against this procedure do not consider the possibilities of operative analysis, which does not aim at an analysis of the structure of what is evident, but rather, because of the *a priori* structure of knowledge, can show which traits necessarily belong to the objects of experiential knowledge, viz., what is always co-apprehended in what is mediately evident in experience. This is extremely important with regard to a metaphysics of objects of experience as well as a theory of experiential knowledge. Therefore, it must be shown that this is the only way of demonstrating the universal objects, and universal possibilities, of a grounded experiential knowledge. Whether or not in particular cases we have a grounded knowledge of experience is a matter which can be decided critically only in conjunction with the elements of intentional analysis.

We have given a careful examination of the objections which

have been raised against the transcendental method in order to clarify the essential elements of the basic structure of the transcendental method. Now we shall turn our attention to several philosophers who have attempted a systematic reconstruction of philosophy on the basic of the transcendental method.

PART THREE

TRANSCENDENTAL SYSTEMATIC OF PHILOSOPHY

Its all-pervasive character enables the transcendental method to ground particular domains of objects through reference to the conditions of possibility of their knowability and to mediate their position in the order of being and the universal structure of their objects. This, along with the demands of contemporary philosophy to mediate the fundamental insights into essence through transcendental deduction, has led to the attempt to ground philosophy in, and to develop it systematically through, the transcendental method. Whereas Maréchal only attains the starting points of metaphysics and the theory of knowledge without actually developing these disciplines as such, Grégoire formulates (at least in its essential traits) a natural theology and André Marc completes a whole system of philosophy, including ontology, psychology and ethics. Lotz has attempted to work out a complete theory of the transcendentals and Rahner has worked out a philosophical anthropology broad enough to serve as the foundation for a fundamental theology. Lonergan, finally, moves from the reflection on the act of knowledge to a systematic foundation and thorough development of the theory of knowledge and the philosophy of science, ontology, cosmology, natural theology, ethics and fundamental theology. Just as comprehensive, although developed in a completely different fashion, is Coreth's metaphysics. In this section of our study we shall consider the three most thorough attempts at a systematic development of philosophy as grounded in the transcendental method.

11. ANDRÉ MARC

The first extensive system of philosophy in the tradition of the transcendental method was that of André Marc.[1] According to Marc, we arrive at the conditions of possibility of the act of knowledge from the antitheses which are to be found in the phenomenological givenness of this act. The investigation of the conditions of possibility which this givenness occasions leads to a dialectical development of philosophy which is in essential agreement with Thomism in terms of its results, but which goes much deeper with respect to its foundation.

THE STARTING POINT

The starting point for the methodical development of philosophy is what is given in the human act of knowledge. This requires a phenomenological analysis (MD, p. 63; EE, pp. 12) which confronts the phenomena of consciousness not merely as

[1] As representative works by Marc we refer to: *Psychologie réflexive* (Museum Lessianum, sect. philos. 29, 30), 2 vols., Paris, 1948/49; *Dialectique de l'affirmation: Essai de métaphysique réflexive* (Museum Lessianum, sect. philos. 36), Paris, 1952; *Dialectique de l'agir* (Problèmes et doctrines 6), Paris, 1949; *Raison philosophique et religion révélée* (Textes et études philosophiques), Bruges, 1955; *L'être et l'esprit* (Museum Lessianum, sect. philos. 44), Paris, 1958; "Méthode et Dialectique," in *Aspects de la Dialectique,* Paris, 1956, pp. 9–100; "La méthode d'opposition en ontologie thomiste," *Revue néoscolastique de philosophie,* vol. 23 (1931), pp. 149–169. Cf. also J. Racette, "La méthode réflexive et dialectique du P. A. Marc," *Sciences ecclésiastiques,* vol. 10 (1958), pp. 91–94; Gerald A. McCool, "Phenomenology and Dialectic: The Philosophy of André Marc, S.J.," *The Modern Schoolman,* vol. 40 (1963), pp. 321–345.

something given, but as rooted in the subject and intentionally related to objects. From the very beginning, consciousness implies the fully developed subject-object relationship (EE, p. 13).

We are aware of this implication since we encounter true reality in an act of self-transparency (*autotransparence*). Marc indicates this spontaneous self-consciousness with the term "reflective." This is a spontaneous self-reflection which appears neither as a problem nor as an object of discursive mediation. We are dealing here with something that cannot be exhausted through abstract concepts, viz., something which, in a projective sense, is concrete, singular and present to being as well as to itself (EE, pp. 13f.). Before the intellect (*Geist*) can reflect theoretically on the object, it is spontaneously reflective (EE, p. 19).

Intellectual perception, in which the active, thinking and willing self attains itself and posits itself as being, is not exhaustive, but reflective and objective to the extent that it remains true to the original phenomenon (EE, pp. 26–28). If then an explicit reflection describes this phenomenon and also presents the knowing and willing intellect with what is objectively given (insofar as it is the subjective source of the acts as well as the self-presence of the intellect), such reflection does not close off access to ontology, but opens it all the more (EE, pp. 14f., 25).

The domains of the various problems of philosophy can be viewed as questions about the understanding of what is given at the very beginning as they appear in the human act of knowledge. In psychology the concern is with the clarification of human activity in terms of the conscious structure which characterizes it. Ontology investigates the nature of the affirmation of being as such. Ethics sheds light on the freedom of human activity and on the analysis of the intentions which ground it (cf. MD, pp. 63f.).

Not only are the problems of philosophy formulated as the development of what is given at the beginning, but also the principles which regulate the discussion of the problems and

248

lead to their solution (MD, p. 64). In the phenomenological analysis of what is given in the act of knowledge, the antinomy of the one and the many constantly recurs in different forms. For example, reflective analysis shows that the given act is constituted through the particular and through the totality. This antithesis is precisely what draws forth the problem. The *problem of knowledge* is possible only to the extent that the differentiation of the knower and the object known is comprehended in the unity of reflective thought (cf. MD, pp. 12, 20f.). The problem of ontology arises from the fact that *being* (*das Seiende*), as the object of judgment, is confronted in its particular content of being, but also as a being among beings, viz., in the comprehensive order of being (MD, pp. 27, 66). Human *consciousness* emerges through its unique structure and in its activity, above all in judgment, as dependent on sensibility, but in thought it transcends and comprehends this dependence and duality (cf. MD, p. 28). The *freedom* of choice presents activity in its self-limitation and self-determination as constituted by a striving which transcends these limits (cf. MD, p. 66).

"The interaction of antinomies, however, does not bring reflection to a crisis without prescribing the directrix with which to handle and solve these problems. Since the one and the many are connected and at the same time distinct, the many must be known precisely in its uniqueness but must also be considered in terms of unity to the extent that this procedure is repeated with the necessary gradations at every level where it imposes itself. Since the unity of human activity is asserted to be dominant over the many, the ultimate unity in human being corresponds to the original unity of human activity such that everything is contained between these two poles. They must be distinguished without being separated, unified without being confused. The deciding principle will be to direct our attention to human activity in its totality in order to give a systematic division of its elements while preserving its completeness. The analysis employed begins with what is explicitly given in order to discover all the included pre-conditions" (MD, p. 17).

DIALECTICAL DEVELOPMENT

This analysis initiates a movement in reflection, through what is given in the beginning, which proceeds under its own power and develops the implicit totality (the starting point) dialectically to an explicit totality (MD, pp. 64, 66f.). The dialectic attains its goal if the explication which results gives a full account of the implicit core of the beginning (MD, p. 67). The dialectical development maintains its ties at every stage with what is phenomenologically given at the beginning while deepening it and developing its conditions of possibility (MD, p. 67; EE, pp. 26–29, 43). In this way the logic actuated in the human mind expands in a fully developed system (MD, p. 10). The dialectic makes real progress, not by moving from point to point, but by remaining within what is given and deepening it (MD, p. 29), which appears in its progress as a continually new reference to what is given in the beginning (MD, p. 27). Therefore, to the extent that the dialectic brings the totality into play from the point of view of what is given in the beginning, it is necessarily circular in the sense of describing a path around the starting point while deepening it through explication (MD, p. 77).

To say that the dialectical process of development is initiated through the antithesis in the starting point does not mean that the starting point represents being to be self-contradictory because the successive activity of being must be dialectical. Rather, precisely because contradiction must be avoided, thought is led from the antitheses to the conditions without which these antitheses cannot possibly be free from contradiction. Because the human act of knowledge, as constituted through its orientation to the totality, survives the internal contradiction which persists at the level of the particular, it is thus shown to transcend the level of the particular. Insofar as the particular, because of its limitedness, constitutes a (partial) negation of the totality in which it is itself grounded, it would be contradictory to remain at the level of the particular, viz., it would be the identification of pure positivity with the negation

250

ANDRÉ MARC

of pure positivity, or an absolutization of the limits with respect to the whole, a denial of the possibility of a ground in the absolute, an absolutization of negation as opposed to positivity. Affirmation and denial cannot be maintained at the same time because they exist as objectivization only through a positive act, viz., self-positing, or self-affirmation. Thus affirmation bears ontological significance, viz., that which characterizes being as such, while negation has only methodological significance; in other words, negation is that which brings into relief the essential affirmation contained in every affirmative, as well as every negative, judgment. The interaction of the antithesis and the demonstration of the contradiction which they involve, if considered in themselves, do not prove contradiction to be an essential property of reality; rather, they expose the non-contradictory comprehensiveness that negates the contradiction as soon as the parts of the contradiction are conceived to be made possible not in themselves, but from the very point of view of this comprehensiveness. If the parts of the contradiction were not grasped from the point of view of such an absolute position, the very affirmation of the antitheses would not be possible. Thus the reflective analysis of what is phenomenologically given spills over into a dialectical deduction of the absolute position that makes it possible, i.e., in terms of which it can be properly understood. Phenomenology, reflective analysis and dialectic continually interact with each other. Without such interaction dialectical reflective analysis would be a protracted phenomenological description. It is supported by phenomenological description and never moves completely away from it, but it moves to an understanding of what is given in terms of its conditions of possibility, which are not open to phenomenological description (cf. MD, pp. 30–33, 72, 76–80, 99; EE, pp. 25f., 29).

Marc sees in this procedure the philosophical method par excellence since it leads to a solid theory of knowledge, gives a foundation to an independent ethics, grounds metaphysics in spite of Kant (EE, p. 52) and develops philosophy through the self-exposition of human activity. Dialectic thus prevents itself from absolutizing itself illegitimately without rejecting

251

itself as a philosophical method which considers the totality of thought in function of the totality of being because insofar as it concludes to the fact that not everything can be concluded to, viz., that besides its *a priori* procedure there are still *a posteriori* methods of knowledge, it does not acknowledge limits outside of what is contained within itself (MD, p. 68).

This will have to suffice as a description of the method with which Marc attempts to develop the most important domains of philosophy. We find here again the essential elements of the transcendental method, viz., self-consciousness of the act of knowledge as the starting point and the analysis of the conditions of possibility of this act in terms of which the act itself is determined. The retorsive, or deductive, element does not come through as clearly as it does elsewhere, but it is referred to in the essential inclusiveness of the totality through which the act of particular knowledge is first made possible. This is clear especially if the priority of the positing of affirmation is comprehensively accentuated as affirmative and negative judgment and if it is shown that in the act of knowledge every manifold is grounded in a unity.

It should also not be surprising that transcendental analysis occurs as a dialectical development. Maréchal made use of the dialectical component in the development of what is implicit. What is particularly striking about Marc's method is the deliberate application of this *dialectical development* as the fundamental method for the construction of a philosophical *system*. In this regard, scarcely anyone would harbor doubts which first would concede the fundamental possibility of a transcendental deduction of the modes of knowledge which have essential relations or other conditions of possibility of the human act of knowledge as objects and which, secondly, considers only those parts of philosophy which include only such modes of knowledge. With regard to other parts of philosophy for which modes of knowledge include fundamental statements of historical or scientific fact, the *self-limits* of the dialectical method must concede that only the systematic context of such modes of knowledge, as well as the *a priori* conditions of their possibility, are determined, while their results must await experience.

THE SELF-LIMITS OF THE *A PRIORI*

By this description we mean that the transcendental self-exposition of the human act of knowledge can lead to the demonstration of the historical components in human thought about the concrete and their significance for scientific philosophy. It can also supply the means for a philosophical understanding of past thinkers, viz., the foundation for the understanding of the philosophical problems and sources of error which infect the philosophic thought of mankind. It is not intended to replace a fruitful evaluation of the history of philosophy for systematic philosophy, nor the historical scholarship which such evaluation demands; rather, it requires this evaluation while making it possible. The essential structure of man and of experienceable being, as conditions of possibility of the human act of knowledge, can be derived in the same way. It can also be shown that a philosophical understanding of concrete man in a concrete world is possible only upon the inclusion of the grossly experienceable. The essential relatedness to God intrinsic to man attains its concrete historical self-communication in the appearance of Christ, the necessity of which is not philosophically derivable but can only be accepted by man. This is the point of transition from philosophy to fundamental theology.

It should be obvious that the philosophical understanding which concrete man strives for in the world requires a philosophical understanding of his world-view as expressed in scientific and pre-scientific experience. This world-view is co-constituted through man's *a priori* understanding of the world and cannot be understood without it, but it also requires *a posteriori* elements. Here again philosophy is seen to be related to the sciences of experience, the foundations of which it must justify but the results of which it has to accept.

This is extremely important because the *a priori* elements which enter into the constitution of the results of the sciences and into this world-view can only be conceived in terms of this constitutive function. That something is *a priori,* or a condition of possibility, does not mean that it can be known independently of the *a posteriori* elements together with which it constitutes concrete knowledge, but only that it is not as such grounded in the *a posteriori* elements and is therefore independent of them. However, the *a priori* element can be transcendently disclosed in concrete knowledge. Thus the human *a priori*, to the extent that it makes possible the scientific world-view, cannot be properly disclosed unless this world-view is brought under transcendental analysis. Once the *a priori* structural elements have been attained, then we can develop the *a priori* understanding of man's world.

12. BERNARD J. F. LONERGAN

The foregoing discussion makes it clear why Lonergan[2] undertakes an extensive phenomenology of the act of human knowledge in mathematics, physics and common-sense thought before he investigates its character as knowledge and develops it into the foundation of metaphysics, ethics, natural theology and the possibility of faith. The structure of his book, *Insight,* is clearly indicative of this procedure. The first of the two main parts investigates the mode of human knowledge known as insight as an *activity* of man, viz., as a process which takes on different forms in various similar circumstances. Facts are described here which are commonly accessible, viz., which can be determined in the lives of individual men and in this history of science free from serious epistemological difficulties and which easily lead to common consent once we have given them our attention. After this *quaestio facti* comes the second main part, the *quaestio juris,* in which insight, as activity, and its product, as described in the first part, are investigated insofar as they are *knowledge.* Here the claim of knowledge to dis-close a world of beings, with reference to determinate conditions, and to apprehend that which is unconditioned, is carefully examined and shown to be valid.

[2] B. J. F. Lonergan, "The Concept of Verbum in the Writings of St. Thomas Aquinas," *Theological Studies,* vol. 7 (1946), pp. 349–392; vol. 8 (1947), pp. 35–79, 404–444; vol. 10 (1949), pp. 3–40; 359–393; *Insight: A Study of Human Understanding,* New York, 1958; "Insight: Preface to a Discussion," *Proceedings of the American Catholic Philosophical Association,* vol. 32 (1958), pp. 71–81. Cf. F. E. Crowe, "The Origin and Scope of B. Lonergan's 'Insight,'" *Sciences ecclésiastiques,* vol, 9 (1957), pp. 264–295. The two Lonergan essays cited above, as well as others, have been brought together in B. J. F. Lonergan, *Collection,* ed. by F. E. Crowe, New York, 1967.

At least in the case of the self-affirmation of the knower (which occurs in each performance of the activity of knowledge), this claim is shown to be fulfilled, i.e., the acceptance of the legitimacy of the claim is shown to be absolutely necessary. However, this means that the activity of knowledge does not remain fundamentally outside of the goal toward which it tends, but that it can actually apprehend what is unconditioned and is thus capable of legitimate insight. This capability, prepared by the structure of the activity of knowledge demonstrated in the first place, leads to necessary results for the fundamental validity of knowledge and for the conditions of this validity with respect to the universal structure of what is known. From the viewpoint of the necessary structure and the fundamental validity of knowledge, the objects of knowledge are determined by means of operative definition leading to the derivation of the universal relations between the structural elements of knowledge. This process yields the fundamental concepts and principles of ontology and ethics and ultimately the elements of a natural theology and the principles in terms of which the concrete relations between man and God can be determined. In short, the characteristics of the two main parts can be summarized as follows: "The first part deals with the question, What is happening when we are knowing? The second part moves to the question, What is known when that is happening?" (Ins., p. xxii).

STRUCTURAL ANALYSIS OF THE ACTIVITY OF KNOWLEDGE

The interest is not with what is known, but with *knowing*. While what is known constitutes an incomprehensible manifold, knowing possesses a recurrent structure which can be brought to light through a series of carefully chosen examples (Ins., p. xvii). Thus the first part of *Insight* deals with the reflection on human knowing in mathematics, physics and common-sense knowledge. The scientist places his trust not merely in the system, or the results, of his science, but in the scientific method as such. "But what ultimately is the nature and ground of method but a reflective grasp and specialized application of the object of our inquiry"—including Lonergan's inquiry in *Insight*—"viz., of the dynamic structure immanent and recurrently operative in human cognitional activity? It follows that empirical science as methodical not merely offers a clue for the discovery but also exhibits concrete instances for the examination of the larger, multiform dynamism that we are seeking to explore. Accordingly, it will be from the structural and dynamic features of scientific method that we shall approach and attempt to cast into the unity of a single perspective such apparently diverse elements as:

(1) Plato's point in asking how the inquirer recognizes truth when he reaches what, as an inquirer, he did not know,

(2) the intellectualist (though not the conceptualist) meaning of the abstraction of form from material conditions,

(3) the psychological manifestation of Aquinas' natural desire to know God by his essence,

(4) what Descartes was struggling to convey in his incomplete *Regulae ad directionem ingenii,*

(5) what Kant conceived as *a priori* synthesis, and

(6) what is named the finality of intellect in J. Maréchal's vast labour on *Le Point de départ de la métaphysique*" (Ins., p. xxiv). We shall now take a look at the result of the investigations of the first part, which covers more than three hundred pages. This will show us how Lonergan, from the analysis of knowledge in science and common-sense as related to the dynamic structure of the act of knowledge which slowly becomes manifest, can expect an answer to the philosophical problems which he has introduced.

NOETIC STRIVING

Deep within us is a *drive to know,* to understand, to see the why, to discover the ground, to find the cause, to explain. "Just what is wanted, has many names. In what precisely it consists, is a matter of dispute. But the fact of inquiry is beyond all doubt" (Ins., p. 4). This psychological pressure, which finds its release in the joy of discovery, constitutes the original "Why?" Whatever it is called, it is familiar to all.

Just as familiar is what Lonergan calls *insight,* the resolution of tension, recovery, understanding, the answer. "It is not any recondite intuition but the familiar event that occurs easily and frequently in the moderately intelligent, rarely and with difficulty only in the very stupid" (Ins., p. ix). As a consideration of this situation shows, insight comes suddenly and unexpectedly. It is not a function of external circumstances, but of internal conditions, moving between the concrete and the abstract and entering into the habitual relations of thought (Ins., pp. 3–6).

The desire to know finds fulfillment in insight. "This primordial drive, then, is the pure question. It is prior to any insights, any concepts, any words, for insights, concepts, words, have to do with answers; and before we look for answers, we want them; such wanting is the pure question. On the other hand, though the pure question is prior to insights, concepts, and words, it presupposes experiences and images" (Ins., p. 9). This is apparent in any analysis of instances of human knowing.

LEVELS OF KNOWLEDGE

If this analysis is pursued we ultimately come upon a universal structure proper to each direct process of knowledge as reflected in inner experience. "In both of these we distinguish three levels: a level of presentations, a level of intelligence, and a level of reflection" (Ins., p. 272). "Inquiry presupposes elements in knowledge about which inquiry is made. Understanding presupposes presentations to be understood. Formulation expresses not only what is grasped by understanding but also what is essential to the understanding in the understood. . . . The level of intelligence, besides presupposing and comple-

258

menting an initial level, is itself presupposed and complemented by a further level of reflection" (Ins., p. 273).

What is meant by *levels* can be made clearer if we distinguish between two kinds of questions. There are questions for the understanding, e.g., "How?," "What?," "Why?," "How often?," etc. They presuppose the first level and lead to the second level, which is concerned with the answers to these questions. But there are also questions which relate to the answers to questions such as "Is it so?" These are questions of reflection, which belong to the third level. "It is on this third level that there emerge the notions of truth and falsity, of certitude and the probability that is not a frequency but a quality of judgment. It is within this third level that there is involved the personal commitment that makes one responsible for one's judgments. It is from this third level that come utterances to express one's affirming or denying, assenting or dissenting, agreeing or disagreeing" (Ins., p. 273). The question thus incorporates the attitude of the mind which operates in the passage from one level to another. The questions of understanding lead from the level of what is given in perceptual images to the level of understanding and conception. The critical attitude of mind expressed in questions of reflection lead to the third level (Ins., p. 274). Thus the striving for knowledge is the dynamic orientation which manifests itself in questions of understanding and of reflection (Ins., p. 348).

This means that the *striving of knowledge* leads beyond what is given to further levels. "The level of intelligence is the level of discovery and invention, of catching on and learning, of grasping problems and coming to grasp their solutions, of seeing the point made in each of a series of mathematical statements and then seeing how the successive points hang together. The level of reflection is the complementary process of checking. One understands and now one wishes to know whether what is understood is also correct. One has grasped the point and one asks whether it is right" (Ins., p. 310). Nevertheless, what is attained at both levels, what fulfills the desire to know, is insight.

THE FUNCTION OF THE *A PRIORI*

However, every insight is "both *a priori* and synthetic. It is *a priori,* for it goes beyond what is merely given to sense or to empirical consciousness. It is synthetic, for it adds to the merely given an explanatory unification or organization" (Ins., p. x). This is also the conclusion of a thorough analysis of scientific knowledge. "Scientists achieve understanding, but they do so only at the end of an inquiry. Moreover, their inquiry is methodical, and method consists in ordering means to achieve an end. But how can means be ordered to an end when the end is knowledge and the knowledge is not yet acquired? The answer to this puzzle is the heuristic structure. Name the unknown. Work out its properties. Use the properties to direct, order, guide the inquiry" (Ins., p. 44).

In pre-scientific knowledge that which is known when understanding is attained is known as the "nature of . . ." Since similars are understood in similar fashion, it is expected that the "nature of . . ." will be the same for similar modes of givenness. This leads to classifications on the bases of sense similarities, e.g., the nature of light, of heat, etc. (Ins., p. 44).

We also find similarities in scientific thought. The persistent distinction is grounded in the fact that *scientific thought* works out the relationship between things themselves while *common-sense* views things in relation to us (Ins., p. 294). Thus scientific knowledge attains more precise anticipations. "What is to be known inasmuch as data are understood is some correlation or function that states universally the relations of things not to our senses but to one another. Hence, the scientific anticipation is of some unspecified correlation to be specified, some indeterminate function to be determined; and now the task of specifying or determining is carried out by measuring, by tabulating measurements, by reaching an insight into the tabulated measurements, and by expressing that insight through some general correlation or function that, if verified, will define a limit on which converge the relations between all subsequent appropriate measurements" (Ins., p. 44).

260

This allows us to specify the anticipations which lie behind the scientific discoveries from Galileo and Newton to Clerk-Maxwell and Einstein. Lonergan refers to this as the classical *heuristic structure*. "It is named heuristic because it anticipates insights of that type and, while prescinding from their as yet unknown contents, works out their general properties to give methodical guidance to investigations. It is named a structure because, though operative, it is not known explicitly until oversight gives way to insight into insight" (Ins., p. 45).

Further explanation of the "heuristic structure" clarifies the relation to the *a priori*. "Of themselves, heuristic structures are empty. They anticipate a form that is to be filled. Now just as the form can be anticipated in its general properties, so also can the process of filling be anticipated in its general properties. There exist, then, canons of empirical method" (Ins., p. 103). "Whether one likes it or not, heuristic structures and canons of method constitute an *a priori*. They settle in advance the general determinations, not merely of the activities of knowing, but also of the content to be known" (Ins., p. 104).

This leads to a universal *principle of isomorphism* "between the structure of knowing and the structure of the known. If the knowing consists of a related set of acts and the known is the related set of contents of these acts, then the pattern of the relations between the acts is similar in form to the pattern of the relations between the contents of the acts" (Ins., p. 399). "The pattern of relations immanent in the structure of cognitional acts also is to be found in the contents of anticipated acts and still will be found to obtain when the heuristic contents of anticipated acts give place to the actual contents of occurring acts" (Ins., p. 485).[3]

---

[3] The principle of isomorphism should not be misunderstood in the sense of ultrarealism. It should be taken in conjunction with the Thomistic position: *Intellectus in actu, et intellectus, sunt idem*. The principle of isomorphism is given with the position of the operative analysis of the noetic act. Only in this sense is it not only correct, but analytic. However, if it is freed from this methodical context and considered in itself (which Lonergan attempts to do), then it can create the appearance of an invalid transfer from forms of thought to forms of being. Thus it would appear that the following reviews of *Insight* do not do justice to Lonergan's intention: James Collins, *America* vol. 97

FORMS OF EXPLICIT KNOWLEDGE

Lonergan goes on to show how different forms of knowledge relate to each other: classical and statistical physics, science and common-sense. We cannot go into this interrelation in detail here, but it should be remarked that the same fundamental structure of the three levels of knowledge appears in all these forms. Knowledge, in its various modes of expression, is a *progressive process* advancing from narrower to broader points of view and leading, through experiences within the same viewpoint, to an expansion and more exact consideration of knowledge. Thus new points of view are indicated and drawn together while at the same time preventing unwarranted universalizations and prejudiced restrictions in perspective so that knowledge becomes a *self-corrective process of learning*. It is within this context that Lonergan attains his instructive insights into the relationship between expressly formulated knowledge and the original striving of knowledge.

This leads to a discussion of the function of *concepts*. Lonergan begins his explanation with an example. " 'This is a dog.' 'What do you mean by a *dog?*' The question supposes that the term *dog* has a precise meaning outside the series of statements in which it occurs. But in fact what comes first is the series of statements and what comes only later, and then only if one goes in for analysis, is the determination of the precise meaning of the single, partial term. What the average man means by a dog is

(1) what he would with certainty pronounce to be a dog in any concrete situation with which he is familiar,

(2) what he could learn to be a dog, and

(3) what he would be willing to believe is a dog" (Ins., p. 307).

"Hence it is that a dictionary is constructed, not by the Socratic art of definition, but by the pedestrian, inductive proc-

---

(1957), pp. 591–592; A. J. Reck, "Insight and the Eros of Mind," *Review of Metaphysics*, vol. 12 (1958), pp. 97–107; G. G. Grisez, *The Thomist*, vol. 21 (1958), pp. 554–560.

ess of listing sentences in which each word occurs in good usage.

"It may be objected that one cannot make a brick house without first making bricks. But one is only arguing from a false analogy if one claims that the mind develops in the same fashion as the wall of a house is built. Prior to concepts there are insights. A single insight is expressed only by uttering several concepts. They are uttered in conjunction, and reflection pronounces whether the insight and so the conjunction is correct. The isolation and definition of concepts is a subsequent procedure . . ." (Ins., p. 308). This point of view is essential for Lonergan, who goes behind ". . . concepts and affirmations to the grounding acts of direct and reflective understanding" (Ins., p. 314).

In order to define *judgment,* Lonergan begins with two possible modes of relation with respect to a proposition. A proposition may be the object of conceiving, defining, supposing or considering, as when someone considers what the propositions which he is reading are supposed to mean. But it can also be the object of affirmation or denial, of agreement or rejection, because the expression is the content of an act of judgment (Ins., p. 271). In conjunction with the previous distinction between questions of reflection or of understanding, according to whether they are to be answered with a "yes" or "no" or not, it is necessary for judgment to include an answer with a "yes" or a "no" with respect to a question of reflection (Ins., pp. 271f.). This means that judgment includes personal responsibility. The variety of possible answers makes full allowance for the misfortunes and shortcomings of the person answering and at the same time closes the door on possible excuses for mistakes. Consequently, judgment is bound within the responsibility of the one who judges (Ins., p. 272).

How can this responsibility be assumed? How is the legitimacy of judgment actually known in knowledge? This occurs in that mode of *insight* which relates to the third level, the level of reflection. We experience insights of which it holds that if we express a determinate judgment without such an insight, then it is a mere supposition. If such an insight is present, it would be foolish to deny the judgment. Such an insight is sufficient even if it is not entirely clear what actually occurs. Thus we must investigate what exactly is meant by the *sufficiency of a mode of evidence* (Ins., p. 279). "To grasp evidence as sufficient for a prospective judgement is to grasp the prospective judgement as virtually unconditioned" (Ins., p. 280). Other considerations show that ". . . a prospective judgement will be virtually unconditioned if

(1) it is the conditioned
(2) its conditions are known, and
(3) the conditions are fulfilled.

"By the mere fact that a question for reflection has been put, the prospective judgement is a conditioned; it stands in need of evidence sufficient for reasonable pronouncement. The function of reflective understanding is to meet the question for reflection by transforming the prospective judgement from the status of a conditioned to the status of a virtually unconditioned; and reflective understanding effects this transformation by grasping the conditions of the conditioned and their fulfillment" (Ins., p. 280). The grasping of the fulfillment of the conditions should not be taken to be a mode of deduction. This is only *one* form of this mode of grasping. "Far more general than the form of deductive inference is the form of reflective insight itself. If there is to be a deduction, the link between the conditioned and its conditions must be a judgement, and the fulfillment of the conditions must be a further judgement. But judgements are the final products of cognitional process. Before the link between conditioned and conditions appears in the act of judgement, it existed in a more rudimentary state within cognitional process itself. Before the fulfilment of conditions appears in another act of judgement, it too was present in a more rudimentary state within cognitional process. The remarkable fact about reflective insight is that it can make use of those more rudimentary elements in cognitional process to reach the virtually unconditioned" (Ins., p. 281).

The analysis of the process of knowledge, as it functions in the various domains of knowledge, shows that the bond between what is conditioned and its conditions is a law immanent to the process of knowledge, such that an insight is correct if it poses no further pertinent questions (Ins., p. 284). "So it is the process of learning that breaks the vicious circle. Judgement on the correctness of insights supposes the prior acquisition of a large number of correct insights. But the prior insights are not correct because we judge them to be correct. They occur within a self-correcting process in which the shortcomings of each insight provoke further questions to yield complementary insights. Moreover, this self-correcting process tends to a limit. We become familiar with concrete situations; we know what to expect; when the unexpected occurs, we can spot just what happened and why and what can be done to favour or to prevent such a recurrence; or, if the unexpected is quite novel, we know enough to recommence the process of learning and we can recognize when, once more, that self-correcting process reaches its limit in familiarity with the concrete situation and in easy mastery of it" (Ins., pp. 286f.).

Perhaps the conception, or rather this clarification, of what is evident will appear somewhat strange and uncommon. Is not *evidence* nothing but a look into things? At first glance this is the way we would describe the *experience* of what is evident, but we do not thereby grasp the *function* of evidence as it actually occurs in knowledge. If evidence is taken merely as the glance at an object without further clarification, then it would have to be admitted that this glance could be deceptive. "But if the first look is erroneous, the second, third, fourth, or *n*th may err in the same or in some different fashion" (Ins., p. 634). If, however, we take flight to a privileged mode of evidence, viz., to the evidence of the act of consciousness, then we shall have presupposed and completed what Lonergan has described; in other words, the object of judgment will have been so restricted that there could be no further pertinent questions. Therefore, Lonergan offers the ground upon which such modes of direct evidence in knowledge grant absolute certainty. Lonergan then classifies the function of this unique mode of evidence within the process of human knowledge, which contains a whole series of modes of evidence. They are distinguished from each other with respect to the way in which the bond between what is conditioned and its conditions and the fulfillment of the conditions can be apprehended. Consequently, we can distinguish between the modes of evidence of various classes of judgments: the conclusions of formal arguments, judgments over the correctness of a mode of insight, judgments of fact, universalizations, probable judgments, analytic judgments and principles (Ins., p.'315).

Lonergan emphasizes the grounding of judgment in the process of knowledge and approaches judgment from this point of view, viz., on the basis of the analysis of the process of knowledge and the interaction of the elements which are demonstrable in it in the various forms of human knowledge. This permits Lonergan to grasp human knowledge in its concrete *totality,* not merely with respect to some of the fundamental logical relationships through which judgments which are only indirectly evident can be connected with directly evident judgments.

The consideration of the position of judgment in the process of knowledge shows that judgment, as distinct from other elements, must be described as the full result, the total increment, of the process of knowledge. Each element is at least a partial increment. "But the judgement is the last act in the series that begins from presentations and advances through understanding and formulation ultimately to reach reflection and affirmation or denial. Thus, the proper content of judgement, the 'Yes' or 'No,' is the final partial increment in the process. But this proper content is meaningless apart from the question it answers. With the question it forms an integrated whole. But the question takes over a formulation from the level of intelligence, and that formulation draws upon both insight and presentation. It follows that the judgement as a whole is a total increment in cognitional process, that it brings to a close one whole step in the development of knowledge" (Ins., p. 276). "It is true that prior to judgement there are other components in knowledge; but it is not true that the components of knowledge prior to judgement are complete as knowledge; before one denies that P is Q, one must have evidence for denying; but having the evidence is one thing; grasping its sufficiency is another; and assenting to the denial is a third. Only in the act of judgement itself does one posit the absolute; only in positing the absolute does one know being" (Ins., p. 489), only here do we reach the termination of a distinct process of knowledge.

Although judgment appears as the termination of a distinct process of knowledge, and therefore as the full form of knowledge, this does not exclude the possibility that the *contextual aspect of judgment* is essential to judgment. "Though single judgements bring single steps in inquiries to their conclusion, still the single steps are related to one another in a highly complex fashion" (Ins., p. 276).

"The most general aspects of cognitional context are represented by logic and dialectic. Logic is the effort of knowledge to attain the coherence and organization proper to any stage of its development. Dialectic, on the other hand, rests on the breakdown of efforts to attain coherence and organization at a given stage and consists in bringing to birth a new stage in which logic again will endeavour to attain coherence and organization" (Ins., p. 276). The relationship between classical and statistical physics serves as an example of two such stages.

Within this universal schema of *logic* and *dialectic* the *contextual aspect of judgment* appears in three ways: "There is the relation of the present to the past. Thus, past judgements remain with us. They form a habitual orientation, present and operative, but only from behind the scenes. They govern the direction of attention, evaluate insights, guide formulations, and influence the acceptance or rejection of new judgements. . . . Hence, when a new judgement is made, there is within us a habitual context of insights and other judgements, and it stands ready to elucidate the judgement just made, to complement it, to balance it, to draw distinctions, to add qualifications, to provide defence, to offer evidence or proof, to attempt persuasion.

"Secondly, there are the relations within the present. Existing judgements may be found to conflict, and so they release the dialectical process. Again, though they do not conflict, they may not be completely independent of each other, and so they stimulate the logical effort for organized coherence.

"Thirdly, there are the relations of the present to the future. The questions we answer are few compared to the questions

THE TRANSCENDENTAL METHOD

that await an answer. Knowing is a dynamic structure. If each judgement is a total increment consisting of many parts, still it is only a minute contribution towards the whole of knowledge. But, further, our knowing is dynamic in another sense. It is irretrievably habitual. For we can make but one judgement at a time, and one judgement cannot bring all we know into the full light of actual knowing . . . It cannot be both comprehensive and concrete . . . The business of the human mind in this life seems to be, not contemplation of what we know, but relentless devotion to the task of adding increments to a merely habitual knowledge" (Ins., pp. 277f.).

Thus human knowledge is both cyclic and cumulative. "It is cyclic inasmuch as cognitional process advances from experience through inquiry and reflection to judgement only to revert to experience and recommence its ascent to another judgement. It is cumulative, not only in memory's store of experiences and understanding's clustering of insights, but also in the coalescence of judgements into the context names knowledge or mentality" (Ins., p. 375).

Lonergan's procedure can best be understood from the point of view of the contextual aspect of knowledge. Lonergan begins with the description of particular modes of knowing and strives for a comprehensive viewpoint which makes the total context of human knowledge clear down to its fundamentals. Consequently, if noetic activity is directed to mathematics, physics or common-sense knowledge, then it is conceived within a subordinate context. It approaches a higher context if it investigates mathematics, experimental science or common-sense knowledge in order to apprehend the nature of this noetic activity. If it comes to understand and to affirm what understanding and affirmation are, then ". . . it has reached an upper context that logically is independent of the scaffolding of mathematics, science, and common sense. Moreover, if it can be shown that the upper context is invariant, that any attempt to revise it can be legitimate only if the hypothetical reviser refutes his own attempt by invoking experience, understanding and reflection in an already prescribed manner, then it will appear that, while the *noêma* or *intentio intenta* or *pensée*

pensée may always be expressed with greater accuracy and completeness, still the immanent and recurrently operative structure of the *noêsis* or *intentio intendens* or *pensée pensante* must always be one and the same" (Ins., p. xxvi). If we understand exactly what understanding is, then we will not only understand the broad outlines of everything that can be understood, but we will also possess a solid foundation, an invariant schema, which is open to the further development of understanding (Ins., p. xxviii). According to the principle of the isomorphic relationship between knowledge and what is known, the structure of the acts which necessarily interact in the process of knowledge corresponds to the structure of the elements of the object which is known through this act.

THE COMPREHENSIVE ORDER

The investigation thus leads to a *universal point of view* which is ". . . a potential totality of genetically and dialectically ordered viewpoints" (Ins., p. 564). The totality is only *potential* because it only contains the heuristic structure of the totality. It does not, for instance, replace historical scholarship, which is necessary if the ideas of a particular thinker are to be understood. Second, this universal viewpoint is a *totality of viewpoints* insofar as it opens the possibility of understanding other points of view and holds the key for the understanding of special viewpoints. Third, it is an *ordered* totality of viewpoints, because, as we shall see later, it is grounded in a complete self-knowledge of the knowing subject, viz., in the structure of its process of knowledge and in the structure of the knowable contained in this process, i.e., in a metaphysics which follows from the structure of knowledge. From the point of view of the conditions of the process of knowledge, this clarifies the various stages of the development of knowledge, the dialectical expansion of the manifold formulations of the discoveries of man's multiple consciousness as well as the appeal to further development which lies in correct points of view and to self-contradiction which lies in the positions adopted by false points of view. Finally, it aids in the discovery of those elements of true experience in terms of which the persuasive power of opposing positions with respect to different thinkers can be understood. However, because this totality is potential, viz., a heuristic structure, its contents are results of the unknown, and the relations which hold in the unknown are not specifically, but generically, determined. Thus not only that which orders, but that which is ordered, are involved in the development from the universal to the particular, from the undifferentiated to the differentiated, from the vague, global and spontaneous to the fluid, exact and methodical. Fourth, the universal viewpoint is not universal through abstractness, but through *potential completeness,* since it maintains its comprehensiveness not by stripping objects of their peculiarities but by specifying the necessary relationships of the subject (Ins., pp. 564–566).

In order to attain this goal, Lonergan was forced to write the whole book, especially the first part, from a *flexible point of view.* He had to begin with a completely subordinate point of view and a minimal context and manipulate them so that further questions would arise which would expand both the point of view and the context. This alters the foundation as well as the relational components of his investigation, which is developed until the universal viewpoint and the full concrete is reached which comprehends every aspect of reality (Ins., p. xxiv). The object of concern in this whole investigation, however, is the knowledge which underlies the development of this whole process. "In other words, not only are we writing from a moving viewpoint but also we are writing about a moving viewpoint. Not only are earlier statements to be qualified by later statements, but also the later qualification is to the effect that earlier statements tend to be mere scaffolding that can be subjected to endless revision without implying the necessity of any revision of one's appropriation of one's own intellectual and rational self-consciousness" (Ins., p. xxvi). Consequently, we eventually become aware of and familiar with the activity of true reason and become capable of seeing, more easily and with more conviction, the distinction between the purely intel-

270

lectual modes of noetic activity and the many other "existential" affairs which penetrate intellectual activity and become mixed with it to the extent that its expressions become ambiguous (Ins., p. xix). The crucial issue consists in ". . . one's own rational self-consciousness clearly and distinctly taking possession of itself as rational self-consciousness" (Ins., p. xviii). This is the central aim of Lonergan's book.

SELF-AFFIRMATION OF THE KNOWER

Now we have prepared the foundations for the second part of Lonergan's work. After the analysis of the process of knowledge, its implications and its climax in judgment, we naturally come up against the question of the legitimacy of judgments as an actual value. The answer consists in making one (Ins., p. 319) The judgment of awareness, "I am a knower," serves to this end. The guarantee of this value is attained through the following demonstration.

(1) The statement is conditioned insofar as I question its actual legitimacy.

(2) The connection between what is conditioned and its conditions signifies that I am what is meant by "I am a knower," viz., that whoever makes this judgment is someone who is an identical whole, i.e., that he performs an internally related process of activities which are experienced in the dynamically conscious state of awareness as experienceable, namely, (a) in inquiry, which leads from objects to insight, (b) in insight, which leads to formulations, (c) in reflection, which leads from formulations to the apprehension of the unconditioned, and (d) in apprehension, which leads to affirmation or denial (Ins., p. 338).

(3) The conditions are fulfilled (a) since they are given in consciousness, (b) since the attempt to deny the question of whether I am a knower negates itself and (c) since the self-affirmation of the knower is a condition of possibility for the occurrence of factual judgments. These points will have to be explained more carefully.

By *consciousness* Lonergan means neither a kind of internal perception nor an act in which we focus our attention, but an awareness immanent to cognitional acts (Ins., pp. 320f.), which Lonergan explains in connection with the contexts for the various acts of knowledge (Ins., pp. 321–328). However, anyone who asks whether he is a knower, in the sense intended here, is aware of the fulfillment of the conditions required because he only knows what the terms in the question mean inasmuch as he can find this in his own consciousness (Ins., p. 328).

Furthermore, the vindication of the self-affirmation of the knower appears through the self-negation of the denial of the question: Am I a knower? "The answer, Yes, is coherent, for if I am a knower, I can know that fact. But the answer, No, is incoherent, for if I am not a knower, how could the question be raised and answered by me? No less, the hedging answer, I do not know, is incoherent. For if I know that I do not know, then I am a knower; and if I do not know that I do not know, then I should not answer. . . . It is this conditional necessity of contingent fact that involves the talking skeptic in contradiction" (Ins., p. 329). Lonergan here refers to the rebuttal of the skeptic, viz., to *retorsion,* which gains its effectiveness ultimately from the conditioned necessity which belongs to contingent facts and from the natural spontaneity and inevitability which we identify with the activity of knowledge (Ins., p. 329). This inevitability does not enter into the proof of the possibility of knowledge in premises, but pragmatically, inasmuch as one enters into the process. Contradiction arises as soon as the skeptic makes use of the process of knowledge in order to deny it (Ins., p. 332). Self-affirmation thus shows itself to be a law immanent to the process of knowledge.

Ultimately, the self-affirmation of the knower is an *a priori condition of possibility* of every factual judgment, for an analysis of the conditions of a factual judgment shows that it can have its own proper structure only if the conditions upon which the unconditionedness of the self-affirmation of the knower depends are fulfilled. As judgment it is the rational and absolute answer to the question, Is it so?, and thus it presupposes an apprehension of the virtually unconditioned in order to make the transition from question to answer possible.

In this question the "it" is related to the domain of activity, which extends to the question for reflection and in which the conditioned is apprehended as related to its conditions, viz., the level of understanding, i.e., of the positing of systematic unity and relations which, on the one hand, demonstrate a fixed independence from the field of realized conditions but which, on the other hand, are nevertheless related to this field. Since conditions and what is conditioned are strictly correlative and reciprocal, however, there must be a field which contains something that can be a fulfilling condition because it is neither conditioning nor conditioned with respect to the factual knowledge present in the question, i.e., it is what is merely given. Since possibility is ultimately concrete, it also includes the conditions for the conjunction of the various components which are required for the possibility of factual judgments. This above all else belongs to the concrete unity which poses the question, Is it so?, viz., the self.

If the conditions of possibility of factual judgments as such are taken into account, then the existence of these conditions is established by the appearance of a factual judgment and its content. These, however, are precisely the conditions on which the vindication of the self-affirmation of the knower depends. Consequently, the vindication of the self-affirmation of the knower is a condition of possibility for factual judgments as such (Ins., pp. 337f.).

In a reflection on these grounds for the vindication of the self-affirmation of the knower, in which the fundamental structure of human knowledge is affirmed, Lonergan introduces the nature of the theory of knowledge as he understands it. "It is that other theory reaches its thing-itself by turning away from the thing as related to us by sense or by consciousness, cognitional theory reaches its thing-itself by understanding itself and affirming itself as concrete unity in a process that is conscious empirically, intelligently, and rationally. Moreover, since every other known becomes known through this process, no known could impugn the process without simultaneously impugning its own status as a known" (Ins., p. 338).

COMPARISON WITH KANT

Lonergan sees the realization of the essentials of a *transcendental deduction* in this sort of grounding of the validity of knowledge. "We have performed something similar to what a Kantian would name a transcendental deduction" (Ins., p. 339). Therefore, Lonergan tries to show where the essential differences are through which his method of proof is distinguished from Kant's.

The first difference concerns those components of the conscious act of knowledge which are the starting point for the question concerning the conditions of possibility. Kant begins with the question about the conditions of the knowledge of objects. Lonergan, however, distinguished between two parts of the question. The first is the *problem of objectivity* (for the time being he does not consider the way in which he had dealt with this problem in the first 'part). The other precedes the problem of objectivity and consists in the *determination of the activities* which are operative in knowledge. Previously, he had only dealt with this part of the question. Therefore, he is only questioning the conditions of possibility for the appearance of a factual judgment, viz., of an absolute and rational "yes" or "no," not the conditions for there being a fact corresponding to this "yes," nor what meaning such a correspondence might have (Ins., p. 339).

The distinction between the thing-in-itself and the thing-for-us is not determined from the point of view of a theory of objectivity, as noumenon and phenomenon, but from the point of view of the modes of noetic activity. A *thing* is a concrete unity-identity-whole (cf. Ins., p. 246) which is apprehended in what is given as individual. If it is *explained* through a determination of the content in terms of which experimentally verified relations are specified with regard to other things, it is a *thing-in-itself*. Whether it is objective or a determination of the act of knowledge are not the central questions for the moment (Ins., pp. 339f.).

A third distinction invades the meaning which universal judgments of necessity have in proofs. While they stand in the foreground with Kant, they are of less importance for Lonergan since the *factual judgment* already indicates noetic increment (Ins., p. 340).

While Kant explains the immediate ground of judgments from the point of view of the schematism of the categories, it is essential for Lonergan that besides the investigation of what is given to the senses or to consciousness and besides the insight into the results of discovery, there is yet a *third level* extending beyond experience and understanding. It is also constitutive for judgment. It not only manifests itself, but is essential for knowledge. It manifests itself because the reflection of reason requires a *virtually unconditioned* and because reflective understanding apprehends this unconditioned. It is essential to knowledge because before I come to judgment, I am merely thinking, but when I judge, I know. Moreover, as the following discussion will show, I know being. This constitutes the rejection of *empiricism;* and since the unconditioned is only virtual, also of post-Kantian *idealism;* and because the meaning of what is given is received, of pre-Kantian *rationalism* as well. Since the analysis of knowledge does not have to be rooted in the knowledge of beings, but only in the knowledge of knowledge, the realism which it comes to is not intuitive, but immediate (Ins., p. 341).

A final distinction concerns consciousness. With Kant, besides the empirical consciousness of inner sense and the transcendental unity of apperception there is no place for the consciousness of the *generative* principle of the categories. Consequently, these are inflexible and opaque. Fichte and Hegel found here a free reign for their notions of intellectual perception and the development of intellectual consciousness. In distinction from Kant, for Lonergan the *dynamic* states of discovery and reflection are given. Discovery leads to understanding and this includes all concepts and systems. Reflection leads to the reflective apprehension of the unconditioned and this includes all judgments (Ins., p. 341).

COMPARISON WITH MARÉCHAL

We shall find in this comparison ideas with which we are already familiar from Maréchal's critique of Kant, e.g., the constitutive function of the unconditioned for judgment, the question concerning the conditions of possibility of judgment as such, the search for a principle in terms of which the apriority of knowledge can be understood in unified fashion and the contingency avoided which infects Kant, the grounding of the formal product of knowledge in the act of knowledge and the operative determination of what is known in terms of knowledge. With regard to the *problem of objectivity,* however, a difference begins to emerge. Maréchal begins his transcendental critique essentially with the relation to the object, while Lonergan, in his brief transcendental deduction, begins simply with the activity of affirmation. Maréchal prepares the reader psychologically through a comparative philosophico-historical investigation for the completion of the transcendental mode of proof, thus familiarizing him with the state of the problem and the fundamental concepts, while Lonergan accomplishes this end in the first part of *Insight* with an analysis of the cognitive stance of man within the various domains of knowledge, which ensures a more personal access to transcendental analysis and which clarifies much of the concrete structure of this method, although it does not deal with its essential form.

However, the difference with regard to the problem of objectivity should not be overemphasized, for ultimately Lonergan's mode of demonstration also arrives at objectivity and being, although not in the first step. The division of the transcendental method into partial steps is already familiar to us and does not affect the essence of deduction. Maréchal attains absolute objectivity and being through an operative analysis, although because of the differences in personal approach and preparatory material it is not so obvious as Lonergan's. However, in the act of knowledge brought under analysis, the object, for Maréchal, appears only as an immanent object, viz., as a determination which distinguishes and specifies the act irrespective of any relation to a transcendent or ontological object. When Maréchal poses the decisive question, viz., how the object in knowledge can be distinguished from the subject and posited over and against it, we can take this to be another aspect of the unconditionality of judgment, i.e., of the concept of the unconditioned, or of absolute positing, as the essential trait of judgment, through which it is the completion of the actual step of knowledge. This shows up in Maréchal to the extent that what brings knowledge to completion is what relates it to the domain in which the partial goals represent a striving toward the absolute. With Lonergan the trait of the absolutivity of judgment is immediately demonstrated, while only later is its relation to willing and to the not merely virtual absolute shown. These remarks will suffice for the moment. Now we shall turn again to Lonergan and try to determine how he arrives at being.

THE FOUNDATIONS OF METAPHYSICS

After determining the fundamental traits of the process of knowledge, Lonergan turns to the clarification of several fundamental concepts. First he deals with the *concept of being*. Noetic striving, which is directed to noetic content, serves as a starting point. That which is known serves as the objective of knowledge. By being we mean simply the objective of pure noetic striving. Since the desire to know is not the same as knowledge, we find that being (1) is everything that is known, and (2) everything that remains to be known. Since knowledge is completed in judgment, being is whatever is to be known through the totality of true judgment (Ins., pp. 348–350).

This definition of the concept of being shows clearly again the characteristics of an *operative definition*. "It assigns, not what is meant by being, but how that meaning is to be determined. It asserts that if you know, then you know being; it asserts that if you wish to know, then you wish to know being; but it does not settle whether you know or what you know, whether your wish will be fulfilled or what you will know when it is fulfilled. Still, though our definition is of the second order, it is not simply indeterminate. For neither the desire to know nor knowing itself are indeterminate" (Ins., p. 350).

Being can be more precisely determined than what is known through the totality of true judgment and thus being has at least *one* characteristic trait, viz., it is all-embracing (Ins., p. 350). It can be shown through retorsion that the desire for knowledge, and consequently being, is unlimited (Ins., p. 350). Other properties of the concept of being are similarly derived. It is, if we consider the concept itself and not some theory about the origin and content of the concept of being, spontaneously active in knowledge (and invariantly so, despite all the theories about it) and as common to all men as noetic striving. It pervades all things and is what is most important to every constituent of meaning (Ins., pp. 352–375).

This permits us to determine the concept of truth. "The true judgement affirms what is and denies what is not. In the true judgment there is harmony between what is intended and what is meant. . . . The false judgment is false precisely because it means a state of affairs that is the opposite of the state one intends to affirm, namely, the state that truly is" (Ins., p. 358). "The definition of truth was introduced implicitly in our account of the notion of being. For being was identified with what is to be known through intelligent grasp and reasonable affirmation and so being is what is known truly. Inversely, then, knowing is true by its relation to being and truth is a relation of knowing to being" (Ins., p. 552).

In the chapter on *objectivity* (Ins., pp. 375–384), the concepts of object and subject are dealt with in the following way. The concept of objectivity is fundamentally contained in a proposition of correct judgments which conforms to the following model: A, B and C are objects if the following judgments are correct:

A is, B is, C is . . .
A is neither B nor C nor . . .
B is neither C nor . . .
. . .

As *subject* an object can be defined as whatever is true when the subject affirms itself as a knower. Thus the essential aspect of the concept of objectivity will have been attained if we add to the judgment "I am a knower" the judgments "This is a typewriter" and "I am not this typewriter." Through the addition of other such judgments an unlimited number of objects can be included.

Now we can derive the important *properties of objectivity*. The absolutivity of objectivity results from the virtual unlimitedness which is grasped in reflective understanding and posited in judgment. Its normative character results from the demand which is connected with noetic striving, viz., to pursue its unrestricted objective. The empirical aspect of objectivity results from the role which the given plays in the process of knowledge.

Lonergan arrives at the development of metaphysics through an interpretation of the fundamental structure of knowledge as confronted and affirmed in the self-affirmation of the knower, of the heuristic anticipations which it contains and of the isomorphism with regard to knowing and what is known. As we have already seen, ". . . while the content of a future cognitional act is unknown, the general characteristics of the act itself not only can be known but also can supply a premise that leads to the act. A heuristic notion, then, is the notion of an unknown content and it is determined by anticipating the type of act through which the unknown would become known. A heuristic structure is an ordered set of heuristic notions. Finally, an integral heuristic structure is the ordered set of all heuristic notions" (Ins., p. 392).

If metaphysics is taken to be the science of being as such in its function within the whole of human knowledge, the result is that metaphysics lies at the base of all other domains and pervades them, viz., it sets them in relation to each other and unifies them. In human knowledge this unification is completed in the process of knowledge, which is grounded in pure noetic striving and which is developed in empirical, cognitive and reflective consciousness. However, this unification also involves the determination of the heuristic structure of that which can be known in this way, viz., the fundamental structure of the objects which confront man. Consequently, the dynamic unity of empirical, cognitive and rational consciousness, to the extent that this consciousness lies at the ground of the other domains of knowledge and pervades, binds and unifies them, is a *latent metaphysics* which is present and operative in human knowledge (Ins., p. 392). A development of the integral heuristic structure of the objects which confront human knowledge would merely fulfill these functions explicitly. "As heuristic, it would underlie other knowledge. As the questions, which other knowledge answers, it would penetrate other fields. As dialectical, it would transform these answers. As integral, it would contain in itself the order that binds other departments into a single intelligible whole" (Ins., p. 392). An *explicit metaphysics,* therefore, is ". . . the conception, affirmation, and implementation of the integral heuristic structure of proportionate being" (Ins., p. 391).

We can, in the same manner, arrive at the fundamental structure of being as it relates to the human mode of knowing. "Proportionate being is what is to be known by experience, intelligent grasp, and reasonable affirmation. The integral heuristic structure of proportionate being is the structure of what is to be known when proportionate being is explained completely. But in that explanatory knowledge there will be affirmation, there will be understanding, and there will be experience of the empirical residue. Let act denote what is known inasmuch as one affirms; let form denote what is known inasmuch as one understands; let potency denote what is known inasmuch as one experiences the empirical residue. From the distinctions, relations, and unity of experienced, intelligible, and affirmed contents, there follow the distinction, relations, and unity of potency, form, and act. From the different modes of understanding concrete things and abstract laws, there follows the distinction between central and conjugate potency and between central and conjugate acts. From the structural unification of the methods by generalized emergent probability, there follow the structural account of the explanatory genera and species and the immanent order of the universe of proportionate being. Such are the elements of metaphysics" (Ins., p. 486). Thus the domains of reality, as grasped through physics, chemistry, biology, the psychology of sense life and the psychology of spiritual life, can be classified under explicative modes and species. The point of view for these lower levels proves to be insufficient since it must view determinate facts as merely accidental yet actually conforming to rules (cf. Ins., p. 256).

This classification results in a relationship to particular modes of knowledge. "Metaphysics does not undertake either to discover or to teach science; it does not undertake either to develop or to impart common sense; it does not pretend to know the universe of proportionate being independently of science and common sense; but it can and does take over the results of such distinct efforts, it works them in to coherence by reversing their counter-positions, and it knits them into a unity by discerning in them the concrete prolongations of the integral heuristic structure which it itself is" (Ins., p. 393).

THE METHOD OF METAPHYSICS

The consideration of the structure immanent to the knower leads to an integration of the known and the knowable in which metaphysics becomes explicit. The mode whereby the implicit passes into the explicit determines the procedure of metaphysics. As Lonergan views it, it can be conceived in its universal form as a deduction with a main premiss and a series of primary and secondary minor premisses.

The main premiss includes the isomorphism of knowledge and what is known. The primary minor premisses have as their object the recurrent structure of knowledge. The secondary premisses are posited in terms of the special sciences, taken in their respectively unique natures, and in terms of common sense. From the main premiss and the primary minor premisses come a series of specific questions which are answered and find their application through the secondary minor premisses.

Such an employment of the premisses leads to the passage from a latent to an explicit metaphysics. If the fundamental traits of noetic activity are ignored, metaphysics is latent. If they are attended to and determined and if the principle of isomorphism is taken into account, then latent metaphysics, with which we are all familiar without knowing it, ceases to be latent and becomes explicit. Such a method, however, is not essential to the attainment of the ultimate results. There is nothing to prevent one from beginning with the secondary minor premises, conceiving them in their necessary and ultimate structure, and then generalizing from the cases examined to the totality of all possible cases. "In fact, this has been the procedure of the Aristotelian and Thomist schools and, as will appear, their results largely anticipate our own" (Ins., p. 400).

Nevertheless, much is to be gained from the method presented here. "Aristotelian and Thomist thought has tended to be, down the centuries, a somewhat lonely island in an ocean of controversy. Because of the polymorphism of human consciousness, there are latent in science and common sense not only metaphysics but also the negation of metaphysics; and only the methodical reorientation of science and common sense puts an end, at least in principle, to this permanent source of confusion. Further, without the method it is impossible to assign with exactitude the objectives, the presuppositions, and the procedures of metaphysics; and this lack of exactitude may result in setting one's aim too low or too high, in resting one's case on alien or insecure foundations, in proceeding to one's goal through unnecessary detours.

"Finally, the misconceptions, in which metaphysics thus becomes involved, may rob it of its validity and of its capacity for development; what should provide an integration for the science and the common sense of any risks taking on the appearance of a mummy that would preserve for all time Greek science and medieval common sense" (Ins., pp. 400f.).

"In theory, it is possible for metaphysics to rest solely on the known structure of the human mind. In practice, it is necessary for the metaphysician ever to bear in mind that scientific views are subject to revision. But neither the theoretical possibility nor the practical restraint add up to the conclusion that the metaphysician does well to lose contact with the sciences; for that loss of contact not only means that metaphysics ceases to play its integrating role in the unity of the human mind but also exposes the metaphysician to the ever recurrent danger of discoursing on quiddities without suspecting that quiddity means what is to be known through scientific understanding. Accordingly, just as the scientist has to raise ultimate questions and seek answers from a metaphysics, so the metaphysician has to raise proximate questions and seek their answers from scientists" (Ins., p. 509).

"If one wants to know just what forms are, the proper procedure is to give up metaphysics and turn to the sciences; for forms become known inasmuch as the sciences approximate towards their ideal of complete explanation; and there is no method apart from scientific method, by which one can reach such explanation. However, besides the specialized acts of understanding in which particular type of forms are grasped in their actual intelligibility, there also exist the more general acts of understanding in which one grasps the relations between experience, understanding, and judgment, and the isomorphism of these activities with the constituents of what is to be known" (Ins., p. 498). The *a priori* structures operative in the special sciences, viz., ". . . heuristic notions and structures, are not discovered by some Platonic recall of *a priori* state of contemplative bliss. They result from the resourcefulness of human intelligence in operation. They are to be known only by an analysis of operations that have become familiar and are submitted to examination. Just as the other departments of knowledge advance by discovering new methods, so metaphysics advances by adding these discoveries to its account of the integral heuristic structure of proportionate being" (Ins., pp. 392f.).

This discussion of the method of metaphysics includes many familiar points, e.g., the fundamental validity of a non-transcendental method but the necessity of the transcendental method with regard to the concrete development of the problem in history, the applicability of this method to problems which touch upon the relationships between philosophy, the special sciences and common sense, the impossibility of conceiving the a priori as a temporal *a priori,* which leads to the necessity of deriving it from the analysis of the concrete act of knowledge.

283

But the mode of relation to the special sciences is worked out here more clearly than before, viz., the complementarity of metaphysics and scientific knowledge and the grounding of the scientific *a priori* in the *a priori* that resides in each act of human knowledge, without which the protraction of the *a priori* structure of the object of knowledge could be derived simply from this structure. The special *a priori* must rather be reductively disclosed in terms of the methodical modes of the special sciences.

Just as metaphysics, for Lonergan, is derived from the cognitive structure of true knowing, so *ethics* for him results from the composite structure of true knowing and acting (Ins., pp. xxix, 595ff.). The nature of God is demonstrated as that which an unlimited act of understanding must have in order to correspond totally with being, viz., God's existence is shown by demonstrating that such an act is the condition of possibility of the act of knowledge (Ins., pp. 634–687). But as soon as the self-appropriation of true intellectual and rational self-consciousness is raised beyond the metaphysics of what relates to the world and ethics to a conception and affirmation of God, the emergence of the problem of evil demands that an understanding which trusts in itself must be transformed into an *intellectus quaerens fidem* (Ins., pp. 731, 688–731).

This brief treatment of Lonergan's suggestive and discerning work could only be expected to draw out some of its fundamental traits and to give some inkling of his method. Much that is important for the concrete elaboration of the method must be passed over, e.g., the discussion of the understanding of the significance of positions adopted in the history of philosophy and the exact structure of dialectic in human knowledge. But we have been able to show that despite his unique viewpoint and terminological peculiarities (which are, of course, direct consequents of the development of his viewpoint), the essential elements of transcendental analysis can easily be discerned while the distinctness of his concrete expression demonstrates anew the extent of the developmental power of this method.

284

13. EMERICH CORETH

As with Lonergan, Coreth is concerned with a radical foundation of philosophical thought which, from the point of view of
the self-certainty of knowledge, evolves the validity of the
fundamental concepts and system of philosophy through the
explicitation of what is implicit. While Lonergan adopts as
his means of explication the determination of the reciprocal
relationships between the fundamental acts which recur in the
multiple instances of knowledge, whose necessity he determines
through retorsion and through the demonstration of their
character as conditions of possibility of the act of knowledge,
Coreth structures his explication of the act of knowledge around
the immediacy of the intentional constituents of meaning and
the transcendental proof of their constitutive function. Both
attain the *a priori* structure of objects which corresponds to
the structure immanent to the act of knowledge. Both distinguish between acts according to their content, which suggests
an intentionality without which the validity of the claim to
intentionality would be a presupposition. But Lonergan is primarily interested in demonstrating the relation in which the
acts stand to one another, and thus it is only later that he
determines the nature of the object to which they are related.
This gives the impression that Lonergan is much too concerned
with reflection without a sufficient assessment of this reflection
for direct knowledge. Although Lonergan develops this "objectification" only for fundamental metaphysical knowledge,
not for a philosophy of nature or special ethics, his principle
of isomorphism at least supplies the methodical key to this
endeavor.

Coreth, along with the majority of the philosophers dealt with so far, especially Isaye, Lotz and Rahner, tries to give at least a preliminary determination of objects and then ascertains the further structures of the act of knowledge and its object. However, Coreth is to be distinguished from most of the philosophers already discussed in that he begins with the question and then not only tries to give a transcendental justification of the statements which he derives and the basic concepts which he employs, but he is careful to mediate the methodical procedure of examining the conditions of possibility and the starting point. Thus we can expect here a further radicalization and transformation of the transcendental method.

THE HISTORY OF THE
TRANSCENDENTAL METHOD

Coreth gains access to the transcendental method through the problematic established by the history of philosophy. In his numerous publications on Kant,[4] the German Idealists[5] and the relation of these thinkers to 'the fundamental-ontological stance of Heidegger,[6] Coreth makes several points concerning

[4] Emerich Coreth, "Kant—nach 150 Jahren," *Wort und Wahrheit,* vol. 9 (1954), pp. 620–625.

[5] Emerich Coreth, *Das dialektische Sein in Hegels Logik,* Vienna, 1952; "Dialektik und Analogie des Seins: Zum Seinsproblem bei Hegel und in der Scholastik," *Scholastik,* vol. 26 (1952), pp. 57–86; "Hegel und der dialektische Materialismus," *Scholastik,* vol. 27 (1952), pp. 55–67; "Die Ernte des Schellingjahres," *Zeitschrift für katholische Theologie,* vol. 78 (1956), pp. 334–351; "Vom Ich zum absoluten Sein: Zur Entwicklung der Gotteslehre Fichtes," *Zeitschrift für katholische Theologie,* vol. 79 (1957), pp. 257–303; "Zu Fichtes Denkentwicklung," *Bijdragen,* vol. 20 (1959), pp. 229–241; "Schellings Weg zu den Weltaltern," *Bijdragen,* vol. 20 (1959), pp. 398–410; "Sinn und Struktur der Spätphilosophie Schellings," *Bijdragen,* vol. 21 (1960), pp. 180–190.

[6] Emerich Coreth, "Das fundamentalontologische Problem bei Heidegger und Hegel," *Scholastik,* vol. 29 (1954), pp. 1–23; Zum Verhältnis Heideggers zu Hegel," *Analecta Gregoriana* (ser. fac. philos.), vol. 67 (1954), pp. 81–90; "Auf der Spur der entflohenen Götter: Martin Heidegger und die Gottesfrage," *Wort und Wahrheit,* vol. 9 (1954), pp. 107–116; "Heidegger und Kant," in *Kant und die Scholastik heute* (Pullacher philosophische Forschungen 1), Pullach, 1955, pp. 207–255.

the results of his investigations into the historical problem and his understanding of the nature of the transcendental method in the diversity of its concrete expressions.

The first point relates to the Kant's *transcendental-philosophical* stance, his great discovery, the fundamental significance of which for philosophy has been recognized by the thinkers discussed in this work. Not only this stance, but even the name, has been universally adopted. Although these thinkers can be understood as transcendental philosophers, or at least in their approach to their topics have assumed the transcendental stance, a deep opposition to Kant is discernible in the concrete assessment of this stance, both as regards their respective starting points and conclusions. As the history of philosophy clearly indicates, we must distinguish between the *nature* of the transcendental method and its various concrete *expressions*.

Second, the various expressions of transcendental philosophy do not stand completely separated from each other. Rather, it is the inadequacies of particular expressions, as they have become known, which have moved later thinkers through the logical force of the transcendental stance to overthrow the limitations and incompleteness of the first attempt. Consequently, we are by no means mistaken to expect a *validation* through the transcendental method itself of the defects in its concrete realizations.

Third, this self-clarification of transcendental philosophy in German Idealism indicates definite positions which do not restrict transcendental thought strictly to the domain of appearance, or to the subject in the sense of a relativization of the absolute character of human knowledge, but recovers the *absolute* horizon of knowledge and advances the claim that absolute thought presupposes an absolute being which is independent of thought (Fichte) and whose free positing is the world (Schelling as opposed to Hegel). This shows that the transcendental question is not necessarily merely critico-noetic, nor restricted to a metaphysics of subjectivity, but that it blends into the ontological question, which is experienced as a distinct deepening and clarification of the transcendental question, because it opens the way (in a reflectively clarified manner) to being as it dis-closes itself fundamentally in me. This *fundamental-ontological* position introduces the relationship of Heidegger to the transcendental stance. However, Heidegger remains too attached to the phenomenological approach and thus succeeds little more than did Hegel in achieving the ultimate understanding of the openness of finite spirit to being in terms of infinite spirit, which is absolute being. From a methodological point of view this development indicates that the limitations of the function of *a priori* determinations have expanded. With Kant they were purely formal determinations of the objects of a restricted domain, viz., the domain of possible experience, and constituted a knowledge of only limited value, viz., phenomena for the human transcendental subject. Fichte discovered the transcendental significance of the performed act of knowledge and the immediacy of intellectual perception in which facts are made transparent. Hegel does not bother with intellectual perception, but in the *Phenomenology of Mind* he sets up the fundament for the dialectical transcendental deduction of the *Science of Logic* through the reductive demonstration of "absolute thought." Heidegger reaches the *a priori* through the phenomenological "exposition" of what is unthematically given, simultaneously and previously, without which what is self-manifesting could not be given. This demonstration has the structure of a transcendental reduction which uncovers the content of the original understanding of being, although Heidegger does not attain a full interpretation of this understanding of being since he disregards the conceptual aspect of this understanding of being.

Even this brief glance at some of the results of Coreth's investigations into the historical problems shows how a reflection on the failures of the transcendental method can yield invaluable hints with regard to its proper use. The historical systems should be approached in systematic fashion so that the valid positions can be gathered together and assessed from a unified point of view. In this venture Coreth is indebted to previous attempts along these lines in neo-scholasticism, especially those by Maréchal, Rahner, Brugger and Lotz, as well as by the further clarification which de Vries' critique has contributed to these efforts.

THE QUESTION AS STARTING POINT

In Coreth's introduction to the fundamental questions of philosophy[7] intended for wider circles, one principle becomes clear: the question is the starting point, viz., the explanation of the understanding of being in terms of the pre-knowledge of the question and the horizon of being, which reminds us immediately of Rahner. He then goes on to give, first, a general outline,[8] and then a detailed study,[9] of how, from an initial nonarbitrary position the whole of metaphysics (or, the system of philosophy) can be grounded and developed.

The starting point is the performance of the *act of questioning,* or more concretely, the question concerning the beginning of metaphysics. Considered in itself it is taken for granted

[7] *Grundfragen des menschlichen Daseins,* Innsbruck, 1956.

[8] "Metaphysik als Aufgabe," in Coreth, *Aufgaben der Philosophie* (Philosophie und Grenzwissenschaften IX/2), Innsbruck, 1958, pp. 11–95.

[9] *Metaphysik: Eine methodisch-systematische Grundlegung,* Innsbruck, 1961. Cf. G. Penati, "Punto di partenza e metodo della metafisica realistica secondo E. Coreth," *Rivista di filosofia neo-scolastica,* vol. 53 (1961), pp. 407–413. Objections, similar to those raised against Maréchal, have been directed against Coreth's starting point. Penati, along with de Vries (cf. "Der Zugang zur Metaphysik: Objektive oder transzendentale Methode?," *Scholastik,* vol. 36 [1961], pp, 481–496), has accepted the apologetic function of the transcendental method (cf. Penati, *op. cit.,* p. 412). Penati holds that an essential alteration of the approach to metaphysics (such as that presented by the transcendental method as opposed to traditional metaphysics) would necessarily lead to a fundamental and deliberate alteration of the concept of reality. He favors the direct insight into being as a starting point rather than the question. However, it is far from Coreth's intention to deny the direct understanding of being. Rather, this understanding, along with the metaphysics grounded in it, must be critically demonstrated and reflectively explained and mediated from the point of view of the act of questioning. The starting point is not merely apologetic, but positively conditioned by the history of philosophy and signifies a definite advance. The result, not the preceding stages of mediation, shows that the methodical starting point does not condition an essentially foreign alteration of the conception of reality.

that it functions as a possible beginning which makes no logical presuppositions. This beginning is at the same time necessary (although not considered in itself) because it has yielded metaphysics without beginning expressly with the question concerning the starting point of metaphysics. This question, then, is unavoidable in the problematic of contemporary scientific philosophy.

We should now ask ourselves whether the question concerning the starting point of metaphysics is itself a starting point which does not make any further logical and critical presuppositions. This turns the question back upon itself and discloses that the question in the beginning is unavoidable and that at least questioning in itself is given as an unavoidable and non-arbitrary beginning, for if the question concerning the starting point were itself improper or meaningless, then questioning the meaningfulness and appropriateness of the question concerning the starting point of metaphysics would be unconditionally presupposed or conceded. This shows that the question of whether questioning is validly given as a starting point (the validity of which does not have to be grounded in some other basis) can be posed thematically. "Insofar as I do this, however, I again ask a question so that the thematically posed question, through the new act of questioning itself and the direct and incontravertible (though unthematic) knowledge concerning the act of questioning, negates itself. The question, with regard to its possibility, cannot itself be placed in question since the question which places it in question negates such a mode of questioning through the very performance of the act. The answer to the question, in its thematically posed intention, is attained in reference to the unthematically co-posited knowledge of the act of questioning which is raised to thematic explicitness through reflection and thus negates the question through a questionless answer. . . . The result is that the decisive position does not lie in the thematically posed intention of the actual question, since each determinately individual question (with regard to its determined content and determined aim) can itself be put in question, but only through the very act of questioning (which cannot be put in question), i.e., through a question that presupposes the possibility of questioning. However, this act is a self-cognitive, or self-certain, act. When I ask a question, I know that I am asking a question, and I know something about the meaning of questioning— otherwise, I could not ask a question (at least not a meaningful question) and could not later reflect on the question and question its meaning. In every question there is an unthematic but nevertheless a *knowledge of the act* of questioning which is certain in and through itself" (Mp., pp. 101f.).

DIALECTIC OF ACT AND CONCEPT

Since we are chiefly concerned with the structure of the transcendental method, we would like to introduce two interrelated notions. The first is that the validation of the starting point occurs through *retorsion,* which makes explicit the unthematic knowledge concerning the validation and meaning of the act in which it is shown that the very attempt to cast this into doubt is only possible through the recognition of the validity and meaning of what is brought to awareness in the act. This retorsion does not grant validity to the knowledge of the act, but only makes it explicit and validates the explicit scientific formulation of that which is brought to awareness in the knowledge of the act.

Insofar as the starting point is validated through retorsion, and insofar as the starting point is the question, Coreth goes beyond Maréchal. Insofar as the act of questioning as such is evaluated, we can see a similarity with Lonergan's evaluation of noetic striving. However, since Lonergan demonstrates this striving through a phenomenology of human knowledge and then later gives a retorsive justification, they must be distinguished. Lonergan tries to demonstrate the knowledge of the performance of the act phenomenologically and to justify it only later. Coreth goes the opposite way inasmuch as he demonstrates the knowledge of the act and what is contained in it as a condition of possibility of questioning and then later attempts a further mediation and differentiation of what is con-

THE TRANSCENDENTAL METHOD

tained in the act of knowledge. However, since Coreth, as we shall see, does not merely demonstrate what is posited in knowledge of the act as something necessarily disclosable in the act, but as something which comes to consciousness in the act, what is co-known is not simply a purely formal determination but something given with content. What is given, however, is not introduced simply in reference to a phenomenological perception, but is demonstrated as necessarily present through its necessary operation in the activity of the knower. This assures the fact that necessary knowledge has content (which explains the similarity here with Fichte's intellectual perception, Husserl's phenomenology and Heidegger's fundamental-ontology), but at the same time the content of what is given is mediated with the structure of the act and is therefore apprehended and critically justified in its rational form. This leads to the validity of the demand for the mediation of knowledge, especially as emphasized by Hegel, without this mediation being restricted to the merely formal.

This clearly shows the nature of the method of developing what is co-posited unthematically in knowledge of the act, viz., a *dialectic* between concept and act, not, as with Hegel, between concepts alone. The dialectic between concept and act is worked out "between conceptually explicit, thematically posited knowledge and pre-conceptually inexplicit knowledge co-posited unthematically in the act. This knowledge of the act co-posited unthematically in every act is direct and incontravertible, but it is grasped explicitly only when, through reflection, it is 'brought to the concept,' i.e., is raised to knowledge fixed thematically and conceptually. However, reflection can never fully comprehend the act, i.e., the thematic knowledge explicitly posited concerning the act and its moments can never exhaust the knowledge unthematically co-posited in the act. It remains behind the lived fullness and unity of the knowledge of the act. The act does not negate or contradict it, but actually replenishes it anew through the appearance of other components which can be drawn together thematically and grasped conceptually, leading to the development of thought" (Mp., pp. 103f.).

292

This reminds one of Marc's treatment of the dialectical deepening of what is given at the beginning. But it would seem to us that this procedure gains a more powerful development with Coreth inasmuch as, first, the starting point comes to a sharper conception and critical foundation through the question; second, the method of dialectical development flows from the starting point itself; third, concepts are attained as conscious products of this process; and fourth, the connections between individual steps are extended much farther. Coreth, therefore, is seeking "to mediate everything that is subsequent derivatively from a strictly transcendental, self-grounding position—namely, the question. This requires the mediation not only of each new insight but of every freshly introduced concept, i.e., they must be concretely demonstrated through the development of the act of questioning itself" (Mp., p. 104).

The reflective explanation of concepts through activity is a trait of the transcendental method with which we are already familiar, viz., inasmuch as it is operative analysis. The important thing to note here is that the *method* is derived directly from the starting point, and that the starting point is the one imposed on the metaphysical question by contemporary philosophy. We could attempt to answer the question concerning the starting point of metaphysics in some other way, e.g., by referring to immediately given being in the concrete act, or by validating judgment retorsively and giving a transcendental analysis of what is co-posited in it. However, these starting points carry the disadvantage that we must first ask why a certain way has been chosen and how criteria are to be selected with which to assess the chosen way, while the starting point from the question itself produces the criteria for the delineation of the direction of the adopted way. For if the beginning were to be called into question, thought would again be involved in questioning the question, and thus we find in questioning the unassailable beginning, in the knowledge of the act of questioning the answer to the question about the validity of questioning and in the process from the question to the question concerning the question which yields the answer to this question through the knowledge of the act which makes the question possible (which, from the point of view of explicit questioning, appears as its condition of possibility, viz., the way to the reflective clarification of such expressions).

In this simultaneous mediation of method and the starting point of the method from the self-development of the initial questioning concerning the starting point of metaphysics, we find the strength of this starting point as opposed to the starting point from judgment. In terms of results, the difference is not that important since basically everything that can be derived as a condition of possibility of the question can also be presented as a condition of possibility of judgment (Mp., p. 97, note 3), for question and answer are related as the basis of judgment and judgment itself.

ANALYSIS OF THE CONDITIONS OF POSSIBILITY

The advance from the question to the question concerning the question indicates that a knowledge not yet thematically developed is contained in the question. If this knowledge is present, the question is possible; if it were not present, the question would not be possible. However, when the concern is with the question as such, which has been shown to be unassailable with regard to its conditions of possibility, we are not dealing with a question which must yet establish its possibility in fact. Nevertheless, if the question is the object of questioning, we are dealing with a further *conception* of this question, viz., how it is possible. Therefore, if the question as such is questioned further, this is a question concerning the conditions of its possibility. It is not the fact of its possibility that is put in question. The corncern is with the conditions operative in the act of the question which has been put into question, i.e., unthematically co-known in this situation but not formulated as such in concepts, without which the question as such could not be fully understood. This is the reason for the further questioning concerning the *conditions of possibility* of the question.

The conditions are not simply ontic conditions, for conditions

294

which would have to be presupposed for the possibility of the existence of the act but which do not enter into the act as self-cognitive, would not explain why the act, in order to be understood, would have to be seen as directly related to them. They could not be gained through an explication of the knowledge of the act. However, they are not logical conditions in the sense that they must first be explicitly justified in order to guarantee the validity of the act. They would then not be co-posited in every act of questioning as such.

"If we ask questions about the conditons of questioning, the concern can only be with the conditions of possibility of the act, viz., with conditions which are co-posited, though unthematically, in the act of questioning itself. A condition of this sort is called a *transcendental condition*. It has this in common with ontic conditions, viz., it is a condition of possibility of the act, not merely, as are logical conditions, a condition of the validity of its positing. In common with logical conditions it enters into the act itself and is co-posited in it, not merely, as with ontic conditions, merely existentially presupposed" (Mp., p. 108). The transcendental condition is, in the strictest sense of the term, a condition of possibility of the act, viz., it is not only presupposed by the act but is co-posited in it and is shown to be fulfilled through the factual act.

Inasmuch as this procedure reflects on the previous conditions of possibility of an act of knowledge, it satisfies Kant's definition of the transcendental (Mp., pp. 69f.). If it is pursued it leads to the double-movement of reduction and deduction as a ground structure (something with which we are already familiar from Maréchal, who derived it from Kant).

Through *reduction* what is directly given in consciousness is demonstrated thematically in terms of the conditions which are implicit in it. It consists in the relation of what is thematically known (or willed) to what is unthematically co-known (or co-willed) in the actual act of consciousness, or to what is pre-known (or pre-willed) as condition of the act. It involves the demonstration of a *"prius"* over and against directly empirical consciousness, to the extent that consciousness is conditioned and determined in this way.

In *deduction* the essence, possibility and necessity of the empirical act of consciousness is derived from the reductively demonstrated *prius,* or *"a priori."* In the concrete application of the transcendental method both movements interact with and condition each other (Mp., 72f.; MA, p. 44).

This double-movement is to be found in the dialectical development of what is co-posited in the act as brought into play through the initial question. The knowledge of the act, i.e., the unthematic knowledge not yet reflectively grasped in concepts, which is co-posited in the act, is direct and incontravertible, but requires the mediation of thematic knowledge insofar as it is unthematic. This occurs through mediative reflection in the double form of reduction and deduction. In order that the knowledge of the act be made thematic, the act must be questioned in terms of its conditions of possibility. We thus discover, as a condition of possibility of the question as such, that what is questioned is known, otherwise it would not be open to question, but that it is not fully and exhaustively known, otherwise it would not be possible to ask a question about it. If both sides of the condition were not satisfied, the question would not be possible.

However, if this *a priori* is attained, the act can be better understood in its factually disclosed structure precisely because what is questioned is known already in a pre-knowledge, but not yet fully known, because questioning is not only possible, but necessary. If questioning is made possible through a relation to what is known, but not yet fully known, inasmuch as what is not known must be elevated to knowledge (which is the result of reduction), the knowledge of what is not known directly includes the question.

When this *a priori* has been attained we immediately have a new question, namely, What is known in this way such that it demands further questioning?, or What is it that is known (corresponding to the question as such) precisely to the extent that it is not known? The answer is anything that can still be questioned. However, it would not be that which corresponds to the question as such if it were not all-encompassing, because every limited domain is, in terms of that which limits it, the object of a possible question. Therefore, the pre-knowledge of the question as such includes an all-encompassing domain (all in one), and only in this way is it possible as the question as such (which, as we have seen, is nothing but the question concerning the question). However, if this is the condition of possibility of the question as such, it follows that questioning, the knowledge presupposed by the question and the knowledge to be attained through the question are related to an absolutely unlimited domain, viz., that every individual mode of knowledge stands in the horizon of what is known in the pre-knowledge of the question as question.

We have introduced this example (cf. Mp., pp. 112–142) in order to show how each partial step proceeds reductively and deductively and then leads to a new step which possesses this very same double structure. The result is a further development of what is co-posited unthematically in pre-knowledge. The means of explication is the evaluation of the tension between what is thematically questioned or known and what is unthematically known, in terms of which the thematic gains meaning and to which the thematic refers as its conditions of possibility. Therefore, it can be raised to explicit knowledge as the condition of possibility of the thematic.

DEDUCTION AND INSIGHT

Since the result attained is a development of unthematic pre-knowledge, we are dealing with original insights. However, the proof of the validity of this knowledge does not come about by referring to this insight, but through the demonstration that the present act would not be possible if it were not supported by this insight, for the very attempt to negate this knowledge requires it and is impossible without this requirement (Mp., pp. 67–69).

Here again we are face to face with the problem of the relation between *evidence* and transcendental deduction. Coreth has seen this problem clearly and, with some similarity to Lotz, holds that far from being a give and take between these two against one another, the transcendental method should be taken to be a means toward the reflectively clarified discovery of the fundamental insights which support thought. Since they are unthematic, and since the mere reference to their thematic formulations as constituted by insight cannot bring the ultimate clarity which is demanded by the contemporary philosophical approach to the problem, a critical mediation of these insights is required through a transcendental development of pre-knowledge. Since transcendental analysis leads to a demonstration of that into which we have gained an insight (down to the very content of the fundamental insights), its result is not purely formal in nature, but pertains also to content. At any rate, it cannot simply replace that which is given as content; rather, it can only demonstrate that these contents are always given in thought and that they stand in determinable relationships to each other.

This explains why Coreth stresses the efforts of Fichte, and also of Heidegger, to make manifest the content of the *a priori,* in opposition to Kant's formalistic conception (HK, pp. 212–214; HH, pp. 94, 97; MA, p. 47; Mp., pp. 37–40). This is only possible if we trace the conditions of possibility to their ultimate stage, viz., to the pre-knowledge of being. From this point of view the absolute character, as well as the existential validity, of the *a priori* becomes clear, so that the *a priori* can no longer be subjectively interpreted. It is then clear how the formal laws originate in the very being of beings, i.e., the content-principle of all concrete contents. This content is given in those insights whose act can be shown to be the condition of possibility of the act of thought.

This is the sense in which we should understand the meaning of the concept of *horizon.* Since the pre-knowledge which makes possible the question as such is a knowledge of the universal contents of objects, viz., of the unity of the domain in which these objects can be objects, a horizon of the question is already given with the pre-knowledge of the question (Mp., p. 115). It is "the totality of a determinate domain of objects which is viewed together under a formally determined reference to its unity of meaning. In terms of the unthematic common view of a totality, corresponding to the essence of the horizon, the meaning of the thematically posited question is constituted and modified in its unique reference to what is being questioned" (Mp., p. 125). The concept of "horizon," according to Husserl, signifies the totality of that which is unthematically perceived or anticipated in thematic modes of particular knowledge, and according to Heidegger, it is the end-point of the projection in terms of which something is understood.

The horizon of the question can be classified more carefully according to the kinds of pre-knowledge. *Pre-knowledge* can be divided into adjacent-knowledge (*Nebenwissen*), co-knowledge (*Mitwissen*) and pure pre-knowledge (*reines Vorwissen*) according to the way in which the question is approached.

Adjacent-knowledge is that mode of knowledge which precedes and enters into the question temporally, not by constituting its content-meaning but by giving it a determinate degree. Adjacent-knowledge enters into the question only as a modifying influence. Its denial does not destroy the meaning of the question, and therefore it cannot be derived from the question through transcendental analysis.

The situation is different with *co-knowledge,* which constitutes the uniqueness of the content-meaning of a particular question as such, is co-known unthematically and is co-posited as something known and therefore can be derived deductively from the question. However, it does not constitute the movement beyond what is known to that which is not yet known, viz., the prehension (*Vorgriff*) of that which is being questioned. Rather it only specifies this prehension.

It is only *pure pre-knowledge* which goes beyond what is already known and is the pure prehension of what is not yet known. As the movement of pure *excessus* it is the constitutive condition of possibility of questioning as such. While the pure pre-knowledge, which is proper to the question as pure question, constitutes the prehension of what is not yet known, adjacent-knowledge and co-knowledge enter into the particular question inasmuch as they determine the unique direction of the question and anticipate the unique nature of what is questioned (Mp., pp. 118–123). This should bring to mind Lonergan's notion of heuristic anticipation.

These different forms of knowledge correspond to different contents of what is known through them. Constitutive and modificative horizons (or rather, constitutive and modificative elements of the horizon) correspond to the distinction between modes of knowledge which enter constitutively or modificatively into the question. Co-knowledge is nothing but that element of pre-knowledge which specifies the question as such as this or that particular question. "The horizon grasped in co-knowledge is thus a *constitutive partial horizon* since it constitutes essentially the unique meaning and the particular direction of particular questions. Adjacent-knowledge, on the other hand, . . . contributes only a superficial modification to the determinate meaning-content of particular questions. Thus the horizon which is proper to adjacent-knowledge can be designated as a *modificative partial horizon*. Both . . . establish a formally determinate relation to that which is questioned" (Mp., p. 125), in which the universal fundamental structure of the content of what is questioned is known. A more exact determination comes through the answer to the question.

The way which has led from the question as starting point to pre-knowledge as the condition of the question as such leads to a further differentiation of this pre-knowledge through which we are once again referred back to the starting point. For in the beginning we do not find the question as such, but a particular question distinguishable from others. This *reference* to the concreteness of the starting point, which requires the development of a component according to its conditions of possibility and thus leads to an understanding of the act in question (but does not suffice as an understanding of the concrete relatedness of the component grasped in this regard with other components), constitutes an advancement of transcendental analysis. Coreth considers the structure of this process as essential, so much so that it supports the development of the whole system and the succession of individual steps. However, this does not mean that we can determine which component is to be designated as successor. It would be possible, most likely, to derive one as well as another from varying components. But if we have preferred one over another then the process leads back to the act understood in this regard and demands some reference to the component which has been de-emphasized. We find here again what we have already discussed with regard to the principle of abstraction and the principle of integration.

THE HORIZON OF BEING

We take up again the notion of the horizon of the question. What is the horizon that corresponds to the question as such, viz., the pure pre-knowledge? This is the horizon in which the all-encompassing domain is disclosed, viz., the domain which includes everything which is open to question and everything which can be brought under judgment, in which every object about which something can be asked or asserted (whether and what it is) attains its ultimate stance, incapable of being negated through some other question or answer. This, then, is the all-encompassing, non-relative and absolute *domain of being*. In pure pre-knowledge of the question as question this is a unified comprehension, such that on the basis of this knowledge individual questions are made possible and such that whatever is the object of an individual question (even if it should be the act of questioning or the questioner as such) can only be viewed as something open to questions and requiring an answer in terms of what is grasped in pure pre-knowledge. A being cannot be questioned, and cannot be known, unless something is known about *being* as such, i.e., as that which makes a being a being, or an object an object, viz., that which is the ground of being. This whole of being, disclosed in pure pre-knowledge as the *horizon of being*, as the end-point of pure prehension, is not merely the subsequent and resultant sum of all beings, but the previously projected and comprehensive totality of all being, which comprehends all beings without comprising them as such. This goal is approached by the succession of particular questions and their

301

answers through the internal development of pre-knowledge and through individual experiences. This being is not yet grasped as the ground of all beings inasmuch as this unity is made possible through absolute being, which is the ultimate ground of all beings and of the entire order of being (this becomes gradually and successively more manifest), but as the previous unity and totality, viz., as the condition of possibility for the fact that within this unity and totality particular beings can be posited and known. This is precisely what is meant by the concept of the horizon of being (Mp., p. 126–142). This horizon is unfulfilled inasmuch as the questions which it makes possible are not yet answered. But it is not a contentless container, or an empty form; rather, it is that which determines the content of pure pre-knowledge, even though this is by no means thematic knowledge. This unthematic knowledge is made thematic, not through objective knowledge and objective concepts introduced from without, but from the very act of questioning and through reduction to its conditions of possibility (Mp., pp. 130–133). This horizon is fulfilled through every mode of knowledge related to the facts. If we wish to see more clearly how such a transcendental analysis through the dialectical self-development of the act of questioning is distinguishable from pantheistic idealism, we must move to the next step in this development. Since the act of questioning and being as the end-point of prehension (which is contained in the pure pre-knowledge which makes the question possible) are reconcilable, we come to the question concerning the relation between *act and being*.

When the act of questioning is set over and against being as open to question, this relationship is mediated precisely through the knowledge which is posited in and through the act, viz., the knowledge of the act. This is how it is possible that the act of questioning is constituted through the knowledge of what is open to question, viz., in a reflection which explicates what is known in the act and thus answers the question posited by the act. In this knowledge the act comes to know itself, i.e., its own being as well as being in the absolutivity of being in itself. The being of this act shows itself to be the self-presence of this being, and each self-presence is the knowledge that is posited in the act. Thus the difference between the questioning act and what is questioned is posited in the unity of being and the unity of the knowledge of being, which constitutes the act. Consequently, the duality of questioner-knower and questioned-known is posited in the knowing act as a mutually limiting relation between *subject* and *object*.

This brings us to the question of the conditions of possibility of difference in identity and of identity in difference, because the identity of the act cannot, as such, be the formal ground of the difference which is posited in it. While Hegel absolutizes the identity of identity and non-identity, viz., the act of knowledge in difference, and does not question this "absolute knowledge" in terms of its conditions of possibility, Coreth derives from the immediate knowledge of the act (which has been shown to be a condition of possibility of the question) that knowledge as knowledge is pure identity, viz., that knowledge is the self-transparent self-presence of being. If this quality is posited in difference, then the self-knowledge of the act is impossible unless it is posited as a condition for the difference. The solution is to be found by referring to the starting point. In questioning, the object is known as what is not known. It is presupposed by my previous knowledge (which makes the question possible) as that which goes beyond this knowledge. That which is known in the pre-knowledge of the question as what is not known and which is not posited in the knowledge of the act as object, but rather which is presupposed, is the object "in itself." Deeper reflection shows that the difference between the subject and object in itself is the condition of possibility for the difference in the identity of the act. This point of view reveals the fundamental dis-closedness of this condition and shows how Coreth is to be distinguished from Hegel, as well as from Kant.

Thus the difference is encompassed by the in itself of being and is known as such in pre-knowledge. This shows itself to be possible only inasmuch as the unity in multiplicity results from a unity beyond multiplicity. However, since this unity cannot result from one of the two alternatives distinguishable from each other as the subject in itself and the object in itself, the interpenetration of identity and difference in the act of questioning is only possible through the identity of an act in which subject and object are fundamentally unified, viz., in a knowledge which has completely grasped the in itself in the act and is therefore not questioning, but the identity of absolute being and absolute knowledge. Thus we come to know the absolute (which is not open to finite differentiation) as the ultimate ground of the unity of the horizon of being, and furthermore, since the knowledge of the horizon of being, as well as its nature (which is nothing but its ultimate condition of possibility) is the condition of possibility of every particular mode of objective knowledge and univocal conceptualization; in other words, the analogous knowability of this absolute is shown to be the fundamental condition of possibility for objective knowledge (Mp., pp. 160–211; 348–375). "If the abstraction and predication of univocally objective concepts is possible only as the product of the intellect as actuated in the horizon of the absolute and through the dynamism toward the absolute, then objective knowledge must necessarily be transparent and transcendent, viz., a pointing beyond itself to the absolute as the ground of possibility of all objectivity. In every concept we grasp a positive content . . . or else we grasp nothing. However, to the extent that we know this content as a finite, limited magnitude (otherwise we could not form a variety of different, mutually exclusive concepts), we grasp beyond limitation and are capable of actuating a conceptual content of pure positivity by thinking the negative of the limit."[10]

Since the act of questioning knowledge has shown itself to be finite and conditioned by pointing beyond itself to the absolute, we ask again how the finite act stands with respect to the finite subject and how it is made possible by it. This leads to the development of being and acting, being and essence, and the universal laws of being. However, not every act is a ques-

[10] Emerich Coreth, "Zum Problem der Analogie: Eine Erwiderung an Erich Heintel," *Zeitschrift für katholische Theologie,* vol. 80 (1958), pp. 430–445, 443.

tion. This leads us to the conditions of the act of intellection in which being as such is disclosed, and to the immanent exposition of being according to its transcendental determinations (in the classical sense). However, this step does not explain why the intellectual act of man is questioning and not simply the possession of knowledge. This void leads to the foundation of a metaphysics of the material world and of sense experience, as well as of human being in the world (including interpersonal relationships and the moral order of human activity). It also leads to the determination of the relations of questioning to the absolute as religion, and this absolute as God.

We have attempted, through a series of brief studies, to become acquainted with the comprehensive and systematically austere development, and the consequent evolution of the self-exposition, of the question which at the same time contains a critical foundation of metaphysics and the chief areas of philosophy. The recurrence of the fundamental elements of the transcendental method should, in the process, have become abundantly clear. The previous forms of realization of transcendental thought in idealism and neo-scholasticism should have suggested its further development, consequent application and ultimate deposit as a foundation of philosophy beginning with the question concerning the starting point of metaphysics as posited within the limits of contemporary philosophy. This does not presuppose the validity of this question because questioning as such, as actuated in the very question about the validity of this question, is taken as the initiation of transcendental analysis. The strength of Coreth's procedure lies in the transcendental mediation of the starting point, of the method, of the concepts and, of course, of the validity of the expressions used. Many other topics which have come to light in the discussion of the transcendental method among scholastic philosophers find a deeper development in Coreth, e.g., the transcendental demonstration of that which comes under insight in the act, the disclosing, content-related and totalizing traits of the *a priori* (which relates only to the horizon which makes particular modes of knowledge possible without replacing them), the dialectic of act and concept as the fundamental law of transcendental analysis and the reiterated reference to the starting point as a continuance and systematic development of transcendental-dialectical analysis.

This completes our study of the main representatives of the transcendental method in neo-scholasticism, beginning with Joseph Maréchal. We could not include the many disciples of these thinkers who have developed the basic ideas of the transcendental procedure in various ways through numerous articles and lectures. We were forced to concentrate on the most characteristic traits of the main representatives, and therefore, in order to complete the structure of the transcendental method as we would view it, we shall, in the final chapter, draw together the elements of the transcendental method as presented by the individual thinkers.

14. THE FUNDAMENTALS OF THE TRANSCENDENTAL METHOD

We have studied various representatives of neo-scholasticism who use a method in their philosophy which is inspired by contemporary philosophy and which is commonly referred to as a "transcendental method." They all agree with each other (and with the essentials of Kant's transcendental stance) with regard to the basic idea that regulates this method, but they distinguish themselves from Kant in their respective concrete expressions of the method and in the results to which this method leads them.

We must, then, in retrospect, question the fundamental idea of this method and determine how this makes possible the various expressions which we have studied. Then we must fix the meaning of this method for scientific philosophy (especially as this is understood in the scholastic tradition). Consequently, we can no longer content ourselves with a description of this procedure in its particular manifestations, but with an accentuation of the fundamental structure and the methodical principles which this method must observe.

THE POSING OF THE PROBLEM

The motives for using the transcendental method are problems which concern the relations between domains of objects, or in other words the relations between object-oriented acts. Therefore, it is not concerned with the latest developments in physics, but with how what physics discovers can be related to other

307

modes of knowledge, e.g., to the developments in biology, or to the modes of knowledge according to which we organize our lives. It is not the particular objective content of our way of knowing that is put in question, but how that which is known in specific modes of knowledge is related to that which is grasped through other modes of knowledge. For instance, it was Kant's aim to explain how the knowledge of experience is related to the kind of thought which cannot be sufficiently discovered through what is fundamentally given in experience, and how theoretical relations between objects (which are contained within experience and thought) can be linked with relations which are necessary in order for moral decisions to be possible.

Such a problematic can appear in different forms. It can be formulated *objectively* as the question concerning the relations between domains of objects, e.g.: How do the results of physics relate to the whole of reality?, or: How can the individual objects which are dealt with in physics be understood metaphysically?

The problematic can be *methodological,* or scientific-theoretic, in the sense of the question concerning the relation between modes of knowledge, e.g.: How do the methods of physics relate to the methods of metaphysics?, or: How can the statements of a science be brought into relation with statements of another science or with statements of everyday language?

If the question of the relationship of a mode of knowledge to its object is posed, then we have an epistemological conception of the problem. Some might ask: How are judgments which depend on insights into universal relations linked with the intended real object?, or: What noetic value do synthetic judgments *a priori* have?

Despite the different formulations of the problematic, all such questions are taken as questions about the relationships of object-oriented acts. The objective problematic concerns the relation of our knowledge of one domain with the knowledge of another and we seek, as much as possible, the self-relations of this domain as its object. This sought-for knowledge, however, is itself an object-oriented act which is related to the first two modes of knowledge.

The ground for the transposability of the objective into a methodological problematic lies in the correlation between the object-oriented act and the object. Because of this correlation it becomes possible to stress the object at one time and the act at another—i.e., the object if we are looking for a result, the act if we are looking for the way to a result. Especially, then, if a mode of knowledge is not sufficient to clarify questions which come up in connection with its objective domain, it becomes necessary to turn to a reflection of the mode of knowledge, its range and its limits. The various approaches to reality through the special sciences and the claim for the verifiability of their relations to each other makes such a reflection necessary today.[11]

The methodological problematic is directly concerned with the relationship between two modes of knowledge. The epistemological problem introduces a translation into the sphere of object-oriented acts which poses difficulties because the act corresponding to the object is questioned in terms of its relation to the object to which it is referred. The answer comes in two steps. First, we can take the question concerning the relation of the act of knowledge to the corresponding object as a question concerning its relation to other intentional acts, because the answer to the epistemological question discloses to what degree the object is known and thus how other object-oriented acts can depend on the mode of knowledge whose validity is under investigation. Second, this question can be absolutized insofar as I can and must conceive of the knowledge of the reality of an object as an intentional act. The question concerning how the act of knowledge relates to its object is thus transformed into the question of how the mode of knowledge whose validity is being investigated is related to the mode

[11] In terms of philosophy's task of relating the variety of special sciences to each other and to metaphysics and common sense knowledge, we have attempted to show the necessity of the transcendental method in our "Methodologie und Metaphysik" in *Coreth–Muck–Schasching, Aufgaben der Philosophie* (Philosophie und Grenzwissenschaften IX/2), Innsbruck, 1958.

of knowledge in which the reality of the object is grasped. If the result of this investigation is given objective expression, then we have what is grasped in reality through the investigated mode of knowledge.

This kind of problematic explains why the transcendental method today is seen by many as a necessary means toward the goal projected by scholastic philosophy, although at the time of high scholasticism a merely initial and implicit attention to the relations which are taken up by the transcendental method with much more systematic comprehensiveness was sufficient. According to the testimony of the authors we have discussed, retorsion and the operative determination of concepts were not foreign to Thomas of Aquin. He also was interested in epistemologico-metaphysical questions. Due to the immense variety of methodically specialized sciences, the concern with methods which this specialization has occasioned, the methodically developed critique of systems and the growing importance of the problem of knowledge, the intellectual milieu in which philosophy must develop and the questions to which it is supposed to give an ultimate answer, has significantly altered. Some may regret these changes (whether this regret is directed to the critique of the history of philosophy or of the history of theology is another matter and not of direct concern here). But in any case the change is a fact, and even if such regret were valid it would not permit a disregard for the fact. The forced attempt to turn back time is futile and would do harm both to the scholastic tradition and its contemporary condition, for only an open philosophical confrontation between the contemporary problematic and the scholastic heritage can make the tradition fruitful for contemporary life and lead to the resolution of its problems. The means to these ends must reflect the contemporary problematic.

THE TRANSCENDENTAL STARTING POINT

The *transcendental turn* revolves around an awareness of the fact that a reciprocal relation holds between the domain of ob-

310

jects and the object-oriented act and consists in the fact that attention is drawn to the act and that the investigation of the act and its structures and relationships is methodically examined with regard to the explanation of the relation between the act and knowledge as well as the relations that hold between objects. Thus it is an indifferent matter whether it is called the question of validity or the question about being.

The consideration of the object-oriented act, with the aim of mediating the total order of reality and the order of approaches to reality from an understanding of the intentionality of the act, is nothing but the contemporary problematic. The apprehension of reality in knowledge, the direction of our attention to reality and the possibility of explaining the noetic procedure through the theory of abstraction, does not go against the methodical stance of the transcendental method, but is rather a result of this method which clarifies its procedure. However, the contemporary problematic does not permit us simply to refer to the givenness of reality. Besides, the reference to evidence does not constitute an ultimate solution, for the question is: What is evident given reality as it is determined by our knowledge? The problem as posed is to be worked out in complete fashion as opposed to the disordered fullness of models of reality, of conflicting meanings, of one-sided points of view and of invalid generalizations. The unifying focal point from which we can initiate a clarification, however, cannot be the not yet explicitly clarified order of reality of which we expect an ultimate clarification, but a human act which is related to everything which can be conceived in its relational order and which itself can be understood only in terms of the total order which makes it possible.

The *correlation between act and object,* as posed by the transcendental turn, is therefore not simply an arbitrary affair. The correlation here is meant only as a description of the fact of the intentionality of acts, not as the meaning of the object of the acts in a comprehensive relation, whether this be only the meaning of pre-scientific everyday realism or the meaning within a system of empirical psychology or metaphysics. Thus we can conceive of the starting point of the transcendental method as the object in the precisive phenomenological sense, viz., as a bracketing of all conceptions with regard to the intended object which goes beyond a determination of the function of the object of the intentional act, which is an act that must be distinguished from other intentional acts. The object is considered only insofar as it is a component of the intentional act through which the act is distinguished from other intentional acts. For the moment we do not consider how the object is grasped in a theory of the relation between the intentional act and the real object. Therefore, the correlation between act and object does not give more expression than an analytic relation that the object-oriented act is directed to its object. To this extent, the transcendental method grasps the concern of phenomenological analysis and functions as a phenomenological method by representing the content of what is given in the act.

In *transcendental reflection,* attention is not completely given to objects, aspects of objects and relationships between objects, but to the corresponding object-oriented acts, the object-oriented components of the acts and the relation between acts insofar as they are related to objects. The objects, therefore, are no longer considered in themselves, by ignoring the conscious relation to them, but only insofar as they are the objects of an intentional act, that is, insofar as they are a differentiation or unification of consciousness. Such a reflection is a fundamental possibility for all objects, since we can be related to objects through object-oriented acts only if we turn our constant attention more to the object than to the relation to the object.

Transcendental reflection is distinguished from other modes of reflection through its presuppositionlessness and through its comprehensive point of view. The conscious act is considered only in its object-oriented function. Further meanings and explanations are not taken into account. *Psychological* reflection, for instance, presupposes an explicit meaning of the act, viz., the act is seen as a mode of relation and the laws and principles of the actual occurrence of this mode of relation are carefully examined. The validity of this meaning is not to be disputed, but logically speaking it comes after transcendental reflection. First, psychological reflection occurs with its object-oriented acts (with which we are familiar) which bear upon transcendental reflection. Second, the psychological procedure depends on the meaning of an object-oriented act which is ignored by transcendental reflection. Only if the meaning and validity of this meaning are clarified (with the help of transcendental reflection) does psychological reflection gain its logical foundation. This is the basis for the logical dependence of psychological reflection on transcendental reflection. Transcendental analysis, however, is intrinsically independent of psychological analysis and therefore it cannot be contradicted by it. Thus psychologism, as an attempt to undermine its own logical foundation, is condemned to failure. This constitutes a fundamental response to all objections which misrepresent the procedure and the result of transcendental analysis in a psychologico-subjectivist sense.

Transcendental reflection is distinguished from *logical* reflection inasmuch as logical reflection functions under the presupposition of the intentionality of a determinate class of object-oriented acts, viz., the forms of discursive thought, and these are only considered from the viewpoint of its consequent relations. The relation of discursive thought to other object-oriented acts and the relation of thought to objectivity as such are ignored. Logical reflection and the resultant development of logic takes place through object-oriented acts treated by transcendental reflection. Therefore, logic is open to a transcendental clarification with respect to its foundation and application. However, the validity of transcendental analysis cannot simply be structured according to logical laws and criticized through them unless these very criteria, at least inclusively, are transcendentally founded. Consequently, objections against the procedure of the transcendental method are without foundation if they begin with the specific logic of a determinate mode of knowledge without having first shown the universal binding force of the logical norms beyond this mode of knowledge.

Now we are in a position to deal with the objection that we are caught up in a logical *circle* in light of the fact that transcendental reflection operates with object-oriented acts because transcendental reflection is set up to justify the validity of these intentional acts.

This objection does not take into account that transcendental reflection is not concerned with a justification of acts. Transcendental reflection merely devotes its attention to intentional consciousness and determines that the object-oriented act knows itself as an object-oriented act and is therefore aware of itself, which is ultimately the reason why we can reflect at all and how the question of the meaning and validity of intentional acts is first possible. Thus self-consciousness, self-transparency, the reflectivity of objective consciousness (or however we wish to refer to this state of affairs), is determined as the true law of objective consciousness. At the same time, we know the necessity of this reflectivity because we would not know an object, that is, we would have no objective consciousness, if we were not aware that we were related to an object. Furthermore, in transcendental reflection we are not concerned (as the principles of a theory of knowledge would be) with the *judgment of consciousness,* or to demonstrate the validity of the statements concerning the true act with reference to the direct givenness of the act which is judged by reflection. If we refer to what is directly given, viz., to evidence, this does not constitute a proof of truth in the sense of a correspondence with reality, but as the determination of a functional dependence of the judgmental relation to an object, or a relation to the object in which the object is directly presented as such. In transcendental reflection only the act, its components and the relation to other object-related acts are important, that is, constitute the true law of the act. All other questions can be classified in the relations of transcendental analysis only inasmuch as they are translated into a question concerning the relations between object-oriented acts.

Thus we see that transcendental reflection is related to object-oriented acts as such, not merely to a special class of them, and that reflection itself is an object-oriented act. To this extent it does not constitute a logical circle, but results from a methodical postulate, viz., that every conception of the object-oriented

314

act, which holds for all object-oriented acts but which cannot be applied to the reflection of the act, does not correspond to the true law of intentional consciousness, for this is essentially reflective.

PRINCIPLES OF
TRANSCENDENTAL REFLECTION

The properties of the transcendental problematic discussed in the last two sections are fundamental for any methodical realization of transcendental reflection and can be expressed in the following principle: "In the context of the transcendental method only those determinations of objects should be employed for which we find a coordination to corresponding object-oriented acts, that is, which can be operatively defined." By an *operative definition* we mean the determination of objective contents taking place through the reversible and unequivocal coordination of objects, or aspects of objects, to object-oriented acts, or aspects of these acts. The coordination, therefore, is such that the objective aspect of each object is that to which the coordinated act is related. The ground for this coordination is the correlation between act and object which is the concern of the transcendental turn. Because this principle guides the transcendental method when it investigates objective relationships by means of the analysis of intentional acts which come into view through transcendental reflection, we shall call this principle the *principle of operative analysis*.

"No determination can belong to the object-oriented act as such, nor can it be attributed to it, which cannot also be applied to reflection of the object-oriented act and thus of the attribution of this property." Reflection and the determination of modifications of the intentional act are instances of intentional acts. This principle is given a methodical interpretation through the fact of the reflectivity of knowledge on knowledge, or of consciousness of our relations to objects. Thus we shall call it the *principle of reflectivity*. Through this principle the invalid restriction of objective consciousness to a particular

315

domain is precluded. These two principles lead to two others which are connected with the relation of transcendental reflection to intentionality.

"If the problematic to which the investigations of the transcendental method are applied appears within the objective framework, then an objective framework must also be sought for the result." This *principle of objectification* results from the methodical character of transcendental reflection and from the fundamental object-orientation of knowledge. An objectification is fundamentally possible because of a correlativity between object-oriented act and object. If reflection of the act discloses an aspect which results from the object-orientation of the act, but for which there is no objective coordination, it is nevertheless possible to introduce a corresponding objective aspect into the objective order as long as it is defined operatively in terms of the act and its relation to other objects is determined by operative analysis. On the basis of these relations it is possible not only to determine the object through its relations, but to see its content in connection with the contents of its objective domain and to formulate it within the language which gives expression to this objective domain, its relations and contents. To the extent that reflection was necessary in order to mediate this objective formulation is dependent on methodical mediation. This leads to another methodical principle.

"Objective formulations within the transcendental method have only the meaning that can be fixed by operative definition and analysis." This *principle of mediation* is another form of the principle of operative analysis under the co-reference of the necessity of objective formulations. Objective formulations are necessary when we reflect because language is just as objectively oriented as thought. In the determination of what is grasped in transcendental reflection, we must employ linguistic modes which contain much that we must presently ignore. Its meaning within transcendental reflection must be restricted, if it is to be communicated, to what is intended in transcendental reflection. Therefore, we must only use the restricted and transcendentally mediated meaning in later operations, not the original, full meaning which is proper to the formulation in the not yet mediated meaning which belongs to the object. By *mediation,* then, we mean the determination of the objective meaning of a concept, or the operative foundation of a judgment of objective relations.

Therefore, the transcendental method, in its strictest sense, can only be spoken of where the principle of mediation is accepted. Without this acceptance we might have a metaphysics of knowledge, or a critical reflection on the immediate givenness of acts through which the correspondence of judgments of reflection with real acts can be directly examined, or a useful phenomenological description which presents the contents which are to be mediated, but not transcendental reflection. Linguistic modes of expression do not provide a sufficient pretext to decide whether we have transcendental mediation or not, for the conceptual framework and the linguistic expression of that which is open to transcendental reflection depends on the initial problematic and appears in objective forms of expression. The decisive factor is whether in the development of the proof, the *restricted* transcendentally mediated meaning is employed, or the *full,* objective meaning. Only to the extent that the full meaning is transcendentally mediated can epistemo-logico-metaphysical considerations be a part of the transcendental procedure. Inasmuch as such epistemologico-metaphysical considerations are necessary for the self-understanding of the act and its structure they must be integrated into operative analysis from the very beginning (although in a very general and undifferentiated form). For instance, Coreth, at the very beginning, not only gives a retorsive demonstration of the validity of the starting point and of knowledge, but also an understanding of the initial question and the knowledge it contains in terms of the being of the act (which has already been mediated). Consequently, from the very beginning the analysis of the act, the mediation of objective knowledge and the epistemologico-metaphysical understanding of the structure of the act and of the mediation of knowledge are organically bound together.

317

WAYS OF APPLYING THE PRINCIPLES

The fulfillment of the above-mentioned principles (which a methodical evaluation of transcendental reflection must satisfy) opens a wide range of latitude. This explains, to some degree, why we have seen such different expressions of the transcendental method. We wish to distinguish some of the fundamental forms of the transcendental procedure according to the various ways of being referred to principles.

According to whether the reference of the principles of operative analysis and of objectification are tightly linked or widely separated in meaning (such that the objective evaluation follows a long process of analyzing the act as a conclusion) we distinguish a *step-by-step* mediative form from a *complete mediative* form. Thus, for example, the application of the transcendental method with Coreth and Isaye is step by step, whereas with Maréchal it is complete. For we saw that with Isaye reflection and objective deduction are much more closely connected than with Maréchal. With regard to its practical application, we must take into account that the more operative analysis and objectification (i.e., reference to the contents given in the act) separate from each other, the greater the danger becomes that we shall be lost in reflection and that reflection will not arrive at a clarification of what is concretely given (although such clarification is the goal of the method). This means that the understanding of the act will suffer. Of course, if the mediative contents can be drawn to an understanding of the act, a more deeply penetrating operative analysis becomes possible. This is excluded according to the complete mediative form. Only with a division into several mediative steps can the mediation arrived at by previous steps be made fruitful for later steps.

The concepts whose meaning is first of all fully mediated at the conclusion of the procedure can, according to the principle of mediation, only be used in the extended investigation only in a restricted and already mediated meaning. This is often given linguistic formulation in the *conceptually developing*

318

form of the transcendetal method so that the concepts are systematically enriched in the course of the investigation. In the *conceptually retrieving* form the concepts of the results (which attain full mediation only at the end) are used already in the beginning. The principle of mediation allows for the fact that use will be made of these concepts in the course of the investigation as permitted by their already mediated meaning. This is often referred to explicitly in a reflection on the procedure. For example, Coreth and Lonergan proceed in a conceptually developing way, while Maréchal and Lotz prefer the conceptually retrieving form. The conceptually retrieving form, in the course of the development, brings forth a precise understanding of the partial steps in terms of a result yet to come and therefore partially balances the disadvantage of the complete mediative form. Because of the methodical ambiguity of the formulations which bind together the limited and the full meanings, the logical structure is not quite so clear here.

The principle of reflectivity can also be taken in several ways. It can mean that the act is analyzed as including reflection and that the necessity of the components belonging to the object-oriented act can be shown through transcendental deduction. However, reflectivity can also be taken methodically in the form of retorsion. The first, most *deductive* type we find with Maréchal, the second, more retorsive with Isaye. While retorsion only proves the necessity of an act, deduction conceives the necessity in the nature of the act. Deduction, however, already presupposes reduction, and the starting point of reduction, which can be mediated by retorsion. We saw that with Isaye (as distinct from Maréchal) retorsion makes possible a very tight connection between reflection and deduction while keeping the demonstration and the understanding of validity separate. With Coreth, on the other hand, an understanding of validity is already possible in the first step, although it is not completely expressed since it is yet to be developed in the following steps.

In order to distinguish these various types of transcendental reflection we must be aware that it concerns *types* which should not be sharply excluded from each other. Most of the time the concern is with a predominance of one sort or another insofar as a principle is referred to. For all forms it is true that they must be referred back to the regulative principles of the transcendental procedure which evolves from the nature of transcendental reflection and its methodical interpretation. However, a *complementary relation* holds between the types; that is, the differentiated understanding of the structure of the act and the differentiated mediation of the contents of objects cannot be co-developed all at once because in operative analysis mediation depends on an understanding of the act. The full understanding of the act, however, according to the principle of objectification, presupposes mediation. Thus the act can be differentiated and then be evaluated for mediation, as with Lonergan, or, as with Coreth, the differentiation of act and mediation can be performed in step-by-step fashion, that is, parallel limitation in and through each other without presupposing a full differentiation in the beginning.

Various typical expressions appear to be conditioned through the special positing of goals. If the concern is with a systematic development of philosophy, then a step-by-step, mediative, conceptually developing form is adopted (e.g., Coreth) which mediates the beginning and the method retorsively (but if possible also makes it deductively understandable). If the concern is with a deepening of metaphysics from the point of view of the metaphysics of knowledge, then the act can be viewed in a metaphysical context which leads to a conceptually retrieving form that proceeds more deductively (Lotz). If the problem consists in the confrontation with an entirely determined explanation of knowledge whose validity is to be interpreted, then a complete, mediative, deductive form has the advantage of a better adaption to the criticized system since a mediation of the starting point and of the method through agreement with the opponent in the discussion is not urgently demanded (Maréchal as opposed to Kant). But the danger here is that the premisses will be unwittingly accepted and that the analysis will not be sufficiently developed. Thus Maréchal's dynamism of knowledge gives a unified answer to all the questions left unsolved by Kant, but noetic dynamism itself is not sufficiently conceived in terms of the very being of finite being. If the self-exposition of the act should be worked out against the background of an epistemologico-metaphysical conception, and if the meaning of intentional acts should thereby be more exactly determined, then the conceptually retrieving form exposes whatever parallels there may be more clearly (e.g., Maréchal in connection with Thomas and Kant, and Lotz and Rahner in connection with Thomas and Heidegger). If a quick demonstration of the validation of the actual affirmation is sought, then we turn to retorsion (Isaye). The long reductive phase in which Lonergan demonstrates the fundamental structure of human noetic activity in terms of a phenomenology of the procedure of the various modes of knowledge ultimately demonstrates, through its striving, not only the mediation of the knowable through insight into noetic activity, but above all the clarification of the methodical principles of speculative thought. Consequently, various concrete expressions of the transcendental method become understandable in terms of the concrete situation.

Further, we must note that the methodical principles of the transcendental procedure are not intended as major premises for conclusions which are then taken to be the result of this method. The particular steps of the transcendental procedure are, rather, drawn entirely from the reflection of the act on itself and from the explication of the intentional act which is thereby actuated. The methodological reflection on this procedure therefore can determine certain principles of this development and thus prevent a confusion with the demands of other methods. This safeguard is provided by the methodical principles. These principles thus do not have a *constitutive* function, but only a *directive* one, i.e., they do not enter into the development of the proof as a logical presupposition, but only draw attention to the important demonstrative components with which methodical reflection attains its goal and checks itself from getting stalled half way there. Thus Kant's expression of the transcendental method can be understood in terms of previously discussed principles. It disregards the principle of reflectivity because reflection is not sufficiently included in the analysis of

321

knowledge. Thus in analysis the whole act is not considered since an essential component remains excluded. The result is that experiential knowledge is not coordinated with the knowledge which relates to the comprehensive domain which Kant refers to as the thing-in-itself. The result (according to Maréchal) is a collapse of experiential knowledge on the one hand and talk about the thing-in-itself on the other (i.e., of theoretical and practical reason). According to Lotz, this collapse leads to the neglect of the very *a priori* which is the ultimate condition of possibility of affirmative judgment and reflection.

PRINCIPLES OF THE
TRANSCENDENTAL SYSTEMATIC

In the discussion of principles above, several structural elements of the transcendental method were mentioned which result from the transcendental starting point. These must be expanded by principles which characterize the structure of the produce of transcendental analysis.

Transcendental analysis is the investigation, proper to transcendental reflection, of the nature of the object-oriented acts, which aims at elucidating the nature of the objects to which the acts are related. It is the completion of the operative analysis which grows from the transcendental turn.

Since transcendental reflection, as an auxiliary function of the philosophical method, should not be restricted arbitrarily, it must be fundamentally open for the resultant analysis of all modes of objective acts and thus must operate above all with the relation to objectivity as such and with the differentiation of the various modes of relations to objects. However, everything cannot be investigated at once, and therefore reflection cannot refer to all the components of all the kinds of objective relations at once. If the comprehensiveness of transcendental reflection is not to be prejudiced and its completion not to be made impossible, then some components must be accepted and others rejected. At the same time, however, the investigation of these components requires that the result must be referred to the starting point, i.e., to the totality of objective consciousness, and integrated with it. Only through such an integration can the necessity of abstraction avoid a falsified isolation. This property of the transcendental procedure permits an understanding of the cyclical advance, or circular thought, which we find especially with Rahner, Marc, Lonergan and Coreth. This relation can be expressed in the following principles:

"Transcendental analysis can and must direct its attention only to some of the traits of objective consciousness." We can call this the *principle of abstraction.*

"Transcendental analysis must relate the results of every partial investigation to the concrete totality of objective consciousness and thus guarantees openness with regard to other partial investigations." This is the *principle of integration.*

These two principles are generalizations of the principles of operative analysis and objectification. Transcendental reflection abstracts by emphasizing the act over the object, which must be distinguished from the kind of abstraction in objectification.

The integration of abstraction in the concrete act and its relation to the object concerns the formal as well as the content side of that to which the act is related. By the formal side we mean the system of relations to other objects, and by the content side what actually presents itself in these relations and especially the horizon in which something is presented. Thus we arrive at further principles which gives expression to the nature of transcendental mediated objectivity.

The *principle of systematic openness* signifies that the transcendentally mediated objective relations are open with regard to further differentiations. Since operative analysis can in fact refer only to some of the traits of the act, they can only mediate some of the traits of objectivity. Insofar as it presents the necessary determinations of the object-oriented act and of objects, these cannot be denied by further analysis, i.e., they offer an insurmountable systematic frame for the determination of objects (although not all of the objective determinations are thereby given). The continuation of the analysis brings new determinations which are integrated into the already considered frame and thereby determine further the previously discovered considerations. The fundamental possibility of the integration is guaranteed by the principle of integration. It should be understood that the determinations of the system must be taken in the limited sense. The system should not then be conceived as a concrete system, i.e., as a subsequent relationship of concrete objects. The system should primarily be characterized as a formal system which begins with the determinate forms of unity under which every differentiation of content must be placed. Through further differentiation and fulfillment of content, however, we begin to see what these forms mean concretely, so that the system discovered becomes essentially open to all further determinations thus preventing a disruption of the system or of what is integrated into it.

The *principle of all-pervasive order:* "Transcendental analysis does not replace partial object-oriented acts but orders them and their object in the totality of that to which human consciousness can be related." It exposes the principles of the ordered totality in which the partial object-oriented act is first capable of confronting its object, i.e., it mediates the structures of the horizon of that to which the act is related. This principle follows directly from the nature of the transcendental turn. Transcendental reflection does not replace the concrete intentional act but only aids in clarifying it and its object. The clarification takes place through transcendental analysis, which investigates the structure of object-oriented acts in a step-by-step fashion without being able to include the partial act in its concrete uniqueness and fullness and without risking the loss of relationship to it. This, in connection with the principle of systematic openness, leads to the transcendental mediation of the principles of a differentiated order of all that to which the acts can be related. This order is thus all-pervasive since it does not merely present a subsequent relation to objects. From the formal point of view it consists rather in necessary objective relations which correspond to the consciousness of objects and specific kinds of objective consciousness, and from the concrete point of view in the horizon, or relation of content, in which every object of an act must stand. Anything at all that can be the concrete object of a concrete object-oriented act must be ordered by these relations. Inasmuch as transcendental reflection mediates these relations, it aids the understanding of the objects, although it is incapable of replacing the givenness and the concrete content of objects.

This principle is connected with the fact that transcendental analysis (as we have seen in the philosophers studied earlier) draws forth universal and necessary objective relations which regulate what is experienced and what is willed and according to which the noetic preparation of experience and the distinction of meaning must be oriented without attempting to replace the concrete act of experience, of knowledge and of judgment. According to the principles of objectification and of integration, the mediated order in which these acts and their contents stand must be referred to in order to understand the concrete acts and their contents in terms of this order. Otherwise, transcendental analysis halts half way and does not lead to the illumination of the concrete act as sought. However, according to the principle of abstraction this mediated order does not exclude the fact that partial steps and partial investigations do not directly involve this relation to the concrete act. But they are partial investigations if they do not hold open the possibility for such a reference.

Because the total order does not replace the partial acts but only mediates their universal relations and contents, this does not mean that the critical reflection which accompanies and introduces the partial act has been replaced. If, through the transcendental foundation of physics, the object of physics is ordered in the total objective order, this does not replace concrete physical knowledge nor does it undermine the accompanying critical attitude. However, the result of the objective domain of physics would not be sufficient if, in a particular case, a physicist did not take into account the inner laws of physical modes of knowledge and thereby fell into error. Thus transcendental analysis does not render the critical attitude superfluous, since it is proper to every scientific mode of knowledge and every objective act as such which claims to be valid. But transcendental analysis can produce the norms according to which every object-oriented act must be directed and it can

325

specify the position of the act which is attained through this act with regard to the totality of objectivity.

PRINCIPLES OF TRANSCENDENTAL ANALYSIS

The principles just discussed have put forth several principles which must belong to a methodical assessment of transcendental reflection and of transcendental analysis, if this is possible. But how does this analysis itself proceed? How is the analysis initiated? This is the concern of the following principles.

The question can be posed in another way. Transcendental analysis is concerned with the nature of objective consciousness. Why is transcendental reflection drawn to the act in order to analyze the nature of the act? Further, what is this nature and how is it discovered?

The problematic which is the occasion for transcendental reflection draws attention to traits in the object-oriented act which bring about a differentiation of the unity of the consciousness of objects which is completed in transcendental analysis. The problematic essentially concerns the relationship of one mode of objective consciousness to another, viz., the ordering of this mode in objective consciousness as such, even if the problematic in particular cases should appear in various forms. In this way the very consciousness of objects shows itself to be a unified plurality or interrelated relations to objects. The unity of the plurality is thus given to the extent that the reflective act can compare and contrast the various modes of relationship to objects. However, the fact that the various modes are related to each other and yet are independent from each other and from unity results from the problem that otherwise the reflective act would not be seen to be effected, i.e., to be concerned with explaining the relation of one mode to another and their ordering within objective consciousness as such.

Thus on the one hand the object-oriented act is separated from others, and on the other hand it can be shown to be related to other object-oriented acts in the unity of objective consciousness. This produces an antinomy between the individual act as individual and the individual act as part of objective consciousness as such. This antinomy can take on various forms, e.g., as the difference in the results of various sciences, as the difference between the special sciences and the philosophical method, as the difference between actuated knowledge and a theory about knowledge. Thus, for instance, Kant was caught up in the difference between synthetic judgments *a priori* (which support the mathematical sciences) and the empirical theory of knowledge (according to which these judgments have no validity) and the difference between "knowledge" and "belief."

In the antinomies particular acts or kinds of acts stand in concurrence with each other, i.e., reflection is conscious of the fact that this difference is alien to unity of object-oriented consciousness. The difference appears as a misinterpretation of the object-oriented act and reveals a deficient consideration of the integration of the unity of objective consciousness. Thus reflection, from the point of view of the object-oriented act, seems to be forced to clarify this order. Transcendental analysis is thereby motivated, through the very power of the act and the reflection proper to it, to clarify the order of object-oriented acts with the goal, and therefore it dissolves erroneous identifications of one objective domain with another or with the totality of objects, viz., through the clarification of the interaction of the particular object-oriented functions in the unity of objective consciousness. If erroneous identifications are resolved in this way the one act can be limited in its claim to the validated core while the other is freed from compromising superfluities. This leads to a critical, a metaphysical and a methodical clarification: *critical* because the validity of acts is determined, i.e., limited and validated; *metaphysical* because the relations of objective domains to each other and their place in the whole is demonstrated; and *methodical* because this leads to the discovery of the correct interaction of various objective relations. We can express this situation in a principle.

The *principle of the antinomy of the starting point:* "Antinomies of the starting point, which appear in the object-oriented act, cause the reflection proper to the act to determine the unity of order of the object-oriented acts in which the antinomies are dissolved." This brings forth the question concerning the unity of differentiation in consciousness.

Nevertheless, the antinomy appears in contradictions which have their ground in the premisses which rest in a deficient self-understanding of the function of the act in the unity of objective consciousness. Because of the presence of these contradictions the possibility of the act is posed in the question. However, since the act is a fact, it seems to be related to something from which it derives its possibility. This is nothing but what we call the structure of the object-oriented acts through which the contradiction is dissolved. Consequently, the act because of the antinomies is seen to be related to the conditions of its possibility. The question concerning the unity of differentiations in the act thus becomes the question of what the unity is that conditions such differentiations.

The *principle of the conditions of possibility:* "The object-oriented act itself reveals the conditions of its possibility, the existence of which is guaranteed through the existence of the act." Transcendental analysis reaches its goal through the realization of the conditions of possibility to which the act itself refers. Insofar as it is this realization it is a *self-exposition* of the act. Antinomies are not given and do not lead to a contradiction if they do not present the alternatives of antinomies in the following form. First, the concern must be with something to which the direct or reflective act relates, i.e., there must be objective contents of knowledge. Otherwise, it would be impossible to have a conception of the contradiction. Second, these contents must be grasped in a determinate conceptual form, i.e., they must be capable of expression. Otherwise, they could not be the object of consequent discursive and contradictory thought. Third, the expressive form must also include relations of the conceptually apprehended contents in the form of judgments. Otherwise, consequences and contradictions would not be possible. We shall call the system of concepts and self-evident judgments used here the *categoreal material* in which these objective contents are given. Normally, this will also involve a determinate conceptual framework. To the extent that it would be possible to grasp the noetic contents in other categoreal material, we can characterize both mutually referential categoreal frameworks as two different *categoreal interpretations* of the content in question in terms of different categoreal material.

The categoreally apprehended antinomies coincide with the initial problematic (which calls for the use of transcendental analysis). However, it can also be the case that the antinomies would only be used as a methodical tool. In this case, through a previous description or phenomenological analysis, the differentiation of consciousness is already determined. However, the mediation of what is determined makes use of the antinomies in the form of an indirect proof, viz., if the determined differentiation should not take place then we would have an antinomy. This antinomy then becomes the object of careful examination. According to the principle of the antinomy of the starting point the categoreally apprehended alternatives of the antinomy must be revised. This revision cannot be introduced *ad hoc* but only through a reduction to the object-oriented acts which lead to the antinomy, i.e., to conditions of possibility. But how does this reduction take place? Through reference to the objectively constituted conditions of intentional acts ("objective" *a priori*) and to the conditions which do not constitute the object as such but only the special categoreal framework ("subjective" *a priori*).

The categoreally apprehended alternatives of the antinomy are related to object-oriented acts or to the objective domains of such acts. The solution of the antinomy depends on the integration of these acts into the unity of objective consciousness. Therefore, the fundamental concepts and the self-evident relations between the contents which are signified by these concepts must be operatively defined in terms of the principle of operative analysis and reduced to the context of object-oriented functions. In transcendental reflection, attention is restricted to the act which has as its object the categoreally apprehended alternatives of the antinomy, for in this way the object-oriented functions of the act can be determined through which the objective differentiation of the categoreally apprehended is attained. Thus the object-oriented functions of the act are related to the forms under which the objects to which the act is referred are conceived. These related functions at the same time offer operative definitions for the fundamental concepts with which these forms are actualized. Furthermore, a corresponding relationship of the defined functions presents the relations under objective forms which are conceived as obviously existent and which gain expression in judgments of necessity.

This reduction of the necessary forms of the unity of the objective differentiation to descriptions of the object-oriented act constitutes *transcendental reduction*. Through it the *a priori* determinations of objects are reduced to a priori determinations of the act. *A priori*, with regard to objects, characterizes the relations which constitute concretely the horizon of the objects of acts and which find their formal expression in necessary judgments of amplification. With regard to the act it characterizes a property of the intentional act through which it is determined to be directed to objects in such a way that the structure in question will belong to them. Drawing this all together we have:

The *principle of reduction:* "The structure of objects must be reduced to a structure of the object-oriented act which serves as a foundation for an operative determination and limitation of the being of the categoreal framework."

The *principle of categoreal development:* "Inasmuch as transcendental analysis makes use of the operatively mediated and (as limited by its meaning) categoreal material of the problematic, it is a self-exposition of the act with respect to this categoreal material." At least three things are accomplished here:

First, the meaning and value of the fundamental concepts and judgments of necessity which underlie the antinomy are fixed within limits so that the antinomy is dialectically dissolved and the act itself becomes conceivable.

Second, domains of objects and relations which are not considered in the antinomy are at least referred to conceptually because otherwise the antinomy would not be dissolved. Inasmuch as the comprehensive connection is intended in the initial categoreal framework in the full sense (although in identification with the limited sense), the categoreal starting point (in abstraction from the limited sense) is given for an analogous determination and specification of what is comprehended.

Finally, all this prepares for an analysis of the conditions which have resulted in misinterpretations, and thus to the antinomies. The task of this analysis is to give an account (within the limits of the demonstration of the conditions of possibility of objective consciousness) of those factors which are independent of the concrete categoreal framework. Consideration of this "subjective" *a priori* leads to a better understanding of the limitation of the act. The danger of invalid generalizations and identifications (which leads to antinomies) is systematically precluded. These three traits can be expressed in the following principles:

The *principle of dialectic:* "Transcendental analysis is developed as a dialectic between act and concept." Inasmuch as the categoreally apprehended (but not yet mediated) special objective relation to which an act is related is regulated through reference to the act (insofar as the categoreal system was not related to the comprehensive relation and this integration disregarded), the integration into the total relation and the foundation of the categoreal system is introduced into its limited mediated meaning. According to principles of abstraction and integration this introduction occurs in an advancing dialectical process which mediates the objective determination of the act step by step. This same dialectic can also be seen as the negation of the opposition by means of the constraint of the reflective act for the categoreal development of the unity that makes it possible (through the antinomy of the starting point).

The *principle of analogy:* "The categoreal framework of the determinations of the comprehensive domain which are mediated through the act by abstracting the limited meaning from the full meaning of categoreal expression." If categoreal expression were in no way capable of aiding the relation to the comprehensive domain, then there simply would not be con-

331

fusions, erroneous identifications, antinomies and problematics. The application of this categoreal expression for the relation to the mediative comprehensive domain must be contrasted in the manner of its application with a less comprehensive relation and its meaning must be fixed through mediative determination in the comprehensive domain. However, the way must be prepared for a mediative analogous application of the categoreal expression.

The *principle of systematic criticism:* "Transcendental reduction strives for an analysis of the factors which determine the concrete categoreal formulation." For on the one hand the object-oriented act is referred to categoreal expression, on the other hand it is not restricted to the limit of a determinate system of categoreal expression. Thus the object-oriented act cannot be taken as sufficient if it is not understood as dependent on the conditions which determine its categoreal form and which include the danger of typical falsifications. Through investigations into the comparative history of philosophy this dependence is quite often at least implicitly referred to (and explicitly so by Lonergan). He examines fully the factors which determine concrete positions and at the same time make them possible.

Transcendental reflection, therefore, reduces objective consciousness to its conditions of possibility and thus limits the meaning and validity of the object-oriented act, viz., through dependence on the comprehensive order of objective consciousness. However, this reduction has another result, viz., it becomes clear, through integration into the total order of the intentional functions of consciousness, how far a particular objective relation fulfills a necessary role in the constitution of objective consciousness (a role which it plays in the relation to objects as such). In other words, insofar as it can be shown from the point of view of the demonstrated conditions of possibility that the intentional function in question is a condition of possibility for the constitution of objects of consciousness, then the meaning and validity of the object-oriented function and the relation of the corresponding objective component to the total order of what is objective are thereby mediated. Thus transcendental reduction prepares the way for a derivation which draws out the meaning and validity of the object-oriented function and the relation of the corresponding objective component to the total order of what is objective is thereby mediated. Thus transcendental reduction prepares the way for a derivation which draws out the meaning and validity of the object-oriented function and mediates the corresponding objective component in its necessary relation to the objective order and thereby abstracts from the falsified meanings of the intentional act.

The *principle of deduction:* "We can derive from the integration of the object-oriented act into the unified order of object-oriented functions in what sense the object-oriented act is the condition of possibility of the constitution of objective consciousness." Deduction determines and validates the meaning of the act and the nature of the object as they are distinguished from erroneous meanings. This leads us to the next principle:

The *principle of the a priori:* "The *a priori* determinations of the intentional act are attained through the concrete act which, as a constituent *objectively a priori,* results in the determination of the objectivity of the act, and as a *subjective* condition (which only determines categoreal formulation) leads to the understanding of, and to the exclusion of erroneous meanings of, the act." Since the *a priori* determinations are gained from transcendental reduction through the concrete act, they are not given as such previously as full expressive knowledge. Their differentiation is dependent on the differentiation of the actual intentional act. To this extent the *a priori* is not known as temporally previous, but is operative only as the inner law of the intentional act. This inner law, however, is not blind, but functions within the actual consciousness of the self-cognitive intentional act, viz., determined by the act.

Because the *a priori* of the act is not the concrete act, but only determines its universal nature (since it still requires the element which leads to the emergence of the concrete act), the *a priori* is restricted to the *a posteriori* in order to be able to work itself out. Therefore, it must be said of the inner law of the act that it is not the full determination of itself. However, this means that the *a priori* of the act is only the co-constitutive element of the act and does not determine objective consciousness alone. This concept can be expressed in several ways, e.g., the *a priori* determines only the necessary forms of objective unity, not concrete content; the *a priori* grounds only essential relations, not the facts in which these relations are concretized; the *a priori* provides only the horizon within which something can be given, viz., the universal structural context which is concretized by what is given: the *a priori* determines only the preparation for what is given *a posteriori,* not the fact of its being given. The *a priori* component becomes operative only in cooperation with the *a posteriori* component and can be shown only in this way. Consequently, the investigation of the *a priori* cannot proceed in *a priori* fashion but must begin with concrete intentional acts as they commonly occur or as they appear in the various sciences.

The *a priori* guarantees the objectivity of the intentional act because the meaning of the act is determined through reduction and deduction and thereby is related to, and integrated into, objective consciousness as such. Through the methodical assessment of the principle of reflection we find that this integration guarantees the objectivity of the intentional act because it can in no way be made more relative. The exponents of the transcendental method whom we have studied also claim that the object which is guaranteed through the *a priori* is not a relative, only so-called "object," but that it is absolute value in the sense of the correspondence with being since that which cannot be demonstrated in terms of the inner law of objective consciousness is a "subjective" notion which does not reproduce being, but only a way in which reality can be represented. In the formulation of the principles ˇof method, objectivity cannot yet be determined as truth in the sense of a correspondence with real being since this correspondence is a result of the act of the method which gives a methodical assessment of the transcendental turn and whose nature can be described through the principles which have been introduced. Concepts such as truth, being, reality, evidence as a criterion of truth and the pre-givenness of real being (which are norms of our knowledge) must first be mediated. This mediation, of course, is a methodical aid which, through the self-reflection of intentional consciousness on its inner law (which itself requires such self-understanding), justifies the valid claim of intentional consciousness and distinguishes it from invalid meanings. Otherwise, the validity of the intentional act could not be produced through transcendental analysis, but merely presented and demonstrated. Since the reflective demonstration of validity (in response to the scientific character of philosophy) is constitutive for philosophical knowledge, the transcendental method has a constitutive function for scientific philosophy.

Further, since the transcendental method begins with the concrete act in which being is already known, it is no wonder that the essential traits of being can be ascertained. It is not grounded methodically in the validity of the insight that being is grasped in knowledge. It only investigates how the being-oriented act is structured and operatively determines through the structure of the act gained in reflection that to which the act is related.

THE SIGNIFICANCE OF THE TRANSCENDENTAL METHOD

The transcendental method begins with a reflection on the intentional human act. It seeks ultimately to understand the various modes of the human act of existence and its objective domains in terms of the comprehensive order of being. This order is not appended to the act from without, but is disclosed as the supporting ground of the object-oriented self-activity of that which man is. This disclosure is introduced in such a way that the comprehensive order is manifested in the act as its supporting ground, viz., that without this manifestation the act would not be possible as the act of which we are aware. Thus the self-cognitive act requires a reduction to its conditions of possibility and can disclose through itself the comprehensive order of being in terms of which the variety of objects of

335

consciousness can be understood in their ordered unity. Insofar as this disclosure is supported by that which is known in the act, we are dealing with a self-exposition of the act.

The total order as such is not given, but is disclosed. The starting point of the disclosure is a member of this order which is possible only in conscious reference to the total order, viz., the human consciousness of objects. This reference, however, is usually not the theme of the intentional act. The thematic is only a special domain which is grasped in a determinate categoreal form. Since the act is possible only in relation to the whole we find the tendency to mistake the particular domain and its categoreal form for the whole. Such false developments result in antinomies which compel the act to reconsider the comprehensive order and the uniqueness of the absolute domain. The various philosophical methods are ways of solving these antinomies. The objective method of realistic metaphysics in the Aristotelian-scholastic tradition includes the connection between the particular domain and the relation to the absolute. Particular domains cannot be taken as the absolute without going against other particular domains. These antitheses demand a differentiation of particular domains and an abstraction from (along with a simultaneous reference to) the absolute. Metaphysics is the development of this differentiation of the modes of being, their reference to the absolute and the determination of the absolute through this reference.

The relations of the products of differentiation among each other and with the absolute and the properties which belong to all members of the order of being through their position in this order, are validated through their openness to insight. Objections directed against the appeal to evidence are in some cases eliminated through reference to privileged insights in which the factors which call forth the objections are excluded.

The *phenomenological* method confronts antinomies by bracketing all interpretations which result from the tendency toward a systematic meaning directed to the absolute. It draws attention to the pure givenness, i.e., the essential contents of the intended objects, and puts together a demonstration and thereby explains this givenness. This method is capable of demonstrating the fullness and structure of the horizons of the experienced contents, but not the final order in which these contents and the acts which are connected with them stand and in terms of which their givenness can be understood.

The methods of the *logical* and linguistic analysis of knowledge resolve false identifications and generalizations through the analysis of the logical relations and differentiations of the language employed. The language and the logical presuppositions which are related to a particular domain are distinguished from languages and presuppositions which relate to other domains. However, the validity of these presuppositions and the relation of categoreal systems to each other cannot thus be grounded.

The *systematico-critical* methods of the comparative history of philosophy, rational psychology and the critique of world-views, of the sociology of knowledge, the critique of ideologies and depth psychology attempt to eliminate antinomies by showing the correlations between the actual appearance of determinate viewpoints and the conditions of historical, social and psychological natures. But this does not resolve the question of value which lies at the base of the claims of these investigations. However, we can understand why a certain perspective has appeared and become absolutized (despite a presupposed orientation to the whole).

In the light of these possibilities of error the demand for a way which permits us to distinguish the valid content of the act from invalid elements becomes all the more pressing. Such a reflection must begin with intentional acts as grasped in particular domains and as dependent on categoreal material and the conditioned standpoint of man. However, so that this reflection is capable of achieving a self-understanding and a self-exposition of the act which presents the act in its openness for everything, no meaning of the act can be introduced in unmediated fashion from without, viz., unless the self-exposition of the act itself requires and mediates this meaning.

In this sense, *transcendental* reflection is distinct from the meaning of the act which is proper to natural realism and which conceives the noetic act as intentional contact with the real thing. Direct insight is considered only to the extent that the relations of the act of insight into what is directly given to other acts is under examination. This precludes the approach which would see the act only as intentional consciousness without pushing toward further implications and conditions which are essential for the act. The limitations of phenomenology are thus overcome as well as the limits of a logical reflection which only reaches the formal side of the categoreal frame, not the content side (and still less the grounding of the categoreal system in the existential act of man). Systematico-critical reflection presupposes the meaning of the act as an extension of life as conditioned by a standpoint and bound by interest such that it is limited in its analysis to this point of view.

All of these methods focus upon determinate components of the self-understanding of the act. But only a method which supplies a comprehensive self-understanding of the act through an assessment of the comprehensive order operative in the act itself can relate the components of the act (as they emerge from particular methods) to each other and thereby draw the methods and their valid conclusions into order. Such a procedure offers an understanding which is sought by other methods (which only partially attain their goals because of the limits conditioned by their starting points) and directs their efforts. Insofar as the transcendental method is directive it unifies the other methods and draws them to completion.

To the extent that in the application of limited methods attention is given to the limits grounded in the starting point, we can, on the basis of this method, refer to an understanding which goes beyond the method and negates its limits. Thus with Maréchal the realistic starting point is transcended in face of the problems which have dominated the development of modern thought, the sufficient resolution of which cannot be attained by the method growing from the realistic starting point. In the second book of the last volume of his five-volume work he exposes the line of connection between traditional metaphysics and its starting point and the transcendental method, which he then develops in the third book.

Likewise, we find a tendency in the later Husserl and in

Heidegger to go beyond the limits of phenomenological analysis to a grounding in the act and its immanent openness for totality (although in Heidegger the limits are not entirely done away with). The integration of the rational element of the act does not succeed. Attention is also given by the exponents of the logico-linguistic methods of analysis to a recognition of the limits of this method and the demand for inquiry into the source of that which can be apprehended in logical analysis. Thus a transcendental or dialectical or a fundamental logic (or however we might refer to a logic of origins) is required. This is also evident with the systematico-critical methods, e.g., when the attempt is made to disclose the all-pervasive order operative in the existential act of man from the negative of the explicable, but conditioned, variations of positions.

The same holds for the transcendental method because insofar as a particular expression of this procedure, by misconceiving the principles which emerge from the transcendental starting point, becomes lost within limitations, the transcendental starting point has within itself the power to overcome these limitations. We can trace this power in the development of the transcendental method from Kant's critical period through his later writings, to German Idealism, as well as in the development of the viewpoints of individual thinkers. Only here the further development does not dispense with the transcendental starting point, but overcomes false interpretations of the human act precisely in and through this starting point.

However, since the particular methods are conceived in terms of the comprehensive order of the act, they are validly (although limitedly) employed in this order. It is precisely through this limitation that they are freed from the burden of unfortunate attempts at transcending limits, which tends to bring discredit upon them. Thus realistic metaphysics finds its transcendental foundation (and at the same time the meaning of its statements are clarified) insofar as misunderstood conceptions which brought discredit upon it are eliminated. Also, its relation to the results of other methods and its universal relevance for the ultimate understanding of all domains of human life are explained.

339

THE TRANSCENDENTAL METHOD

The methods of phenomenological and logical analysis are grounded in terms of the inner law of the act (which actualizes the objective contents in rational form) in its function in the formal and concrete explanation of categoreal systems and domains. The starting point for this explanation is the transcendental explanation of that to which, beyond their limits, these methods are related. In like fashion, the systematico-critical methods receive their foundation through which their critique of validity (which itself lays claim to validity) is introduced into the frame of the order of the human existential act which, in its categoreal formation and actual realization, is restricted to a particular viewpoint but is nevertheless conceived in this dependency and thus can be distinguished from relativizing aspects in such a way that it is not encumbered by them.

Reference to the fact that all human acts are restricted to a point of view, but such that they can be understood within this restrictedness as fulfilling their claim to absolutivity, we avoid two extremes: a *relativism* which underestimates the absolute character of human acts and thereby negates itself, and an *absolutism* which overlooks the perspectivity of the access to the absolute and, by identifying the absolute with the relative, brings discredit upon the validated claim to absolutivity. Although the act is supported by the absolute order and can be understood and developed only through its relatedness and orientation to this absolute order, this order is not given to man in its concrete totality. However, its principles, as operative in the act, can be grasped in distinction from the relative (this is the task of transcendental reduction), and the content of the absolutivity of the act can be derived and understood in terms of its reference to the absolute order (this is the task of transcendental deduction).

This means that the transcendental method satisfies the concern of philosophy, viz., to understand under the most universal point of view everything that man is and does and thus to arrive at an ultimate explanation of man and his world and to give ultimate grounds and meaning to his modes of relation. This is achieved in a way which is unique to man, viz., by not beginning with a false expectation, as if being and the total order grounded in it were given tó man previously and independently of his concrete act of existence. This would only lead to a false identification of the conceived structures of the order with the concrete totality of this order. Such an identification would block the way to further understanding so that the validly conceived traits would be falsely conceived. The transcendental method rather takes into account the relation of this order to the concrete reality of man as it operates and manifests itself in the existential act of man. This order is disclosed in the act insofar as the act and its object are conceived within this order and (as consciously directed by this conception) can and must be developed further. This order, the order of being, is an *a priori* which supports the act. Thus it is the order of objective reality to which the self-cognitive, object-oriented act is related and which comprehends the one who acts, the act itself and the object. To the extent that the expression of this understanding increases, the principles of this order become expressly apprehended. To the extent that the human existential act develops, it is possible to be more explicit about the totality of this order. The explanation of the *a priori* depends on the differentiation of the concrete act, i.e., on the fullness of the *a posteriori*. However, the understanding of the *a posteriori,* of the act and of the objects given in the act depends on the reference to the *a priori*. To the extent that, in the history of particular men and mankind as a whole, consciousness has differentiated, a different development of this order becomes possible as well as a better understanding not only of the principles of the order of being but of that which is grounded in this order. Such a further differentiation of the understanding of the order of being, in terms of differentiated consciousness and the differentiated problematic, is necessary because otherwise the differentiated human existential act would not attain the reflective clarification of the unity of meaning of its differentiated existential development as demanded by its inner law.

This study has shown that the transcendental method can be thoroughly unified with traditional *scholastic* philosophy, not only through an evaluation of the *a priori* (corresponding to the theory of abstraction), but because the transcendental method is capable of presenting a foundation for the metaphysics of being and the critique of knowledge (corresponding to the notion of differentiated consciousness in contemporary philosophy). At the same time, it is capable of viewing the differentiated domains of the development of human existence in relation to the systematic order through which human existence is supported (which is the explicit concern of metaphysics). The transcendental method is thus homogeneous with the philosophical tradition of scholasticism, because to the extent that the transcendental method is compelled to refer to and demonstrate the traditional relationships of human thought, it is bound to preserve a connection with the scholastic heritage. Inasmuch as it examines the relations of the philosophic method while grounding and determining their value it does not disturb the scholastic method but directs thought on this method and on the means proper to it for attaining its goal. At the same time, it protects this method from a false absolutization which would work against it and its results. The transcendental method is a further development insofar as, in conjunction with the goal of the philosophical traditions of the ancient and middle ages, it takes up the problems which concern modern and contemporary philosophy, viz., those concerning knowledge and methodology. Because it is capable of determining the mutual relation between methods and systems, which has developed in confrontation with these problems, it leads to a concrete solution to these problems to the satisfaction of both scholastic and extra-scholastic thought. Thus the transcendental method, as a consequence of such a study as this one, can be seen as an organic expansion of the approach to philosophy which has been followed by the scholastic tradition.

INDEX

343